A Boy Named Shel

Also by Lisa Rogak

The Man Behind the Da Vinci Code:
An Unauthorized Biography of Dan Brown

A Boy Named Shel

The Life & Times of Shel Silverstein

Lisa Rogak

Thomas Dunne Books
St. Martin's Press 🐟 New York

THOMAS DUNNE BOOKS.
An imprint of St. Martin's Press.

www.thomasdunnebooks.com
www.stmartins.com

Library of Congress Cataloging-in-Publication Data

Rogak, Lisa, 1962-
    A boy named Shel : the life and times of Shel Silverstein / Lisa Rogak.—1st ed.
        p.   cm.
    Includes bibliographical references.
    ISBN-13: 978-0-312-35359-9
    ISBN-10: 0-312-35359-6
    1. Silverstein, Shel.   2. Authors, American—20th century—Biography.   3. Artists—United States—Biography.   4. Humorists, American—20th century—Biography.
    I. Title.

PS3569.I47224Z85   2007
818'.5409—dc22

                                                                2007028110

First Edition: November 2007

10   9   8   7   6   5   4   3   2   1

For Don McKibbin, aka "the Don"
You cut the rug better than guys one-tenth your age

Contents

Introduction

When I was growing up in the suburban New Jersey of the '60s, going to diners with my father was my favorite thing in the world. Once we settled into the red Naugahyde banquette, I'd order a cheeseburger—regardless of the time of day—and he'd sit across from me, one hand around a cup of Sanka, the other holding a Kent cigarette.

For other kids, the highlight of the diner meal came with the chance to stand slack-jawed in front of a brightly lit glass carousel that displayed a variety of colossal desserts. But for me it was the moment my father would slide a quarter across the greasy Formica and say I could pick any song I'd like from the chrome jukebox at the end of the booth. I'd grab the coin, spin it into the slot, and stand up on the banquette in my Buster Browns, reaching for the wheel that flipped each page of selections with a metallic click.

After years of camping out in establishments along Routes 4 and 17, we had the ritual down pat. We went through the motions at every diner, even though we both knew there was only one song I wanted to hear: "The Unicorn" by the Irish Rovers. At five plays for a quarter, I'd punch in the same letter-number combination—E-2 or D-4, just like bingo—five times in a row. My job done, I'd settle back down into my seat and wait for the song to begin, my pulse racing until I'd heard my favorite line from the song: "humpty-backed camels and some chimpanzees."

A few of the patrons would inevitably start grumbling around the third or fourth time the song played, but I didn't care. I'd sit with a big grin on my face, my heels kicking the booth to keep time while my half-eaten burger grew cold. All the while, my father sat drinking and puffing, gray tendrils of smoke gathering in patchy clouds above his head.

When I discovered that Shel Silverstein had written "The Unicorn" back in 1962—the year of my birth—I knew I had found the subject of my next biography.

To a majority of the English-speaking world, the man they knew as Shel Silverstein was a children's book author with a special gift for conveying both the frustrations of childhood and the fantasy power trips of ten-year-olds in quirky verse that would have both parent and child laughing out loud. His rhymes were accompanied by squiggly-lined cartoons that always seemed to be drawn by a slightly trembling hand.

But few fans of *A Light in the Attic* and *The Giving Tree* realize that Shel was truly a Renaissance man. Indeed, he created twangy country-and-western tunes, experimental theater productions, drug- and sex-infused pop songs, and semiautobiographical travelogues for *Playboy,* sometimes all in the same week. Regardless of what he did, he never much cared about what other people thought of him, his work, or his unconventional, footloose lifestyle.

Shel was a very private person, which as a biographer, I found to be a real challenge at times and heartening at others. Some of his friends spoke intimately and openly about the times they spent with Shel. Others, knowing his penchant for privacy—he stopped giving media interviews in 1975, making only rare exceptions through the end of his life—declined to speak with me, perhaps thinking that they would incur Shel's great wrath when they met up with him again in the afterlife. He was ultrasensitive about being used for his celebrity, which he always maintained was a figment of other people's imaginations, though he was never beneath using his influence to further the career of a friend who was as much a purist about her art as he was about his.

When it came to his friends, he was fiercely loyal. And he rewarded fidelity in others by giving himself to them—his stories, his attention, his uniqueness. As more than one person told me, "When Shel talked to you, he made you feel like you were the only person in the world."

Then again, his voice just might have had something to do with it. When you hear Shel's voice for the first time, you immediately begin to wonder if the record label executives who rubber-stamped his albums in the 1950s and '60s were partially deaf. One friend compared his voice to that of a creaking door or a rusty gate. "He does sound a little like he'd been chain-smoking for six straight weeks, but he doesn't smoke at all," said his friend William Cole in the liner notes for Shel's 1962 album, *Inside Folk Songs*. "The closest approach I could make to his tonal quality is that it resembles the noise—the yelp—made by a dog whose tail has been stepped on."

"The thing that I like is something else," Shel once said.

His attention span ran from nil to nonexistent. If Ritalin existed when Shel was growing up in the 1930s and '40s, it's doubtful his body of work would have become as rich as it is.

He was determined to cram as much into each day as possible, and every new person he met, every encounter he had with a friend or a stranger, and everything he inadvertently heard come out of someone's mouth was a potential song, cartoon, play, or story. Upon witnessing something that struck him, he'd have to sit down wherever he was, whip out his pad and pen, and start work at that very second. And even if he didn't know what the material would eventually turn out to be, it was at least important enough for him to write down a few notes. If he ran out of paper, he'd start in on the napkins in a fancy restaurant, then move on to the tablecloth. When he had that completely covered, or if he was walking down the street, he'd start doodling on his hands, his shirtsleeves.

He created for the sheer joy of it and couldn't understand people who drew, wrote, painted, or sang for anything but their own pleasure. He did have his doubts and insecurities, like any artist, but his flow was rarely curtailed, and he lacked the internal censors that cause other creative types to sweat over each line, word, or note before sending it through the pen and onto paper, if indeed, they ever did. In fact, Shel was evocative of another artist who was likewise prolific in his own day: Wolfgang Amadeus Mozart. (In the 1984 movie *Amadeus,* Salieri, Mozart's nemesis, describes the wunderkind as composing with such ease and speed, it was as if he were taking dictation from God. More than a few times in conversation, I've described Shel's creative process in identical terms.)

While Shel frequented parties and crowded nightclubs and loved spending time with people, at least in his younger days, he was there primarily as an observer, not as a social butterfly. After all, he never knew what overheard snippet or facial expression might spawn an idea for a new cartoon, poem, or song. It wasn't unusual for him to create fully completed songs out of thin air, start to finish. Indeed, he was known to make up songs on the spot in the recording studio with the producer yelling "Roll tape!" while out of him flowed a perfect song and verse.

He was just as likely to move from one art form to another without blinking as he was to move from one place to another on a whim. "Comfortable shoes and the freedom to leave are the two most important things in life," he said. Shel was an inveterate world traveler, and he considered his success nothing more than a vehicle that bought him his freedom. Being able to pick up and leave on a whim—which he often did, even in the middle of a conversation—was what he valued most.

"Shel was well known for saying 'Take me to the airport,'" said Fred Koller, a songwriter who often collaborated with him.

Settling down in a place only meant adding another house where he could store his vast and cherished collection of old books, especially prewar children's books and short story collections. Shel had homes in New York, Sausalito, Chicago, Martha's Vineyard, and Key West, but they were usually small, eclectic, and historic in some way, and crammed cheek by jowl with his neighbors.

Not only was Shel's voice out of the ordinary, but so was his appearance. The locals in Key West eventually grew accustomed to seeing a rather fearsome-looking, bald, bearded man walking down the street dressed in ratty jeans, a long flowing pirate's shirt, and leather jacket that Goodwill would have rejected; tourists, however, would often be taken aback.

Instead of indulging in drugs or alcohol—it was a common misconception that Shel partook liberally of mind-altering substances, given the people he associated with throughout his life—he instead preferred rich, creamy desserts like pudding and junket, a sweetened custard made with rennet. In fact, the promise of a big bowl of banana pudding was enough to cause him to head for Nashville or New York when his wanderlust hit and he had to decide where to head next.

The promise of women inspired him, too—the more the better. Despite his unusual looks and voice, Shel had no problems attracting beautiful women on his terms, which usually amounted to spending only a night or two with them. He was very open with women, letting them know that that they shouldn't expect more than a passing thing from him.

"He was a babe magnet," said Melanie Smith Howard, the widow of country songwriter Harlan Howard. "Contrary to [what one might think by] looking at him, he had women just falling all over him."

To be sure, there were those women who tried to pin him down or get him to commit, but truthfully, they never lasted long. Those who accepted him usually ended up cultivating life-long, rewarding relationships with him.

Spend enough time with Shel's songs, books, plays, and cartoons, and you very quickly see that they all have one thing in common: There is no such thing as a happy ending. He thought that happy endings tend to alienate the child who reads them. "The child asks, 'Why don't I have this happiness thing you're telling me about?'" he explained. "He comes to think, when his joy stops, that he has failed and that it won't come back."

"He was like a kid on summer vacation," said songwriter and friend

Pat Dailey. "He'd get up in the morning and say, 'What am I going to do today?' He never lost the wonder of being a kid."

Shel was clearly uncomfortable indulging in the beliefs and customs that mainstream America holds dear. In his view, being tied down to a person, place, or thing would interfere with his one great love, the love that would never let him down: his creativity. And that is what he clung to his entire life, from growing up in the Depression to spending the last years of his life in the paradise that was Key West. The work always came first.

When I told people that I was writing Shel's biography, the universal reaction among those in their twenties and thirties was one of great joy and interest. To many, Shel was their hero—saviour even, in some cases. More than a few people told me they spent many late nights in childhood listening to a tape of *Where the Sidewalk Ends* or *A Light in the Attic* in order to drown out the sounds of fighting parents. I then turned them on to my favorite adult album by Shel, *The Great Conch Train Robbery*. The reaction again was unanimous approval. "I'm embarrassed to tell you how many times a week I listen to it," said one friend.

But that's not too surprising. Indeed, *Conch Train* is nothing more than an R-rated version of *A Light in the Attic* set to music, featuring the stories of adults rather than those of kids. Yet, the same motivation appears in both works: the whacked humor viewed through a gimlet eye, the refusal to look down on the reader or listener, and the knowledge that both kids and adults want to feel like they have some control over their lives and that, every so often, they can get away with something.

As for me, researching Shel's life was exhilarating, exhausting, and endearing, sometimes all at once. As I listened to stories from people who had known him, I regretted never meeting the man. One thing hasn't changed for me, despite submerging myself in Shel Silverstein's life and times while writing this book; I can still listen to "The Unicorn" five times in a row without getting even close to sick of it.

A Boy
Named
Shel

1. A Boy Named Shel

When he was five years old, Shel Silverstein taught himself to draw by tracing over the comic strips in the newspaper. His favorite was *Li'l Abner* by Al Capp.

He placed a sheet of paper over the strip and traced over the faces, the hands, the buildings, the scenery, everything. "The first thing I did was copy Al Capp," he said. "He really influenced me. It was the most wondrous thing for me. Al Capp knew how to draw people, shapes, bodies, hands. He knew how to draw well, so I learned how to draw well."

He also began to think up stories to go with the cartoons. "I didn't have a lot of friends," said Shel. "I just walked around a lot and made up stories in my head. Then I'd go home and write them down. That's how I got started."

Shel also loved books. Because he was lonely, he turned to books for companionship. "One of the things that made me happy was to go to old bookstores and look through the books," he said. "I would hold them, smell them, and even hug them. They were my friends."

But he didn't have the money to buy the books he wanted. So he vowed that when he got older and had money, he'd spend it on books. He dreamed of a day when he would have so many books on his shelves that he couldn't read all of them in a year if that was the only thing he did.

Drawing cartoons and reading books gave him something nothing else could: They gave him comfort.

"He was a lonely kid," said songwriter Drew Reid, an old friend. "He was always aware that he was different from the other kids around him. Let's face it, musicians, artists—anybody who's creative—we're all kind of wacky because we don't look at stuff the way other people do. And Shel always knew that."

On March 3, 1891, twenty-nine-year-old Sigmund Balkany, a laborer from Bohemia, arrived at the port of New York aboard the *Aller* passenger ship along with thousands of other European immigrants who wanted a better life in America. He spent a few years in New York before moving to Chicago.

Rae Goldberg was born in Hungary in March of 1876 and immigrated to the United States at the age of twelve. She met Sigmund Balkany in Chicago, and they married in 1897 or 1898. Helen, their first child, was born on January 5,1899.

In 1900, Sigmund found work at a tannery, and the family of three rented a house at 911 Milwaukee Avenue near Wicker Park, in a section of Chicago known as West Town. Eastern European Jewish immigrants flocked to the neighborhood, known as a community rich with political radicalism. However, the Milwaukee Avenue corridor also had its share of gangs and violence, which author Nelson Algren described in his 1949 book, *The Man with the Golden Arm,* the story of a heroin addict released from jail who returns to his old neighborhood and fights to keep from succumbing to the drug again. "Louie was the one junkie in ten thousand who'd kicked it and kicked it for keeps," wrote Algren. "He'd taken the sweat cure in a little Milwaukee Avenue hotel room, cutting himself down, as he put it, 'from monkey to zero.' "

By 1910, the growing Balkany family had moved less than a mile west to 2235 West Potomac Avenue, still in West Town but closer to Humboldt Park and in a more residential area. It was a definite step up for the family, since the neighborhood had newer and more spacious housing stock and apartments.

Sigmund had left the tannery and opened a small grocery store, where Rae worked alongside him. Their family had expanded with two more daughters: five-year-old Esther, and Martha, who was three.

In 1916, seventeen-year-old Helen began clerking for her father at his grocery store located at 2659 Evergreen Avenue, a relatively new building built in 1912 about a mile from their Potomac Avenue home. That move didn't last long, for Sigmund consolidated his family and grocery store and moved them both to 1458 North Washtenaw Avenue the following year, a few blocks away from the previous store. The two-story building was built in 1914 and had five apartments on the second floor and the store at street level. By 1923, Helen was in charge of running the grocery store, and she enjoyed the autonomy it gave her. At the age of twenty-four, an old maid by the standards of the day, she was in no hurry to get married.

On December 23, 1924, everything changed when her father, Sigmund Balkany, died.

Nathan Silverstein was born on July 1, 1890, in either Russia or Poland, the second of five children born to Abraham and Fannie Silverstein. Harry was born a year earlier, and Julius and Jack were born in 1899; a sister, Frieda, followed in 1902.

The Silverstein family's journey to America took the form of a chain migration, where one child at a time traveled to the United States—typically, the sons went first—and once he earned enough funds to send back to the old country, another could afford to come over. Harry arrived in the United States in 1906, and Jack immigrated in 1911. Julius followed in 1913, and Nathan was the last son to immigrate, in 1915. The family initially settled in the Bronx before heading west to Chicago.

It was common for brand-new immigrants to enter the military as World War I was raging. Both Julius and Nathan signed up for the military in

1917 and were discharged in April 1918. However, the war interrupted the migration of the family, and Fannie and Frieda didn't arrive in the United States until 1920.

By 1923, Jack and Nathan had started a bakery known as Silverstein Brothers and lived with their older brother Harry at 2601 Walton Street. Now established in their own business, they set out to find wives.

Nathan found his future wife living about a mile away.

There was little time to lose. When Nathan's engagement to Helen Balkany was announced in the *Chicago Tribune* on June 6, 1926, he was thirty-six and Helen was twenty-seven; the couple was unusually advanced in years during an era where getting married at the age of nineteen meant you were over the hill. They were wed five months later on Halloween 1926, by Rabbi Julien Gusfield at the Hotel Windermere East in Hyde Park. The choice of wedding venue was unusual for a couple from the northwest side of Chicago. The Windermere, hotel residence of Pulitzer Prize–winning author Edna Ferber among others, was a pretty swanky location for a 1926 wedding.

They may have picked it because the brothers had grand ambitions for their business amidst the heady glamour and free-flowing money of the 1920s. They changed the name of their bakery from Silverstein Brothers to the Service Cake Company and began to plan for the construction of a 105,000-square-foot, one-story brick building at 834–38 North Western Avenue, which would be completed in 1930.

After they were wed, the new Mr. and Mrs. Nathan Silverstein moved in with Helen's mother, her sisters, and a new brother-in-law at 1458 North Washtenaw. The widowed Rae Balkany was no longer running the grocery store, and instead, husband and wife Isadore and Eva Hershberg operated the store and lived with their family in one of the apartments on the second floor.

Sheldon Allan Silverstein, Nathan and Helen's first child, was born on September 25, 1930. From the time he was an infant, Shel was surrounded by people and nonstop noise, from the families living in the other apartments to the chaos on the street below outside the store to people constantly clomping up and down the stairs and knocking on the Silversteins' door to see if the young family needed anything.

Helen was thirty-one years old and Nathan had just turned forty when Shel was born, and his parents' mature years—especially his father's—profoundly influenced Shel's childhood. The boy had to walk on eggshells around the house and tamp down the typical manic energy of a naturally curious young child whenever his father was home. He had a surplus of energy, and even as a kid he didn't need much sleep, which would be true all his life.

The Silverstein brothers had the misfortune to open their new bakery during the first full year of the Great Depression, and the financial stress made Nathan tense and short-tempered during the few hours he spent at home each day.

With money so tight at the onset of the Depression, most days the Silverstein family ate whatever Nathan could bring home from the bakery, supplemented by Helen and Rae's creativity. (Since they were no longer running the grocery store downstairs, they couldn't scrounge off the shelves when things got tight anymore.) Wasting food was just about the biggest sin in the world. Nathan provided his family with day-old bread and pastries from the bakery, but of course, being a kid, Shel wanted what he couldn't have: the rare treats.

Shel's favorite food growing up was any creamy type of dessert, especially pudding and the custard known as junket. He was raised in a household filled with other people, where neighbors showed up unannounced for dinner because they had no food, and portion control was the rule.

"I never had enough junket," he said. "When I was a kid, my mother used to make junket and put it into little glass dishes and put them in the refrigerator, and maybe there were six little glasses and I would get to eat one or two of them, but that was never really enough, and in my whole life I have never really had enough junket."

Shel also wanted something more than the wax lips and bubble gum that were all most kids could afford to buy during the Depression at a penny apiece.

"When I was a kid and I had a box of that lousy stinking wax candy, I really wished I had enough money for a Hershey bar or a Mars bar instead," he said. "That would really knock me out because I wanted that nickel candy, not the penny candy and baseball cards with bubble gum."

Privacy and quiet grew even more scarce after Shel's sister, Peggy, was born in 1934. It couldn't have been easy for Nathan, having another mouth to feed during the depths of the Depression. But his son began to retreat more in order to forget about the tension and strife that surrounded him. He buried himself in books, especially fantasy books, comic books, and Little Big Books that he borrowed from the library. Arthur Rackham, a Victorian British fantasy children's book illustrator whose paintings appear in the book *The Romance of King Arthur and His Knights of the Round Table,* was a particular favorite, and Shel also loved stories about cowboys and Indians and others that were set during the Civil War.

Young Shel also listened to the radio, particularly the country-and-western stations. His favorite artist was Ernest Tubb, a pioneer of country music who was a regular on the *Grand Ole Opry* radio show in the 1940s. Tubb's first big hit, "Walkin' the Floor over You," came out in 1941.

"Shel once told me that when he bought his first Ernest Tubb record, he wore it out playing it over and over again," said songwriter Fred Koller.

Shel became a student at Charles R. Darwin Elementary School in 1935 around the same time Nathan decided it was time to move his family out of his mother-in-law's house and into a place of their own. Unlike many businesses that had been driven into bankruptcy by the Depression, the Service Cake Company survived the worst of it, so Nathan moved his family to an apartment building at 2853 West Palmer Street.

Once Shel entered school, in addition to drawing constantly at home, he was bored with the subjects and started doodling in class. As much as he could, anyway, without getting rapped on the knuckles with a ruler or worse.

Drawing became his escape: It helped block out the constant noise from the tenants, but most important, he discovered that it also stopped the voice in his head. That voice was his father's, who totally disapproved of Shel's artistic efforts. Nathan would regularly berate Shel, calling his drawings and cartoons garbage. Nathan would say that he didn't puke his guts out in steerage to make it over here and then serve for a year in the war only to have his son throw his life away by drawing cartoons and day-dreaming.

His father and mother were constantly arguing, and most of the time it was about Shel. Drawing also helped Shel to ignore his parents' fighting.

"His mother and father warred continually," said Judy Henske, a folksinger who met Shel in the late 1950s. "His mother told him he could do anything he wanted while his father expected him to join the family business."

As long as he was drawing cartoons, reading books, or listening to the radio, Shel was able to keep the doubts and insecurity at bay. The moment he stopped, everything came rushing back, the negativity and noise, louder than before.

It was all a matter of control. While he couldn't control the world that existed away from his pencils and sketchpads—including World War II, which began to ratchet up the angst in his household even more—he could control the world in his imagination. And so he began to retreat to that world more often, away from the noise and constant conflict.

Once he had mastered copying Al Capp cartoons, studying them from every angle, Shel began to study the work of Virgil Partch, who went by the name of VIP, an avant-garde cartoonist popular from the 1940s through the 1960s. Partch's work resembles Hanna-Barbera characters like the Jetsons and the Flintstones, except he was drawing in that style at least two decades earlier. Partch drew for Walt Disney Studios for four years during the Depression, where his style was most clearly shown in the Donald Duck cartoon *Duck Pimples*. He came to disdain the three-fingered style common to Mickey Mouse and other symbols of the Disney empire. "I draw a stock hand when it is doing something, such as pointing, but when the hand is hanging by some guy's side, those old fingers go in by the dozens," he once said. Shel would later follow VIP's example in always striving to draw a five-fingered hand.

Shel was in good company in studying the top cartoonists of the day, because the vast majority of them were Jewish: VIP, Stan Lee, and Shel's hero, Al Capp. Plus, Max Gaines had founded DC Comics, and such top comic superheroes as Superman, Batman and Robin, and Captain Marvel were created and drawn by Jewish cartoonists. Although Shel knew he only wanted to be a cartoonist and not pursue any of the other graphic arts disciplines, other Jews at the time didn't have a chance to break into the generally gentile fields of advertising or the fine arts, and newspaper comic strips were all but closed to them. But because comic books were a brand-new field—and most of the publishers were Jewish—they were the only viable avenue into the field for a kid who wanted to draw—and who happened to be Jewish.

In addition to cartooning, Shel also loved baseball, specifically the Chicago White Sox. Like millions of other boys his age, Shel dreamed of playing third base for his beloved team, but he was an unathletic, gawky kid. The closest he would get to his dream was as a vendor at the baseball games, where he roamed the aisles of the bleachers to hawk peanuts and hot dogs to fans.

Later on, he would consider his lack of physical agility a blessing in disguise. "If I had my choice, I would have been a great third baseman with three girls on my arm," said Shel. "By the time I could get the girls, I already knew how to write poems and draw pictures. Thank God I was able to develop these things, which I could keep, before I got the goodies that were my first choice."

Shel was not a particularly good student. His classes bored him and his mind wandered as a result, making up stories in the middle of class that were vastly more entertaining than what was going on in the lesson. He also was a poor speller; today, he might be diagnosed as dyslexic, but the truth was that Shel's mind was operating at such a pace that he couldn't write quickly enough to get everything down on paper. In fact, in later years, editors and art directors at *Playboy* and his book publishers would bitterly complain about Shel's surplus of misspelled words. When he applied for a Social Security card at the age of fifteen, he actually misspelled his middle name, crossing it out before writing it down correctly.

When World War II broke out in 1939, the curriculum at public schools across the country was retooled toward the war. Teaching basic military skills was the rule when Shel entered Theodore Roosevelt High School in September of 1944. The high school was one of the largest in the nation, covering two city blocks, and was one of the best equipped as well. Its capacity was just over four thousand students and contained ninety classrooms and a variety of sewing rooms, music rooms, auto shops, three woodworking shops, science laboratories, gymnasiums, swimming pools, auditoriums, and a cafeteria that could seat one thousand.

One of the programs at Roosevelt was the Reserve Officers' Training Corps (ROTC). Shel signed up for that program when he turned fourteen. During his tenure, he received several honors, including an Officer Eagle Medal and a medal of General Excellence. Despite his ROTC accomplishments, others at Roosevelt High remembered Shel as a combative and uncooperative student.

Art Paul, *Playboy*'s first art director, said he later heard some gossip about Shel's high school days. "Apparently, a lot of people thought he would never succeed in life, because he didn't get along too well with the other students," said Paul. "They said he was such a character and had such an unusual outlook on life that they were surprised that the Shel Silverstein whose work was all over *Playboy* was the same Shel Silverstein they went to school with. I could see where he'd have trouble because his mind was very active, and creatively so. And he said things like he felt them. I think that he had a problem being normal."

Indeed, Shel hated conformity. "When I was a young kid, about once a year we had to buy some new clothes and I'd pick out a new coat or suit," he said. "Someone would always ask if I was sure this is what they're wearing this year. Well, who is this 'they' and what difference does it make what they're wearing? I'll wear what I want to wear!"

Of course, conformity was what his father wanted, to be safe. After a life filled with strife and uncertainty and the difficulty of adjusting to a new country, all Nathan wanted was to work hard and come home to a hot meal and a roof over his head at the end of the day. Shel wanted the opposite. He wanted excitement and adventure, and early on he made a promise to himself that he would never get married, if his parents' stormy relationship was what marriage meant. He kept that childhood vow, remaining single for his entire life.

Above all, Shel wanted nothing more than to draw, to earn his living from it, not to work sixteen hours a day in a hot bakery ordering other people around in a job he hated. A big reason for the discord between Nathan and Helen was because she supported her son in whatever he wanted to do while her husband thought Shel should work in the family business, on weekends at first and then later full-time.

Once the war ended, Shel's father turned up the heat. "I'm grateful I have a job," Nathan would berate Shel. "I'm grateful I'm even alive. If I didn't get out, you wouldn't even *be* here, and yet all you do is daydream all day and scribble cartoons that don't make sense." Nathan held out high hopes that Shel would join the family business after graduating from high school or college. Even though Nathan belonged to a generation that wanted their children to do better than themselves— "Why do you think I came over? It wasn't for me, it was for my kids" was a common defense—he also came from the old country, where sons didn't dare question the issue of joining the family business. Shel, of course, did nothing *but* question those expectations.

Nathan was only looking for the business to continue. After all, he was fifty-eight years old when Shel graduated from high school, and it was important that his son take his place in the family business.

Chris Gantry, a Nashville musician and songwriter who would later collaborate with Shel on a number of songs, grew up in a family similar to Shel's. "My father was the same way," he said. "He wanted all his kids to be involved in the family business. He worked sixteen hours a day at his business, and to do anything else was alien to him. I can't tell you how many times I heard him say, when I was a kid, 'Goddammit, what do you care about banjos and ukeleles?'" Shel's father didn't think that writing songs and drawing cartoons were legitimate things to do in life.

Shel graduated from Roosevelt High School in June 1948, and he went on to college in the fall. In interviews, Shel said that he attended the University of Illinois at Navy Pier—now known as the University of Illinois at Chicago—and that he was kicked out. While no records show that he was a student at Navy Pier campus, they do indicate that he attended the University of Illinois at Urbana-Champaign from September 1948 through June 1949, successfully completing his freshman year.

Why did he fib about the college he attended, even though both schools are part of the same university system? The Urbana-Champaign school was and still is considered the more prestigious of the two, while the Navy Pier campus was strictly a commuter school for working-class students and for veterans attending on the GI Bill.

Nathan may have insisted that he attend the Urbana-Champaign campus since it was a definite step up classwise from Navy Pier. It could also have been due to a Jewish quota at the university. Most state universities during this period had restrictive policies about Jewish admissions; the quota at the Navy Pier campus might have been filled while the Urbana-Champaign campus had some openings.

The year he spent at Urbana-Champaign was undoubtedly Shel's first exposure to a gentile hierarchy based on money, father's occupation, and family connections, and he must have been profoundly uncomfortable there, a real fish out of water among the privileged class. Also, Urbana-Champaign was a very fraternity-oriented campus and Jews were excluded from mainstream fraternities.

It was very early on, then, that Shel began to create a mythology and false history in rejecting the intellectual and "snobby" Urbana-Champaign and creating a false association with the student body at Navy Pier. He never wished to be mistaken for the kind of Jew who wanted to be upwardly mobile, which meant shoehorning himself into the gentile world.

"The first semester they put me on probation," he said. "The second semester they threw me out." This statement only augments the mythology of Shel as a combative student and a free spirit. After finishing his freshman year, he enrolled in the Chicago Academy of Fine Arts, known today as the Art Institute of Chicago, one of a handful of schools in the United States that taught cartooning.

But even there, he didn't fit in. He worked differently from other students, whether he was writing or drawing. While other students would first scratch out a few ideas, scribbling, drafting, crossing out, erasing, and finally crumpling the paper in frustration and tossing it into the wastebasket, Shel's ideas always came out fully developed. He'd turn the idea over in his mind before committing it to paper. And then, when it finally came out, it was done. He knew so in his heart.

But his teachers didn't agree. They were there to provide guidance, and Shel steadfastly refused their help. After a year, he left.

His next stop was Roosevelt University. He'd stay for almost three years at Roosevelt, which he credited to Robert Cosbey, an English teacher who saw the talent beneath Shel's defiance and began to work with him to develop it. As a result, Shel began to blossom.

"Bob Cosbey was the most important influence on my writing, and on many other people's writing," said Shel. "He was the only good thing I got out of Roosevelt University."

"We went to Roosevelt because we could afford it," said Jay Lynch, a cartoonist who would later work with Shel at *Playboy*. At the time, Roosevelt—which was founded by Eleanor Roosevelt—cost only six hundred dollars a year, and it was right in the city, which was convenient for Shel, who was still living at home. "It was a very socialist school, where most of the students were minorities living in the inner city. But nobody ever graduated from Roosevelt," said Lynch.

Shel worked at the school newspaper, *The Roosevelt Torch*. He helped to lay out the paper and wrote a number of one-panel cartoons that generally poked fun at campus life. One cartoon showed a couple of men walking out of a classroom, and one of them is dressed in a bathrobe, pajamas, and slippers. The caption: "I always fall asleep during that guy's lectures." Another cartoon is set in a lecture hall, a professor standing at the podium with his arm around Groucho Marx. "And here, to speak on the philosophy of Marx, we have . . . ," reads the caption.

Shel also wrote a column called "The Garbage Can." In the February 16, 1951, issue, he wrote a piece called "Recipe for Beating the Draft," in which he instructed readers to gather a sharpened pencil, a garbage pail, and one "stout heart." Then he got down to business:

"Insert the pencil into your ear and push until you hear your eardrum go 'Pop!!'"

In the same column, he wrote, "Attention Freshmen! What are you doing here? The tuition at Wright [College] is only ten dollars a semester."

The staff was supposed to get paid, but the newspaper typically lacked the money to spring for much beyond the printing bills. Instead, Shel and other staffers were compensated in typewriters.

Despite Cosbey's influence and encouragement, Shel didn't graduate from Roosevelt, because Uncle Sam came calling. But even if he hadn't gotten drafted into the army, he would have left anyway. "My grades weren't that good, but I'd had too much college anyway," he said. "I should have been out working and living life. Imagine: four years you could have spent traveling around Europe meeting people, reading all you wanted to anyway, and instead I wasted it at Roosevelt. I didn't get laid much and I didn't learn much. Those are the two worst things that can happen to a guy."

Shel received his draft notice in September 1953. He spent a few days in Fort Dix, New Jersey, heading next to Fort Riley in Kansas for basic training. Next he went to Fort Belvoir in Virginia before being sent overseas.

Bob Sweeney, who would turn out to be a lifelong friend, met Shel when they were traveling to Yokohama, Japan, on a troopship right after basic training. They were both working on the ship's newspaper and started churning out cartoons the first day on board, even though Shel was battling a nasty bout of seasickness.

Once he arrived in Tokyo, Shel was assigned to the *Pacific Stars and Stripes* to paste up stories and photo features for the paper. When his work was done—which he performed as quickly as possible—he turned his attention to drawing cartoons using the material that was right in front of him: the military. Shel roamed the streets of Shinbashi, a neighborhood that GIs frequented that once served as the end of the line of Japan's first railroad. He spent hours each day wandering the streets taking note of the activities of his fellow soldiers, which would invariably end up in one of his cartoons.

He initially did it for his own amusement, though within a few weeks, the paper began to print his work. After spending six months juggling newspaper paste-up with cartooning, he convinced his editors to take him off layout duties and allow him to wander the Far East and send back reports in the form of one-panel cartoons. They agreed.

Even with his freedom, Shel had a hard time dealing with the restraints of army protocol. Corky Alexander, the late editor of the English language *Tokyo Weekender,* first met Shel at *Stars and Stripes.* "He was an Army corporal and was perhaps the worst soldier in the history of armed might, down through the ages," he said.

"On base or off base, today's G.I. isn't a very important guy," said Shel. "Civilians don't seem to like soldiers anymore. There's no war now, no casualties, no rationing, and no immediate danger. With no war to fight, [soldiers] dragged through two years, cleaning the grease traps, bugging out of detail, and forgetting their general orders."

MPs used to specifically look for Shel to catch him committing offenses that usually involved his uniform. One day, a couple of MPs stopped him and checked him out from head to toe, but couldn't find anything out of place.

Then one told Shel to lift the cuffs of his pants. He did, and was cited for wearing argyle socks.

Of course, he turned it into a cartoon.

"First he thought of an object, say, his first sergeant," said Bob Sweeney. "He'd concentrate until he would come up with twenty or thirty gags on the one subject. Out of it came situations peopled by his long-nosed characters, his little men, his giants, the animals, and the strange creatures for which he has a special affection."

The cartoons were mostly G-rated, with none of the raciness and double entendres that would later characterize his efforts at *Playboy*. For instance, one cartoon shows an inductee with tattoos of different women all over his chest and arms being asked by an officer, "Do you like girls?" Another shows an officer sitting in an easy chair at home while his wife holds his baby out to him. The caption: "I want to see that safety pin SHINE!"

One of his more notorious cartoons came out one April Fool's Day, where Shel drew a cartoon of a soldier in a mess line with a slab of toast on his plate—what GIs called a "shingle"—as a cook spooned something dark over the toast. Known as chipped beef on toast, a military staple, soldiers and officers alike referred to it as "shit on a shingle." The caption: "Today it REALLY is."

When the paper received complaints about the cartoon, Shel's editor asked what it meant.

"Powdered milk, powdered eggs," Shel replied. "Today it's the real thing. April Fool. Get it?"

His favorite overall targets were the officers. "They even made zebras off limits to me because they had stripes," he said.

While his complaints about the army were legion, Shel always acknowledged the debt and gratitude he had toward the military, because the organization gave him the chance to live life as a full-time cartoonist.

"The army was good to me," he said, "and except for my first and last months, I was given almost complete freedom to say what I had to say. There was a lot about the military that I thought was pretty silly, but these cartoons weren't meant to take a poke at anybody or anything. They were meant to make people laugh."

Even though he stayed in the army for only two years, the amount of work he produced for *Pacific Stars and Stripes* was prodigious, as he cranked out three cartoons a week. In 1955, *Stars and Stripes* published *Take Ten,* a book collection of his cartoons that was sold through military PXs and commissaries. It was his first book.

Shel's humor had struck such a nerve, and soldiers based in the Pacific shared his cartoons with their families and other civilians to show them what life in the military was really like, that a larger audience for his work was a natural consequence. In 1956, Ballantine Books published a thirty-five-cent mass-market paperback edition of *Take Ten* called *Grab Your Socks.*

But working with Shel wasn't easy. When Shel visited the paper's Seoul bureau, Bob Brown, another *Stars and Stripes* colleague, said, "He stays up all night chewing pencils, drawing cartoons and writing ideas on little scraps of paper he never finds again. In the first twenty minutes he was here he had our little office more cluttered than the convention hall in his native Chicago."

The army would serve as a formidable influence on Shel's work patterns, for it was in the military that he began the lifelong habit of having more than one place to work and live. While the other soldiers were content with staying in the barracks, Shel rented a small room, known as an *uchi,* a five-minute walk from the newspaper's offices. He'd stay up at night drawing, writing gag lines and captions, letting the experiences of the day flow through him and onto the paper, then crash for a few hours before getting up to go to the newspaper offices for the day.

It was also in the army that he developed his taste for travel and the desire to get on a plane at the drop of a hat. As his cartoons became more popular with soldiers stationed in Japan and Korea, his editors gave him more leeway on content. And so, just like a reporter or correspondent at the paper, Shel began to travel on assignment to talk to soldiers and use their experiences in his cartoons for the paper.

"He knows the people he draws," said Brown. "He's lived through the same experiences and heard the same lines. In Korea, he spent time in the outposts and the squad tents with the fellows he wanted most to please."

And it was in Japan that he first began to wear loose-fitting clothing. He discovered a loose-fitting caftan known as a *yukata* that he would always wear during his long nightly sessions or whenever he didn't have to be in uniform. A *yukata* was an informal kind of kimono for summer, made of cotton instead of the silk of more formal kimonos.

He also had his first taste of what developed into a lifelong passion for sushi. He loved sushi, and when he came back to the States one of his major complaints was that he couldn't find decent sushi, while in Japan he could eat it three times a day, and often did.

He was discharged from the army in the fall of 1955, after fulfilling his two-year commitment. Shel returned to Chicago, and he moved back in with his parents, planning to make it a very short stay. He also began to grow his hair and his beard.

Almost immediately he suffered culture shock. In a few short weeks, he had gone from a globe-trotting cartoonist whose work and humor had turned him into a virtual celebrity among his fellow soldiers to a no-good worthless son who was wasting his life. Nathan was never able to recognize his son's unconventional military accomplishments, because he still believed that Shel's rightful place was at the bakery, which had failed in the interim, something that Nathan perhaps blamed on his son.

So Shel hit the streets, bringing his portfolio of cartoons from *Pacific Stars and Stripes* to show to art directors at magazines in Chicago. He'd had a taste of what it was like to work full-time doing something he loved, and he was determined to continue on that path.

2. *Wild Life*

The highs of 1955 quickly turned into lows the following year, and things were looking pretty grim for Shel. As much as he hated the regimentation and pomposity of the officers in the army, at least while he was enlisted, he was able to travel, meet women, and do what he loved most in the world: draw cartoons.

He continued to show his portfolio to magazines around Chicago and was also submitting cartoons to magazines in New York on a speculative basis, but wasn't having any luck.

Meanwhile, his father was losing patience with him, and as a result, Shel was having a terrible time at home. His father insisted that Shel forget about cartooning and get a real job. While he wasn't haranguing his son to work at the family business anymore, he was just as adamant that Shel forget about cartooning. Nathan thought he was a failure because he hadn't graduateed from college, and if he wasn't going to buckle down and get a regular job, his only son should have stayed in the army, and done something real, rather than just drawing a bunch of worthless cartoons. Shel, however, dug in his heels and resolved to follow his own path.

He'd leave the house early in the morning to wander around the city and not return until late at night, partly to escape his father's wrath but also because he thought he'd be able to come up with a solution to his predicament if he just kept moving. After all, keeping his pen moving worked for him. He'd walk the streets, watch people rushing by with things to do and places to go, and putter around the old bookstores. When he saw or thought of something that struck him, he'd stop wherever he was, take out his pen, open his sketchpad to a fresh sheet of paper, and start to draw.

His altercations with his father made for some very stormy and tense times at the dinner table. Once spring arrived, Shel turned to his old job as a hot dog vendor in Comiskey Park just to be able to tell his father he had a job.

"In Chicago, if you're an artist or a painter your family has no respect for you," he said. "In Chicago, I feel guilty if I don't wake up every morning at nine and carry a lunch bucket. The fact that I'm working until five in the morning doesn't have anything to do with it, if you don't go to work you are a bum in this city and that's all there is to it."

Between his father's antagonism and Shel's inability to land at least a couple of decent freelance assignments—especially after his almost two years of admiration from his *Stars and Stripes* gig—Shel had turned into an angry young man, lashing out at anyone who got in his way or, worse, keeping it inside.

"When I was younger, I wasn't making it and I was mad at everybody who was," he said later. Even though Shel had resolved to carve out a living as a cartoonist and to prove his father wrong, he was admittedly on shaky ground.

He was making the rounds of magazines in Chicago yet again, when one afternoon Shel wandered into the offices of a new magazine for men. The first issue of *Playboy* was published in December 1953, but no date appeared on the cover, since its founder, Hugh Hefner, didn't know if he'd sell enough copies to warrant publishing a second. Hef, as he would come to be known, had put together the first couple of issues on his kitchen table, and the response to the first issue was so positive that he immediately went out and rented office space nearby and added staff.

All this happened when Shel was overseas, so if he had heard of the groundbreaking new magazine while he was traveling around Asia, it's likely he thought nothing of it.

Like Shel, Hugh Hefner was also born in Chicago, though he was four years older than the cartoonist. One of his first jobs was as a copywriter at *Esquire* magazine, which he quit after he didn't get a promised five-dollar raise. He had studied the then-cutting-edge research on human sexuality conducted at the time by the Kinsey Institute, and decided to start his own magazine for men.

Arthur Paul was the art director at *Playboy,* and when Shel first dropped by the office to show his portfolio, Paul was impressed. Hef had included some of his own cartoons in the first issue, and since Hef was the cartoon editor, Paul led Shel into his inner sanctum. "Hef was as taken with him as I was," said Paul, "but it almost seemed like Shel was feeling his way around. I don't think he had a tremendous amount of experience freelancing."

Indeed, Shel seemed insecure about his work and how it would play in the marketplace. "From some of our conversations [I could tell] he didn't think he was a very good artist," said Paul. "A couple of times, he told me that he couldn't draw, but it's not unusual for artists to feel that way at times. His line was very sure and I didn't see any of that insecurity in his work."

Shel and Hef immediately clicked and discovered they had a lot in common. They had both served in the army—Hef enlisted in February 1944 and was discharged after two years—and he was also a cartoonist, teaching himself the ropes when he was a kid. And like Shel, Hef also drew cartoons for a couple of military newspapers.

Shel left some of his work for Hef to review, and if he didn't hear back from the magazine within a few weeks, he was to return to the office to pick them up, the custom at that time.

A month went by with no response. Shel assumed that the relatively new magazine had gone out of business. Even though he had hit it off with Hef, Shel did have his doubts about the man who called himself the publisher and dressed in silk pajamas at the office. "I really thought, at the time, that I was meeting a guy who [had] just woken up, which is a legitimate concern," said Shel. At that point, his main priority was getting his work back. He dropped by the magazine, expecting the office to be cleared out and empty, but thought he could find out where they had gone so he could get his cartoons back.

To his surprise, the offices were still occupied. Hef met with Shel, but instead of handing him back his work, he told Shel he was buying several cartoons and would write out a check on the spot.

Shel was ecstatic. He grabbed the check, shook Hef's hand, and then ran out to find a bank to cash the check because he wasn't totally sure it wouldn't bounce. After all, he'd dropped off—and picked up—work from other magazines, and showed his portfolio to other art directors, and none of them looked like they were run the way this outfit was.

"I thought it wasn't just a coincidence that he happened to give me the check at five minutes to five on a Friday," said Shel. "Of course not only will the check not be good, but when I get back, he won't be there."

Shel found the bank, cashed the check, and that night he went home to his parents' house. At dinnertime, when his father started his usual diatribe about how Shel should get a normal job and how he should stop scribbling those worthless drawings, Shel had had enough. He reached into his pocket, pulled out the money, and threw it as hard as he could on the table in front of his father.

He then told his parents that he was going to be a professional cartoonist and that he was moving out. He left that night.

For years afterward, Shel and his father were at an impasse and rarely spoke. His relationship with his mother was a different story. They kept in touch, and she always supported him in his quest to become a cartoonist.

Hefner's acquisition of Shel's cartoons and his desire to publish more of the artist's work gave Shel the boost he needed not only to move out of his parents' house, but also to strike out for New York, where he knew the action really was. Chicago was fine, but it was almost too familiar. He couldn't reinvent himself in his own backyard. And besides, New York wasn't known—either fondly or pejoratively—as the Second City. Hef's commitments to him for future issues of the magazine provided Shel with some security to strike out on his own. And if *Playboy* went under after all, at least he would be in the center of the publishing industry.

After he stormed out of his parents' house, Shel crashed with friends in Chicago for a while, and then began what would become a lifelong habit of shuttling between different homes. He used his clips from *Playboy*—which was vastly more successful than he had originally assumed—as his entrée at other magazines. He began to spend time in New York, again initially crashing with friends he had known from Chicago as well as with old army buddies, and commenced the life he knew he was destined to live. After first answering to his parents and then to Uncle Sam, one thing was clear: From now on, Shel would answer to no one. His art would always come first.

Shel's old army buddy Bob Sweeney had recently married and moved into a small studio apartment on East Eightieth Street, and so he invited Shel to stay with them until he could get settled.

"My father knew exactly what [Shel] wanted to do—work full-time at a magazine—but Shel didn't have a job waiting for him," said Sarah Sweeney McCann, Bob Sweeney's daughter. "It was literally like Dad's kid brother lives with him until he finds a job." During those times, Mc-Cann said Shel was constantly submitting new cartoons to *Playboy* and to other magazines in New York as well.

The two army buddies who grew up during the Depression assumed that housework was women's work. "Uncle Shelly and my dad were both pretty big slobs," said McCann. "My poor mother had apparently had enough, and one night, Dad and Uncle Shel came home late to find a note on the door, stuck there with a carving knife, that said clean this place up, or else. They cleaned it and Uncle Shelly drew a picture of a person with a really long face, and a tiny little body that said 'Joanie, why the long face?' My mother framed it and we grew up with it in the house."

Shel lived with the Sweeneys until the end of the year, and then he looked for his own apartment. The tony Upper East Side didn't feel right to him, so he looked for a place downtown in Greenwich Village, where he was beginning to spend a lot of time, hovering around the edges of the beatnik and folk community.

His first *Playboy* cartoons appeared in the August 1956 issue in the form of a cartoon booklet. The characters largely resembled those he drew for *Stars and Stripes,* with the same missile-shaped bodies and big noses, and the humor was pretty tame. One cartoon shows a man at a hot dog stand, where a sign next to the buns says "Dine and Dance." The caption has the vendor saying, "Well, you *can* if you *want* to." Another shows a mother talking with her son, who's in jail. Through the mesh screen, she says, "If only you'd listened to your old mother. How I begged you, have the getaway car overhauled . . . But no."

Hef wanted more of his work, and Shel was happy to oblige. In addition to submitting more cartoons, which he delivered in droves, Shel wanted to travel again. Going back and forth between two cities was great, but it wasn't enough. He was itching to go overseas again, so he suggested what turned into an ongoing travel series, some with photographs, others with cartoons, executed in the same irreverent style as his cartoons, to give readers a taste of what they might encounter if they were to follow in Shel's footsteps, at least when it came to traveling to foreign countries.

Hef gave his blessing, and the first travelogue, "Return to Tokyo," appeared in the February 1957 issue, the first travel feature in the magazine. While he was in Japan, he seriously started to consider living there on a permanent basis. But he was restless, and his itchy feet pointed him in the direction of Europe. Eleven more travelogues appeared over the next three years, and only a couple of his one-panel stand-alone cartoons

were published in *Playboy* during that time. He and freelance photographer Larry Moyer would pick a destination and set off to bring back a
combination cartoon–photo essay about a place as it could be seen only
through the eyes of Shel. He made the series his focus for the magazine
during that time, traveling to places as diverse as Switzerland, Paris,
Moscow, Italy, and Africa. Hef began to refer to Shel as the magazine's
"house humorist."

Hef suggested that Shel include himself in the panels and scenes, a
suggestion that Shel initially did not agree with, believing it was too vain
but also mostly because he didn't think he had the talent to pull it off. "It
was the utmost expression of confidence, more than I had in myself," said
Shel. However, he gave it a try, both readers and Hef loved it, and the
travelogues became the second most popular part of the magazine based
on reader response, after the centerfold, of course.

Shel worked in a way that was foreign to other cartoonists. Instead of
penciling out a few preliminary sketches or taking photographs while
tossing around a few themes for the multipage spreads that featured his
travelogues, Shel would spend several weeks traveling around a new place,
gathering up possibilities in his head, and when he knew what he wanted
to accomplish, only then would he sit down and draw.

And instead of standing on the sidelines and observing, as other cartoonists did, he repeated what he did when he was cartooning for *Stars and
Stripes* and jumped right into the middle of things. When he was in Den-
mark, he signed on as vocalist with a band called Papa Bue's Bearded Viking
New Orleans Danish Jazz Band, a tenure that ended once he completed the
last of the sketches for the "Silverstein in Scandinavia" feature that appeared in the July 1957 issue. In Moscow, he attached himself to a summer
youth festival as a Red Party impostor for the March 1958 *Playboy.*

He was starting to use his position at *Playboy* to gain access to places he
wanted to visit, but also to meet people whose work he respected. Because
of his increasing visibility at the magazine, sometimes they approached
him first.

Just as Shel had shared similarities with Hef, when he first met Herb Gardner, it seemed like they were cut from the same cloth. Gardner was a cartoonist producing a regular strip called *The Nebbishes* that was nationally syndicated to newspapers, *and* he'd grown up in a Jewish neighborhood on New York's Lower East Side. The strip was controversial for its time yet also very popular. *The Nebbishes* were squat, shapeless cartoon figures prone to witty one-line pronouncements, and are often cited as the 1950s version of *The Simpsons*. Gardner wrote the strip for six years and then decided to stop in 1960 at the height of his success—by that time, the characters were produced in great profusion, available on cups, ashtrays, and greeting cards—because he wanted to write plays instead. Of course, Gardner's decision to follow his heart meant instant affinity with Shel; at the same time, he led Shel to explore the theater world.

Shel started to develop a tendency to forge friendships in totally disparate circles, where those in one world rarely met those in another. First, there was his *Playboy* world. Then once he settled in New York, he forged a downtown world with Gardner as well as other artists who were working to establish themselves in the artistic community, which included Gardner's actress wife Rita, radio humorist Jean Shepherd, *Playboy* cartoonist LeRoy Neiman, *Village Voice* cartoonist Jules Feiffer, *Voice* writer William Price Fox, and Norman Mailer. In the late 1950s, actress Lois Nettleton was the longtime girlfriend, later the wife, of Shepherd, who had a popular late-night show on WOR in New York. It was broadcast starting in 1956 from one to five thirty in the morning. Shepherd—aka Shep—ad-libbed, working totally unscripted the entire show, where he talked about his childhood and played jazz records on air. His eclectic mix was totally unconventional for the time, and late night audiences ate it up.

"Shep and Shel were best friends," said Nettleton. "I think they were the two closest of the group. They'd go out drawing together because Jean was a good artist in his own right. Shel would show Jean how he did his line drawings and what he was working on at the time. They were doodlers. You could always count on the fact that they would be sitting in a restaurant or club or coffee shop, just doodling."

She says that while Jean started out being a writer, after he started hanging out with Shel he became increasingly interested in cartooning and Shel gradually became interested in writing. "They almost took on a little bit of each other," she said. "They learned from each other, maybe unconsciously."

But they didn't look like each other, and indeed, of all the regulars who hung out in the group, Shel stuck out the most.

"He was our own personal beatnik, he was crazy and strange with that voice of his," said Nettleton. "We'd walk down the streets of Manhattan and people would turn and look at him with the long hair and the beard. He enjoyed being a little outrageous in the way he looked and the way he dressed."

Though publicity stills for *Take Ten* and his later *Playboy* photos show him with neatly combed hair and dressed in a standard-issue dress shirt and slacks that would fit into any office, Shel was beginning to push the limits of what was acceptable and what wasn't when it came to his clothing. Obviously, the time he spent hanging out in the Village influenced him, as well as the years he lived in Tokyo, but it soon became clear that he didn't have to follow any dress code but his own. The more casual, the better.

Even back then, whether it was with his work or his clothing, Shel considered it his moral duty to shake things up for people who otherwise were in lockstep with conformity in all its guises.

"When people are sitting around and some oddball walks in who's dressed atrociously, they'll say, 'Wow, look at that!' But they're delighted to have it because someone has brought something new and fresh into their buttoned-down world," he said. "Don't you think you owe that to other people, to bring them a little bit of excitement, something goofy and strange?"

In addition to redefining his wardrobe, Shel started to search for a carryall bag that would fit everything he could possibly need over the course of a long day wandering the streets of Chicago or New York, or wherever he happened to be overseas. That's how he came up with the idea of an oversized leather mailbag. Though Shel would be spotted in future years with what would be described as purses and knapsacks, the mailbag remained his favorite overall. It was roomy enough to fit his sketchpads, pens, and other drawing equipment.

On their various jaunts all over Manhattan wandering the city on foot, Nettleton says that Shel was rarely without that mailbag. "Shel and I hung out together during the day when Jean was down at the radio station getting ready for that evening's show," she said. They'd shop for themselves, but Shel also liked to buy things for Jean. He'd see a sweater he thought Jean would like, and he'd buy it. Now that he had a little money to spend, there was nothing he liked more than to spend it on his friends.

Books, however, he'd buy for himself. The mailbag came in handy when he needed to carry a load of books that he happened to buy on an unscheduled stop to a used bookstore; and now that he was making some money, he was living up to his childhood promise to buy as many old books as he could. His favorites were all the fairy tale books he didn't have as a kid. He began to build up a collection that would later fill his homes across the country. Nettleton said that Shel's knowledge of fairy tale figures, artists, and stories was extensive.

"One of his favorite things was fairy tales, and he taught me a lot because I always loved them, too," said Nettleton. They'd often spend hours scouring through used bookstores all over Manhattan, and he'd often buy so many books, he couldn't carry them all. "All of it was second-hand, I never saw him buy anything new."

In fact, he bought so many books in just a few years that his Hudson Street apartment—which he moved into after leaving the Sweeney's studio—was soon crammed full of books and little else. It had twelve-foot-high ceilings, and old books filled the bookshelves that lined every wall and reached to the ceiling.

Though Shel would camp out in old dusty bookstores as often as he could, it's curious that few people ever saw him reading one of those books. But when Shel was with other people, he was a social creature, talking, interacting, observing. Why would he read when there were other people around? On the flip side, when he was alone, he was either working or reading, and didn't want to be interrupted. He wanted to keep distinct boundaries between the different parts of his life.

Nettleton occasionally caught a glimpse of Shel's flip side. "He spent lots of hours alone," she said. "He probably had a million women in his life, but there was a certain loneliness about him. He wasn't turned inward, he was turned more outward, but while the time he spent with people was very outgoing, he had a sad side of him. I think when he was alone, he might have turned that melancholy side into his art."

As *Playboy* became more established, both Hef and the other staffers began to experiment with the format of the magazine, which in keeping with other publications of the time, at first used a text-heavy layout of three columns per page with one accompanying picture or a cartoon or joke unrelated to the article. Shel didn't always agree with the changes.

"He wasn't too happy when I put some blocks of color behind his cartoons, because he liked the purist effect of it," said Arthur Paul. "He just told me he didn't like it. I agreed with him, but I felt it was important to get a little color in there since the magazine was rather thin in the first few years, and I felt that my responsibility was to the whole magazine and not to one particular artist."

But Shel never held it against him, since Shel and Paul began to occasionally get together to draw with each other. They'd sit down with their sketchpads and they'd throw out an idea to each other, scribble it out, and then compare the drawings, their execution, why this turned out that way, and so on.

"Shel would tell me to draw a man sitting down, or a woman hanging up clothes or riding a bicycle, and then we'd both do it," said Paul. "It was almost like playing a game with a child. Basically, I was trying to show him that I could draw, too." This friendly collaboration would later play out in the other artistic venues that Shel would explore—songwriting and theater among them—and Shel would typically encourage his writing or drawing partners to go beyond what they thought they could accomplish.

At the same time, he realized not only that *Playboy* had its limitations in terms of his creative expression, but so did cartooning. In a few short years at the magazine he had moved leagues beyond what he had done for *Stars and Stripes* both thematically and in his drawing style, primarily because Hef put few restrictions on him, unlike the military brass that had kept him on a short leash. But still, one-panel cartoons were pretty limited. He was beginning to sift through the pros and cons of each medium, but he was setting a lifelong habit in motion in which the medium didn't much matter as long as the idea in his head wormed its way out onto paper, in words or drawings.

"I think if you're truly creative, you can work in certain related fields," he said. "For instance, a man who works well with words might work as a writer and as a poet and as a lyricist. But if he tried to work in sculpture, he might get absolutely nowhere."

As a variation on this theme, Shel would later frequently adapt the story first expressed in a cartoon or song into another form while altering it in some fashion. For example, in the case of the original version of "Everybody's Got Some But Me," in the December 1966 issue of *Playboy,* the word *some* referred to a sexually transmitted disease, while in the version that appeared in the *Dirty Feet* songbook that came out two years later, *some* meant the measles.

Again, he understood the limitations of each medium. "The cartoon form will reach more people, but probably won't make as lasting an impression," he said. "You don't have enough time or space to do it. You'd better get your laugh while you're making your point, or you won't be doing it very long."

Despite the fact that his work was being regularly published in a magazine that was garnering attention on an international basis, Shel remained insecure about his work. Of course, since Hef ran the show, he dictated what would ultimately appear in the magazine. "Hef's opinion of your work was intensely important because your future relationship with the magazine depended on whether or not Hef liked your work," said Larry DuBois, a *Playboy* staff writer. Occasionally, after Shel delivered a new batch of cartoons for Hef to review, he couldn't work up the courage to ask Hef if he had seen the cartoons yet, and since Hef was so preoccupied with the magazine, he didn't bring up the cartoons either. A curious passive standoff occurred, at least in Shel's mind. "He'd get intensely insecure and paranoid and do everything short of curling up into a little ball, he was so frightened," said DuBois. "Then he'd get angry, and then he'd get alienated to the point where he was ready to give up his career. The next time he saw Hef, he'd explode and yell, 'What about my work?' Hef would look at him like he was crazy and say, 'What about it?' because he hadn't seen the latest batch. Once Shel realized that was the case, he'd breathe a huge sigh of relief.

"*That* was Shel," said DuBois.

During his early years at *Playboy,* Shel began to frequent the Gate of Horn, a folk club in Chicago that had opened in 1956. The Gate, as it was known, quickly became the place in town for folkies to hang out around the same time that Shel began to hang out in the folk scene in Chicago, and it started to attract some headliners, both on stage and in the audience, including Judy Collins, Joan Baez, George Carlin, and Bob Dylan.

"That bar was really the social center for the hip crowd," said Shel, "and Gibson and Camp were the social directors."

Bob Gibson and Bob Camp—who would later change his first name to Hamilton—were the first folksinging duo to garner a national reputation in the late 1950s. Camp got his start in show business as one of the child stars of the "Our Gang" comedies. In addition to singing folk tunes, Gibson was an early ambassador for this new old form of music and traveled around the country to spread the word wherever he could. He caught the ear of others who were immersing themselves in folk songs, namely a young unknown singer by the name of Robert Zimmerman.

"[Owner] Allan Ribback told all the bartenders to give [Bob] Dylan free drinks while he copied down Bob Gibson's chord changes," said comedian George Carlin. Later on, there was a good deal of resentment among some in the group that Dylan followed Gibson's songs and methods and provided both the spin and the swarthy good looks and distinctive delivery that would make him famous. At the time, though, they were all in it together, helping each other, making music, and having a hell of a good time.

The Gate soon became a regular hangout for Shel. He'd catch the show and then stay for hours afterward at the bar, singing, making up songs on the spur of the moment, sometimes riffing on currently popular songs, but also creating original songs from scratch. Between his notoriety as *Playboy* cartoonist, his rapier-sharp wit, and his ability to pull stories and songs from thin air, he was soon one of the more popular nonperformers at the bar.

The creative energy at the Gate of Horn was so contagious that he began to think about branching out into other creative outlets than drawing and writing. According to Gibson, Shel wrote his first song, "The First Batallion," at the Gate's bar with Bob Camp. As Camp explained it, Shel's propensity for churning out songs overnight was evident from his initial effort.

"I had this tune, and I said, see what you can do," said Camp. "[Shel] took the tune and came back the next night. It was written on a paper bag. I Scotch-taped it to the mike and introduced it."

The response was encouraging, so Bob Gibson tried the same thing with Shel. "Bob had a song that was about half finished," said Shel.

"He'd heard that I'd written something, so he tossed it to me and said, 'You can try this.' I finished it, and then another Bob Gibson song, and we started to write some songs together. Then I was able to write some songs alone," he said. Soon, the two of them writing songs at the bar at the Gate became a regular occurrence.

According to Gibson, Shel was always very big on tying things up in a song. He always wanted conclusions to the songs, the poems, and if they involved a clear moral to the story, so much the better.

Shel and Gibson became fast friends. Among other interests, they shared one thing in common: When it came to music and art, the older the better. They were particularly enamored of music from the second half of the nineteenth century, and indeed, late 1950s folk music drew heavily on songs from the battlefield, particularly from the Civil War. Many of the early songs that Shel wrote were about the Civil War, including "In the Hills of Shiloh," which he cowrote with Jim Friedman and was first covered by Judy Collins in 1963.

Movies about the Wild West also served as an early inspiration for both Shel and Gibson. Bob Gibson wrote a song that turned out to be one of his most popular songs but also one that greatly inspired Shel later on. "Abilene" was written the day after Gibson had seen *Abilene Town,* a Western starring Randolph Scott. Shel would later draw on the feud between Scott and Lash La Rue, another Western movie star of the era, in his song "The Great Conch Train Robbery," which appeared on the album of the same name in 1980.

There was also an unexpected benefit to collaborating with Gibson: women. *Lots* of them. Shel studied his buddy's techniques closely and took advantage of those girls who wanted to talk with him just because he knew Gibson.

"When Gibson and Camp were singing together, there was a social life around him, and all the girls just swarmed to him," said Shel. "It wasn't so much you wanted to play like him, you wanted his life! You wanted girls to come around you. At that time, not many girls came around when you were sitting alone in a room drawing pictures of naked women."

The women, whether they were at the Gate of Horn or *Playboy,* were a novelty to Shel, and he was giving himself a crash course. They were a mystery to him in ways that growing up in a household with women from three different generations would never be, since the women who visited the *Playboy* offices and spent time at the Gate were exotic creatures not only because of the way they looked but also because of another reason:

For the first time in his life, women began to look his way, to flock to him. They wanted him. *Badly.* Though the types of women at the Gate and *Playboy* were different from each other—beatniks and long-haired folkie chicks frequented the Gate while the *Playboy* women ranged from the fresh-scrubbed girl-next-door types to glamour girls—Shel didn't play favorites. He welcomed their attentions and affections, and began to carefully navigate this strange new land. He regarded women the same way he viewed the fairy tale books in the used bookstores: He wanted as many as he could get. Settling down had little attraction for him now that he was just starting to live the life he had dreamed of, and he knew the trouble some of the *Playboy* executives ran into after they promised a girl their undying love and affection when all they wanted was a one-night stand.

Shel decided to take a different stance: Be clear with a woman from the start that his work came first and that he just wanted a little fun; in other words, don't promise more than you can deliver. He had no patience with people who lied, were insincere, or were outright fakes. After all, he'd be no better if he fed women the same lines. Though some undoubtedly turned him down for his bluntness, he was surprised and delighted at how many took him up on his offer. It was a philosophy he would maintain throughout his life, and though he did occasionally fall hard for a woman, it didn't last long. If, on the other hand, a woman fell hard for him and didn't let go, he managed to extricate himself with as much grace as possible. However, in a few cases, he had to have friends run interference.

Second, when it came to women, he had to be the pursuer. "The conquest was very important to him," said Judy Henske, a folksinger who hung out with Shel and regularly performed at the Bitter End and Village Gate. "He didn't mind being rejected, but he had to be the one to make the first move." She recalled a woman back in the early 1960s in the Village who really liked him. She had three strikes against her: She avidly pursued Shel, she was Jewish, and she was over twenty-one.

Henske thought it was hysterical. "There she was, this tiny woman who chased him all over the Village, and Shel would tell me to tell her I hadn't seen him. He was terrified of her," she remembered. "Plus, he preferred these young corn-fed *shiksas* from the Midwest, the younger the better."

If there was a third strike, it would probably be that she *acted* like a woman and not like a girl. "He'd never go around with anyone—man or woman—who acted like a grown-up. The women he liked were more like arrested-teenager women," said Henske. Indeed, Shel thought that once a woman reached the age of twenty-nine, she was pretty much done. He could be extremely chauvinistic, but that wasn't a surprise, taking into account his roots and the fact that he cut his professional teeth at *Playboy* and spent years camped out in the Mansion. In fact, the hothouse environment of sex he indulged in during his twenties and thirties probably helped protect his talent and cultivate it.

"He guarded the child inside of him very, very jealously," she noted. "He was very innocent in many ways. And although he was *shtupping* women left and right, he didn't seem wise to the ways of the world."

He also decided not to waste time pursuing a woman who obviously had no interest in him. After the second strike, he turned to the next in line. "I deeply believe that if she rejects me at first, then I will never create the magic in her," he said.

No matter how quickly he strived to make up for lost time with women after his drought throughout high school and college, women were still a mystery to him. All it would take was to see a woman paint her nails or wrap her hair in a turban and he would sit dumbstruck, drinking it all in while also considering it material for a cartoon or song.

Shel became great buddies with a number of other regular *Playboy* contributors, among them artist LeRoy Neiman, and they weren't above using their connection with the magazine to have some fun. "We'd go out and see a knockout girl walking down the street, and we'd tell her we represented *Playboy* and ask if she wanted to be a Playmate," said Neiman. "Most of the girls told us to get lost. But if they were at all interested, we'd pull out a tape measure and tell them we had to measure them on the spot to see if they had the qualifications. Shel was a master at that."

While the years 1957 and 1958 were filled with travel, music, and women, 1959 was the year Shel first got a taste of what it would be like to live different parallel lives at once: music, theater, art, and travel. But just as he was beginning to revel in the lifestyle, what started off with a bang ended in a tragic accident that forever changed his life.

One day toward the end of 1958, Shel was in the Village hanging out with Shep and a few others at one of their usual hangouts—the White Horse Tavern, the Lion's Head, and the San Remo—when somebody yelled out, "Hey, let's put on a show!"

A moment of silence, and then they were off and running with everyone talking at once. Jean's radio show was very popular at the time, and they realized this was the key to staging a successful show. "Everybody had their own talents, and we just got together and did it," Lois Nettleton remembered. After a couple of months of madcap brainstorming, a script was haphazardly put together, using Shepherd's rambling nostalgic radio narratives as a springboard, and *Look Charlie: A Short History of the Pratfall* opened at the off-Broadway Orpheum Theatre on Second Avenue on the Lower East Side in January of 1959.

The show was generously described as a disorganized mess, surreal at best, a variety show built around Shep's humor and monologues with period musical interludes by a few of the members of the Red Onion Jazz Band, a group formed in 1952. The band consisted of Bob Thompson on washboard, Frank Laidlaw on cornet, Carl Lunceford on banjo, and Steve Knight playing the tuba. Their music was along the lines of a New Orleans Dixieland band. Shepherd had used a few recordings by the band as musical background on his radio show, and hired them for the performances. All the shows were on a Monday night, when the theater could be rented on the cheap, and the stage set used lights and props left over from previous productions.

When the curtain went up, nothing happened initially. After a minute, the audience began to fidget when suddenly there was a big explosion on stage and Shep emerged from a castle. The lights came up to reveal Shel sitting on the side dressed in English mourning attire. Band members sat in the background with no illumination and each faced in a different direction, which made it difficult to perform on cue.

Herb Gardner did a juggling act, and the band had to follow him with appropriate noises as he dropped balls on the floor, Rita Gardner was dressed in an old-fashioned white gown, sitting on a swing, holding a parasol as she sang the old Bessie Smith tune "Electric Chair Blues." Jean performed his crowd-pleasing routine where he would thump out the rhythm on his head, open his mouth before the microphone, and out would come "The Sheik of Araby." Shel would occasionally stand up and croak out a song like "Sister Kate."

The show ended with Shel on stage bellowing some tune. In the middle of it, Shepherd came out and shouted, "Stop! Stop! What is this? This is total insanity!" He then turned to the audience and announced that he was going across the street to Ratner's Delicatessen, and they were invited to join him and the other members of the cast.

Critic Robert Perlongo, in his "In Person" column in the February 1959 issue of *Metronome* magazine, reviewed the show:

Subtitled "A History of the Pratfall," *Look Charlie* strongly reaffirmed the necessity for individual men to persist in being simply what they are. Invectives were hurled, at the world's 'official people'—those who measure success in terms of the cut of their grey flannel suits and the resonance of their official sounding names.

Shel wrote, drew, and designed the program for the show, populating the front cover with tiny recognizable images of each of the performers, producers, and girlfriends of everyone involved in the show, even crediting "the maker of the strudel, Mrs. Max Feinberg." Shel's poor spelling persisted. "Shel couldn't spell worth a damn," band member Frank Laidlaw said. Indeed, he misspelled the words *conceived, receding,* and *Dorothy* in the program, and even the front cover is the result of Shel's bad spelling. He had inadvertently left out the *a* in *Charlie* and so had to draw the letter lying on the ground, being hoisted up by a few of the characters.

One of Shel's downtown acquaintances, Jac Holzman, caught the show and liked the idea of having the Red Onion Jazz Band record an album with Shel as lead singer for his fledgling label Elektra Records, even though the late Al Ricketts, entertainment editor of *Pacific Stars and Stripes* during Shel's time at the paper, characterized his buddy's voice as sounding as if "it were screened through a Brillo pad." Nevertheless, Holzman decided to greenlight what would become *Hairy Jazz,* Shel's first album.

"At the time Elektra was experimenting with jazz and I knew that Shel would deliver an off-the-wall album and that he would be a blast to work with," said Holzman. "I like larger-than-life people, and he certainly qualified. The sessions were fast, furious, and great fun. We did the album in two sessions and it had all the rawness and 'hair' one could hope for."

Neither Shepherd nor Herb Gardner were involved in the album, and the four-piece Red Onion band was augmented by a few more players for the recording sessions. Bob Thompson switched from washboard to drums and added Arnie Hyman on bass, Bob Greene on piano, and Joe Muranyi on clarinet while Steve Larner replaced Carl Lunceford on the banjo.

"Shel picked the songs, and most of the material involved women and booze," said Frank Laidlaw. Shel wrote two of the songs, "Pass Me By Like You Don't Know Me" and "Broken Down Mama," and filled them with double entendres and exaggerated winks. After a couple of rehearsals, Holzman reserved studio time for two consecutive nights.

"You never quite knew what Shel was going to do," said Bob Thompson, the drummer and leader of the band. "He might decide to sing another chorus someplace where we hadn't anticipated it." In fact, although the song is listed on the album as "Go Back Where You Got It Last Night," on the record Shel instead sings "Go Back Where You *Stayed* Last Night."

And in a rehearsal for the song "Kitchen Man," Arnie Hyman, who played bass, said that everyone agreed that Shel would more or less talk the words instead of singing because Laidlaw was going to play the melody on trumpet. "It's not good form to step on somebody else's melody," said Hyman. At the recording session, Shel sang the melody instead of speaking it, but Frank didn't hold it against him. They later hung out at Laidlaw's apartment and he gave him a horn so Shel could learn to play the instrument.

The sessions were pretty much a party atmosphere, with the *Look Charlie* performers and various friends and spouses invited to the studio. On the album, there's frequent interaction between Shel and the band members, whether in a call-and-response or grunts that served as the equivalent of agreement.

Joe Muranyi, who played clarinet on the album, didn't take Shel seriously at first. "It was so off-the-wall compared with what we were doing, since he didn't have much of a voice," he remembered. "Even when we were making the record, I had my doubts. But after it was all over, I realized he was like a natural phenomenon. I had been looking for a proper singer, but he just loved the words and the spirit of the thing, and it all worked out in the end."

"Shel had an outgoing manner that put everyone at ease," said Thompson. "A recording session can get tense at times. Somebody who makes a mistake may feel terrible if he spoiled a good recording. But Shel put everyone at ease during those sessions."

In the end, Holzman decided to forgo making any more jazz albums because, as he explained, "I didn't understand or love the music enough." He decided to pursue folk music instead, and in time would produce Judy Collins, Joan Baez, and Carly Simon, later introducing the world to Jim Morrison and The Doors and Queen. However, two years later Holzman capitalized on Shel's growing fame and association with *Playboy* by repackaging *Hairy Jazz* as *Shel Silverstein's Stag Party,* which he reissued on Elektra's Crestview Records label.

After the recording sessions were over, Shel pursued friendships with some of the Red Onion band members. After all, it presented him with a brand-new circle and a kind of music that he had loved since childhood.

He and clarinetist Joe Muranyi immediately hit it off. They lived on the same block in the Village and were both of Hungarian descent, and began to meet regularly for long late-night espresso-fueled conversations. "I recognized him as the kind of Hungarian intellectual who I was familiar with," Muranyi said. "There are a lot of bright, talented people in Hungary who first and foremost live by their brains, not their brawn, though, he was quite American."

Muranyi saw firsthand how Shel actively worked to create a public image that was at odds with who he was inside. "As much as Shel came across as a loud, boorish type onstage by yelling about booze and women, he was sort of a gentle person," he said. "When we talked, he was warm and friendly, and he was never loud."

Shel invited Muranyi to visit his apartment. Inside was one large main room with countless paintings and canvases leaning up against all four walls, with some stacked two and three paintings deep. Shel said they were all his work.

"They were wonderful," said Muranyi, "and they weren't cartoons. These were paintings and portraits in a folksy style, almost in a Shel Silverstein meets Marc Chagall way." Muranyi had studied art history and the work of different artists, and Shel's paintings impressed him. "I was really staggered by how great they were. There were a lot of sepia paintings and dark brown portraits. I don't remember seeing anything in vivid reds and blues. I asked if I could buy any of them, and he told me he was sorry, but they were all sold."

For Shel, painting became a personal pursuit, not one for public consumption except for the self-portrait that appeared on the cover of his 1967 album, *Drain My Brain*.

Nineteen fifty-nine continued to be a watershed year for Silverstein. He would make enough connections, undoubtedly helped by his association and growing visibility with *Playboy,* to branch out into other artistic venues and spread his creativity around, since it was clear early on that cartooning was not large enough to contain his prodigious creative energy.

He began to write liner notes for friends' record albums that in most cases were 100 percent tongue-in-cheek. In fact, some who originally begged him to write their liner notes would later swear off ever asking again, since in many cases, Shel's words simply upstaged the music within. As Bob Gibson put it, referring to Shel's ramblings that appeared on the 1961 live album *Bob Gibson & Bob Camp at the Gate of Horn,* "The liner notes outsold the album two to one."

"People thought I was married to Shel," said Judy Henske about his liner notes for *High Flying Bird,* her second album. "People took it seriously and believed everything they read in the liner notes, but he intended it to be an inside joke with me, and a joke on all the people reading the notes. The artist knows it's a joke, but no one else does."

Here, from Shel's liner notes for 1959's *Jean Shepherd and Other Foibles:*

I first met Jean Shepherd on the South Side of Chicago on a hot July day in 1945. He was twelve years old and I was seven. I remember him as a skinny, freckly-faced, sandy-haired kid, quiet, sensitive, and pensive, always raising hell and always ready for a good fight. I did not know at that time of his part in the atrocious St. Valentine's Day Massacre nor was this to affect our friendship in later years.

In addition to the liner notes, Shel drew a veritable parade of characters marching across the front and back album cover of *Foibles,* incorporating the message, "Jean Shepherd is a dirty rotten, one-way sneaky son of a bitch," spelling it out backwards to escape the censors. It was clear that by this time, the creative license that Hefner gave Shel in *Playboy* had definitely transformed his drawing style. Now, his cartoons and illustrations appeared more animated, less stagnant than his military cartoons, and the tone was more frenetic and complex, perhaps a direct result of how Shel's own life was becoming richer as he delved into several different crafts.

He also created two dozen highly detailed illustrations for *Report from Practically Nowhere,* a book written by one of his buddies from *Stars and Stripes,* writer John Sack. The book was a collection of articles about travels to the smallest, least-known countries in the world that Sack had written for *Playboy.* After the manuscript was accepted by Harper & Brothers, later Harper & Row—which would publish Shel's first children's book, *Lafcadio: The Lion Who Shot Back,* four years later—Sack offered Shel the opportunity to illustrate the book, and he readily accepted, eager to have a book credit that didn't involve the military.

He was well on his way.

In the summer of 1959, Shel was traveling on assignment for his next *Playboy* travelogue—"Silverstein on Safari in Africa"—slated for the

October issue when a split-second error in his judgment changed his life forever.

One day, Shel was driving around in Uganda looking for something or someone that would spark an idea for his story when he was involved in a serious car accident, shattering his leg. He was flown back to the United States and spent the next two years recuperating.

The accident had a profound effect on his life. First and foremost, it slammed the brakes on his world-traveler lifestyle that he loved so much. In the almost three years since he'd started writing the travelogues for *Playboy,* Shel had visited more than thirty countries in Europe, Asia, and Africa. It would be another two years until he could hit the road again.

However, true to form, he told few friends about the accident, and when pressed Shel may even have altered the details, since one friend recalled that Shel told him that the accident occurred in Alabama. Given the general time frame, however, it's most likely that the crash happened in Africa.

He also never got behind the wheel of a car for the rest of his life. "After the accident, he didn't think he was a very good driver," said Melanie Smith Howard, the widow of Harlan Howard, a close friend of Shel's in Nashville. "He chose not to drive, and from then on, he consciously chose to live in places where he wouldn't need to depend on a car." Places like New York, Sausalito, Chicago, Key West, Martha's Vineyard. Even when he visited Nashville, known as a car-oriented city, he still walked everywhere. He also remained leery about being a passenger while someone else drove.

The fact that he chose never to have a driver's license again meant that no one actually knew when Shel was born, a fact that he sometimes used to his advantage to tease his friends and mislead women. "But that was very much in keeping with his character, because he was very private in his own way," said friend, photographer Larry White.

His penchant for privacy led to a few interesting personality quirks, one of which involved answering machines when they came along in later years. He *hated* them; simply, he never wanted to be that accessible. He would also own only rotary phones his entire life, and he hated phone books.

"He had an absolute phobia against phone books," said White. "He didn't want to have them around. If they showed up, he'd throw them out. Shel never fully explained why he despised phone books, but I think the anonymous nature of all those names and all those personalities just overwhelmed him."

Nineteen fifty-nine was also probably the last time in his life that he would see a doctor, according to country singer Bobby Bare, one of his closest friends. Shel had been deathly afraid of doctors and dentists since childhood, which was common among people growing up in the '30s and '40s, when the techniques used in medicine and dentistry were often primitive and extremely painful. Though he was forced to see a physician while he recuperated from his accident, he absolutely resented being told that he had to rein in his activities, because it would mean someone else was essentially calling the shots on how he should live his life. As soon as his leg healed and he could get around again, he vowed that it would be the last time in his life he would ever set foot in a doctor's office.

He was convinced that if he took care of himself, he wouldn't need to see a doctor anyway. While the people Shel was drawn most to through the years—artists, musicians, actors, and writers—weren't particularly known for their squeaky-clean images when it came to drugs and alcohol, he rarely indulged himself. In fact, he was known to nurse a beer or glass of wine the entire night.

Shel refrained from drugs and alcohol because he felt that he had too much talent to waste it by altering his consciousness. Besides, watching his friends when they were drunk or stoned provided him with endless material for stories, songs, and cartoons. He also loved to spend hours on long walks, which couldn't hurt.

With 1960 looming, Shel had a growing reputation as a talented cartoonist, he had friends in many different fields, and he had his first book under his belt. Life was good, and it was about to get a whole lot better.

3. No Grown-ups

In December of 1959, Hugh Hefner bought what would be his first Playboy Mansion on Chicago's Gold Coast, and nothing in his life, his magazine empire—or Shel's life, for that matter—would ever be the same.

"Being at the Mansion in the middle of the night was like putting your finger in an electric socket," said Larry DuBois, a writer for *Playboy*. "It was really alive. And Shel loved it."

The Mansion consisted of two interconnected buildings at 1336 and 1340 N. State Parkway, two blocks from Lake Michigan. Built in 1899, perhaps the most notorious aspect of the seventy-four-room Mansion was the infamous directive written in Latin that appeared on a small brass plaque at the main entrance, just in case anybody wasn't clear about what they would encounter on the other side of the door.

SI NON OSCILLAS, NOLI TINTINNARE. Translation: "If you don't swing, don't ring."

Since Hef was notorious for never leaving the Mansion, he wanted the world to come to him. To ensure that they did, he made it nearly impossible to refuse. Hef not only peppered the crowd with celebrities and half-naked Playmates and Bunnies, but the entertainment he provided was top-rate, ranging from singers like Sammy Davis Jr. and Sonny and Cher with songs at the top of the charts to party games that included playing strip poker with the current centerfold, several swimming pools, and an underwater bar in the basement accessible by sliding down a fireman's pole. Hef also liked to have a few of the era's more controversial figures attend the parties, including Dick Gregory, Lenny Bruce, and even William F. Buckley. Any kind of gourmet food was readily available, and the drinks of course flowed nonstop, but in Shel's eyes, the main attraction of the parties was the chance to watch the ever-changing dynamics of the crowd.

The parties were held in a giant ballroom on the main level, up a staircase from the front door, large enough to hold a full-size basketball court, and then some. Hef needed little excuse to throw a party, and when word got out and invitations were issued, it wasn't unusual for several hundred people to show up.

Right off the ballroom were four guest rooms: the Red Room, Blue Room, Yellow Room, and the Black Room, named for their color schemes. Whenever he was in town, Shel always had first dibs on the Red Room, which shared a bathroom with the Blue Room. Hef opened the first Playboy Club in Chicago in February 1960, and remodeled one section of the Mansion to serve as the "Hutch," a dormitory for women working as Bunnies at the Club. Rent was fifty dollars a month.

Hef wanted visitors to the Mansion to feel pampered, so he instituted a policy that short- or long-term guests could get anything they needed or desired twenty-four hours a day, 365 days a year—as long as it was legal— and staffed it accordingly. Ordering a five-course meal at three in the morning was not unheard of, especially when Hef normally didn't stop work for the day and start socializing until ten at night. Many nights the festivities— which included watching movies, playing Monopoly, swimming in the underground pool known as the grotto, dancing, or just hanging out—didn't end until seven the next morning.

"The things that usually govern us, like the time of day, where and what one can eat, the time you work, didn't apply at the Mansion," said Shel. "There were no guidelines. This was not only an incredible opportunity, but it created a tremendous responsibility to make our own schedule."

He delighted in introducing the unconventional pleasures of the Mansion to friends from his other circles. "Shel took me to the Mansion when I was in town," said Lois Nettleton, an actress married to Jean Shepherd for seven years in the '60s, who made a cameo appearance in a *Seinfeld* episode called "The Gymnast" in the comedy's sixth year. "He had great fun showing me everything. We went into the kitchen and he opened the refrigerator door and there, all lined up, were a thousand ready-made sundaes and foods of all kinds in case anybody had the slightest whim. The Mansion was a lot of fun for him."

But he also spent the majority of his time there working, and like Hef, he spent his days at the Mansion pretty much in solitude, drawing and writing in his room with the door closed. After his car accident, he also stayed at the Mansion to recuperate, and because he couldn't travel for two years afterward, he came up with a new feature for the magazine: "Teevee Jeebies," a "do-it-yourself dialogue for the late late show." He took a photo still from an old movie and made up a caption of a line of dialogue coming out of one of the characters' mouths that could be humorous or slightly risqué. He also began the habit of recycling gags from his earlier work. For instance, in one cartoon from *Grab Your Socks!* he shows an army officer ordering his wife holding their son, "I want to see that safety pin SHINE!" Then, in the first published book collection of "Teevee Jeebies," he took a scene from the movie *Stella,* showing a man and woman sitting at a dining table. He's holding out a spoon and the caption says, "Sure it's clean, but it doesn't shine! I want that spoon to shine!"

In 1960, *Now Here's My Plan,* his first book of nonmilitary cartoons, was published by Simon & Schuster. The cartoon on the cover that provides the book's title would turn out to be one of his most famous and often-cited cartoons.

In the cartoon, two prisoners are chained to the wall of a prison cell about three feet off the ground. Both their hands and feet are shackled. One says to the other, "Now here's my plan." Shel was both fascinated and distressed by the amount of analysis and commentary that almost immediately began to swirl around the cartoon. "A lot of people said it was a very pessimistic cartoon, which I don't think it is at all," he said. "There's a lot of hope even in a hopeless situation. They analyze it and question it. I did this cartoon because I had an idea about a funny situation about two guys."

This was only the beginning. The way his work was continually put under a microscope and examined and used by countless people to further their own agendas or to underscore their beliefs was something that mystified and horrified Shel throughout the years, and it was part of the reason why he would disdain celebrity for himself and refuse to give media interviews later in life.

Because he always wanted people to focus on the work itself and not on the creator behind the work, he refused to reveal to anyone except close friends how he used his art to send a message to himself. When he came up with the idea for the "Now Here's My Plan" cartoon in 1956, it could have been the direct result of the insecurity he felt about his work. He felt that he was literally shackled to the wall, unable to move forward with his art because although he did have a plan, the outside forces opposed him in the form of magazines that rejected his work. At the time, he was back in Chicago living with his parents and having horrific fights with his father. After the book came out, he made a deliberate decision to mine his dark side for future material. As long as the story he presented in his cartoons was tempered with a humorous twist, it would appeal to everyone: Those who shared his dark side would recognize it as such and see the humor in it, while others would just laugh because it was a ludicrous situation.

As he began to garner small successes, his suspicions were confirmed that this was the path he should continue on.

Shel's increased visibility as a result of *Playboy* not only exposed him to new people in other creative fields, but it also reinforced his talents in the eyes of people who had known him for years and who now were also working in fields that could provide yet another outlet for Shel's prodigious creative output. That's how *Uncle Shelby's ABZ Book* came about.

Shel later said that he got the idea for the *ABZ* book while he was standing on a street corner in Chicago one afternoon licking an ice cream cone. Along comes a mother with a young child, who looked at Shel and his ice cream with great longing. Shel informed the child that the ice cream was quite delicious, and out popped the question: "Why don't you ask your mother to get you one?"

The kid got his ice cream cone and Shel got a dirty look from his mother. He also came up with the idea for the book.

Uncle Shelby's ABZ Book was published by Simon & Schuster in 1961. "It's for adults and people who have children," said Shel, "but you better keep it away from children. It doesn't really tell the kids to do these things, it just hints at these things."

He believed this was the result of parents' beliefs that kids in the late 1950s and early 1960s were exposed to too much violence on TV, and instead of restricting their children's viewing time, they chose to focus on defanging fairy tales. He felt the parents were hypocrites while expressing a negative opinion toward television that would last his entire life. "They think the kids shouldn't hear about giants and a wolf eating somebody up, but they let them sit in front of that TV set for twelve hours a day, just to keep them quiet, where they can watch all kinds of horror and cruel murders," he said. "But watch out for those fairy tales."

Uncle Shelby's ABZ Book was squarely aimed at the adult market—at least in Shel's mind—but most adults assumed it was written for kids.

One reviewer who initially cringed at the book picked up on its subversive nature only after watching his own children read it, a pattern that would inevitably repeat itself with Shel's kids' books from then on. Because of the confusion, in the edition that would be reissued in 1985, the tagline *A Primer for Adults Only* was tacked on.

"The children intuitively knew that it was satire, that they were being put on," wrote reviewer Robert R. Kirsch in *The Los Angeles Times*. "Secondly, and perhaps just as important, they realized that merely because something was printed in a book it was not necessarily true. I had to change my mind about *Uncle Shelby's ABZ*."

Satire. To Shel and his friends and his editors, it was clear that in all his work—cartoons, books, songs, and especially liner notes—all he was doing was poking a finger in the eye of American society. It was crystal clear to them, so why did everyone else take it so literally?

Though conservative pundits and critics had ferociously wagged their fingers at Shel's *Playboy* cartoons since they first appeared in the magazine—not because the cartoons were ribald but because of the risqué content in the rest of the magazine—he had already decided to just create and not worry about whether people got it about his art. After all, any time spent worrying about or responding to what others thought was valuable time taken away from creating his art, which could never be replaced. And because of the tone he set, he was beginning to see other artists follow his lead.

At the same time, he stressed the importance of being as clear in his message as possible: "You should never explain the philosophy behind anything you do, it's not important," he said. "If your work is weak and needs to be explained, it isn't clear enough."

When he wasn't staying at the Mansion, and before he could resume his around-the-world jaunts, Shel was entrenched in his apartment in New York.

After spending a couple of years bouncing around a few places and crashing with friends, Shel finally got his own apartment on Hudson Street on the western edge of Greenwich Village where he was far enough away from the hubbub but could easily be in the middle of Washington Square Park in a brisk ten-minute walk. He immediately turned it into the kind of place where he would be able to focus on the two most important things in his life: work and women. He crammed it full of books, a drawing table, pens, sketchpads, a typewriter, and a guitar along with any other musical instruments he happened to be teaching himself at the time. Somewhere in there was a bed up on stilts—he climbed a ladder to get to it—and a kitchen that rarely got used, since Shel ate most of his meals in coffee shops and restaurants.

The bathroom was the apartment's most unusual feature. Behind a secret door was a bathroom that resembled a New Orleans bordello, the walls covered in red velvet. It contained an ornate vanity and a daybed, and it stood out because it was so feminine, as compared with the cluttered workspace that consumed the rest of the apartment.

His phone number in New York was 691-1666, the mark of the devil on his telephone. He always got a kick out of that.

Once his surroundings were complete, he could turn on the spigot of his creativity full blast. Ideas began to pour out of him, fast and furious. His brain switched gears so rapidly, however, that often in the time it took to reach for his sketchpad, the ideas would be gone. So he got into the habit of keeping his pad close at hand. In the event that he couldn't get to it fast enough, Shel would start to write on whatever was nearby. In a restaurant, he would jot something down on a cocktail napkin. Barring that, he would turn to the tablecloth and scrawl his ideas on that. If he was walking down the street, and ideas came floating up, he'd start writing on his shirt, up and down the sleeves, on the cuffs, across the front. He didn't ever want to risk losing an idea.

Shel wasn't always scribbling or doodling in front of his friends, but once the pump was primed, he couldn't stop. One idea led to another, which sent him off on another tangent, and so on. And as he wrote, he remained fully tuned in to the people and conversation around him.

While Shel was not known to be a vain man—after all, how concerned could he be with inked illustrations and words running all over his shirt?—he was starting to worry about his receding hairline. Jo Mapes, one of his friends from the folk scene, suggested that he shave his head and keep the beard. After some hesitation, Shel agreed.

"He was one of the first men in the public eye who could pull off the shaved-head look in the 1960s," said his *Playboy* comrade LeRoy Neiman. "He always complained that Yul Brynner and Telly Savalas shaved their heads because he shaved his."

It also served as an unconscious way for him to work through a problem or increase his focus. Kerig Pope, an editor at *Playboy,* said that Shel rubbed his head frequently while he worked.

"At times he got very pensive," said Pope. "It was hard to understand his moods, he could be angry or happy and I wouldn't know it because he'd be concentrating so hard on something. I couldn't read the mood or the face, but whenever he rubbed his head, I knew he was thinking."

Pope said that when he saw Marlon Brando rub his bald head in *Apocalypse Now,* it reminded him of Shel. "Some people scratch their heads to figure something out, Shel rubbed his head," he said.

It was no secret among his friends that Shel had little patience for kids, as evidenced by the *ABZ* book. But as his friends started to marry and have kids of their own, Shel softened up a little. He instructed them to call him Uncle Shel or Shelly or Shelby, and whenever he stopped by—keeping with his promise to himself to go wherever he wanted whenever he wanted—more than a few of them described it as having Santa Claus stop by.

"When he showed up, it was like Christmas," said Sarah Sweeney McCann, the second child of his army buddy Bob Sweeney. "He was always so great with us, he'd put my little sister on his lap and tell us stories and draw pictures. He was like the world's best uncle. To me, he was so much larger than life, he was always physically the greatest presence in the room, regardless of who else was there."

"I always thought of Shel as a young Santa Claus, a skinny Santa before he turned gray," said Dave Mapes, Jo Mapes's son. "When Shel laughed, he laughed all the way down to his toes, and it would make the room rumble. I could feel the floor shake when Shel laughed."

The fact that he usually showed up totally unannounced added to the children's excitement.

"The phone would ring and Mom would say that Uncle Shel is at the airport or the Mansion, he's in town for all of eleven hours and wants to come by and say hi," said McCann. "There was no such thing as giving advance notice with Shel, he was always riding the crest of the wave, and it took him where it took him."

Since Jo Mapes was active in the Chicago folk scene, when Shel showed up, his visits often turned into an impromptu folk jam in the living room that went well into the wee hours. Some of the singers who stopped by included Odetta, Arlo Guthrie, and Spanky MacFarland. Shel would sit in the living room, play guitar, and sing.

"I remember many times when I'd wake up in the middle of the night to one of those jam sessions going on in the living room," remembered McCann.

However, he did possess a split personality when it came to children, and when he visited the Mapes household, he would occasionally be impatient with one of the kids.

"There were times when he wasn't Uncle Shel and he was kind of curt," said Dave Mapes. "But it wasn't because of anything he said, it was more the way he behaved, his body language. I think there were times that when Shel came to the house, it was to see Mom, and not be Uncle Shelby to the kids."

Mapes said that it didn't really bother him or his sisters, because the times he was Uncle Shelby vastly outnumbered the occasions when he wasn't. And in a way, visiting with the kids of his friends gave him what he needed as far as family without the responsibility. He didn't have to do the heavy lifting; he was just along for the ride. It was as if Shel could get his parental and family needs met by surrogate; he could be a family man strictly on his terms, which is the same way he lived the rest of his life. And once he got his dose of kids, he could walk out the door, hop on a plane, and go do something else.

While kids were drawn to Uncle Shelby, adults were just as equally entranced by his mere presence.

"The adults loved and admired Shel because he was the totally free spirit they wished they could be," said Dave Mapes. "This guy was the consummate bachelor, jet-setter and world traveler. He essentially sailed the world, and I think adults saw him as this Errol Flynn kind of swashbuckler where the world was his oyster. He had no wife or children to tie him down or make him grow up and get a nine-to-five job so they could get the house, picket fence, and station wagon. To the adults, he came off as being carefree and unencumbered by many of the things they were weighed down with, so he appealed to the adults in the room very much."

He encouraged his friends in their artistic pursuits and strongly supported them. And though he held a clear disdain for celebrity of all stripes, he wasn't beneath using his name recognition and influence to help his friends who were talented and needed a break.

For Jo Mapes, that meant writing liner notes for one of her albums and pulling strings whenever there were strings to be pulled. "He was a fan of my mom's, so he supported her and used his influence to help her early in her career," said Dave Mapes. "Shel was a very persuasive guy. He had a strong physical presence and was pretty opinionated, so if he called an agent and told him to listen to a new singer, the agent would usually set up a meeting because Shel was pretty well-respected when it came to spotting talent."

But it could come at a steep price, namely in the form of junket, or pudding. Whenever he went to a restaurant, whether it was New York or Chicago, he'd complain that the waiters always looked at him cross-eyed whenever he ordered the milk-based dessert. "It seems that junket is something that kids eat and that adults don't, and if you go into the Hip Bagel or Sardi's or the Ming Tree and ask for some junket they'll think you are out of your skull," he complained.

Jo had obviously been promising to make Shel a pot full of junket for years, and one day she came through. However, she had invited a bunch of other people—including the jazz musician Pops Foster, who played with Louis Armstrong during the 1930s—to a spaghetti dinner at her house. While Shel thought everyone else would eat spaghetti and he would have the dessert to himself, that was not the case. One of Shel's cohorts—comedian Bill Cosby—also came to the dinner, and his dream of finally being able to gorge himself on junket was not to be.

"Everybody else had some junket and Cosby eats like a horse," he grumbled. "So when it was all over, I had a lot of junket but I didn't really have all the junket I wanted."

Hillary Mapes remembered that Shel would sometimes come to the house, but refuse to eat at the table. "He'd stay for four or five hours but would never take off his coat," she said. "After we finished eating and getting ready for bed, he'd be there in the kitchen, wearing his coat and eating out of the pot."

Greenwich Village in the early 1960s was a very special place, and one that clearly set the stage for the ways in which Shel later designed his life. "Everybody knew who everybody else was, and they were also very aware of themselves," said Judy Henske. "When I was done working, we'd go to the Limelight to hang out where everybody was famous: Cass Elliott, John Phillips, Bob Dylan, even Joan Rivers. I don't know if you could get in there if you weren't. It was really café society and it was really fun because everybody was doing something." Henske said that Shel tended to sit back and observe everything going on around him instead of holding center stage.

But the folksinger and beatnik gatherings that Shel gravitated toward were not all lighthearted singalongs. The politics that would later erupt in the tumultuous years of the '60s were just starting to attract attention in the folksinger community. "Shel and my mom and other folkies, as they were called, would talk about serious stuff, particularly about the civil rights movement in that post-McCarthy time, and how it threatened the creative community," said Dave Mapes.

And then there was Lenny Bruce, who was a good friend of Shel's. They had met at the Mansion as a matter of course, given Hef's campaign to publicize anyone with ideas on the cutting edge, and Shel was in the audience at one of the acerbic comedian's more notorious arrests at the Gate of Horn on December 4, 1962. The Illinois State Supreme Court eventually reversed Bruce's obscenity conviction on free speech grounds, but the damage was done. Shel was livid.

"Fifteen years from now, when people talk about what Lenny said and did on stage, they'll ask, 'What was the big fuss all about?' It's just as disastrous, just as fatal, to be way ahead of your time as it is to be way behind. And yet, what can you do? You can only do the work that you think is right."

But it seems this applied only to artists who practiced the same style of representational art and cartooning that he did. Indeed, Shel was extremely opinionated about other artists who were creating abstract and modern art because to him, they lacked the discipline and training that he had painstakingly taught himself.

"Young artists today don't want to learn how to draw," he said. "When a man throws a can of paint against a canvas and calls it art, you're supposed to appreciate it by the depth of the color. But they're not learning how to draw and so we're losing the art teachers who know how to draw. The art teachers in our universities form a large group of incapable draftsmen. They may be good with color, but they are *not* draftsmen."

As he had garnered a good deal of success based mostly on his own trial and error and countless hours spent practicing his craft, Shel believed that anyone else could succeed in an artistic field given an ambitious self-apprenticeship. And because he was a native in a town where he was a misfit kid and other kids and his parents thought his constant doodling would never amount to much, he was particularly gratified by the success and visibility his association with *Playboy* brought him.

But that didn't mean he was totally comfortable with "making it big."

The simple truth was that Shel was uncomfortable being in the spotlight. In the early 1960s, as his friend Judy Henske's star began to ascend as a folksinger, she got a gig hosting a live morning television talk show in Chicago. To fill the guest roster, she turned to her own circle of ascending stars, which included Shel. His reaction when the camera focused on him caught Henske off guard.

"First, he wore this shiny corduroy suit that made him look like a filing cabinet," she said. "Then when the camera came on, he froze up. He had the worst stage fright I've ever seen. It was like trying to interview an egg. I was very surprised by that, because it seemed that all of a sudden he'd become this whole different person. This was not the Shel I knew. This Shel was absolutely paralyzed with terror, his eyes bulging. It lasted for five minutes, which is an eternity on live TV."

Later, when she asked him why he had frozen up, he never gave her a clear answer. But Henske thought it tied in with his need to always be in control.

First of all, he didn't drink, or else he pretended to. "He'd order a drink and nurse it the whole night in order to pretend he was drinking," she said. "I saw him spit it back into his glass, he just didn't like it. I don't think he ever wanted to get woozy, he wanted to be fully in his mind and in control of himself."

As his appearance on Henske's show proved, he was uncomfortable with television, probably because it was around that time that he began to see the all-encompassing influence it had on people, sowing the seeds of a lifelong contempt toward the medium even as he began to make regular appearances on local and national shows.

"There's a great myth about people who are on TV," he said. "People are always giving you credit for really wanting to say more than you said. This is bullshit. What you've got to say, you say. If you want to find out what a writer or a cartoonist really feels, look at his work. That's enough."

He also reiterated his belief that his work should stand on its own.

"When I talk, what it amounts to is that I'm explaining my work, and I don't believe a man should explain what he does," he said. "I believe he should do it and not explain it. It speaks for itself. You only muddle it by talking about it."

While he was getting a reputation for telling exactly how he felt about a particular issue or person, whether it was in print or to somebody's face, he was also becoming disillusioned with the pretensiousness and complaining he witnessed among the people who performed at the folk clubs he frequented in Chicago and New York.

"I've been backstage around a lot of comics and acts, and it's amazing how many of them come offstage screaming about the audience as though the audience has to fulfill a certain degree of intelligence and enthusiasm," he said. "It's the entertainer's job to work that audience. If they don't get a response from that audience, that's tough shit."

Neither did he have much patience for his fellow artists who couldn't take criticism or who primarily used art as a form of self-analysis.

"A writer should have a notebook to write down his ideas and the things that he sees," he said. But the young people he saw in the Village who claimed to be writers had a different idea. "What's the point of a notebook?" he asked rhetorically. "To put down things that I feel, things that are happening to me. Things that I think and now I am getting better. It's like their eyes have spun around and are looking inside their brains," he complained, figuring they were doing it more for analysis than for the sheer pleasure of creating art, which was Shel's view from childhood.

"They're not concerned with writing or painting, they're concerned with straightening themselves out. They'll try to paint it out. They'll try to sing it out and be healthy. So what can come of this artistically? They are trying to solve the problems of youth. But by the time you solve the problems of youth you are middle-aged. And then you try to solve the problems of middle age and you're old. And you try to solve the problems of old age and you have a good case on your hands because you can't solve that problem."

The endless posturing and whining he witnessed among artists of all stripes often got on his nerves.

"I don't think it's good for a bunch of successful people to hang out with each other, liking each other's stuff and scratching each other's back," he said. "There are guys who stink, whose work is no good because it is trite. It doesn't search for anything. If I don't like a man's work I never want to meet the guy, because you can't separate a man from his work."

He wouldn't insult a person to his face; instead he'd just get up and leave in the middle of a conversation.

Or he'd turn it into art. In 1963, he and Larry Moyer wrote and produced *The Moving Finger,* a movie about the beatniks in Greenwich Village. He hung with these people and enjoyed their company, but he didn't identify with them at all.

"There are people I know who claim to be pretty independent people, in other words, they don't go to work," he said. "They don't earn any money, they don't contribute anything, but they don't really want to and they consider themselves free. I don't consider this freedom. To me, freedom entitles you to do something, not to *not* do something. If a person doesn't want to do anything, I think they have an absolute right to do it, but don't expect people to unzip your fly for you."

And of course, folksingers were not sacred either.

He had begun to sour on the folk scene around the time he made his 1962 album, *Inside Folk Songs,* which contains the first recorded version of "The Unicorn." However, as Shel screeches and recites it, the song bears little resemblance to the version made popular six years later by The Irish Rovers. Jerry Wexler, who was responsible for producing Ray Charles and Aretha Franklin, was brought on as producer. "That record only sold about five hundred copies, but all of them were purchased by aspiring songwriters in Nashville," said Wexler.

The album title is actually a scathing indictment of the entire folk and beatnik scene, which becomes all the more obvious with one line from the song "Folk Singer's Blues": *What do you do if you're young and white and Jewish?*

"You hear a chain gang song sung by a man who has been on a chain gang, and when he sings about it, it means something," said Shel. "You see a pimply-faced eighteen-year-old Protestant kid up there belting out about a chain gang and you wonder what it's all about. I think they should shut up and sing something that more fits what they know.

"You've got to face it, we are not moonshiners," he said. "We were not born in East Virginny. Most of the guys are Jewish, I don't know what there is about folk music that hangs up city-born Jewish cats. As a group, folk songs are the dumbest things in the world."

Mike Settle, a songwriter and folk musician who wrote some songs with Shel later on, remembers "Folk Singer's Blues." "Shel wrote the song about people who wished they'd done this or wished they'd done that," he remembered. "We were all writing about stuff that never happened in our lives." Settle was amused, but others on the scene weren't, which expedited Shel's departure from the folk scene.

He had just as little patience for those who were signing on to the burgeoning peace movement. He characterized them as a group of uninformed young people who run around saying, "Ban the bomb and let's have peace and clasp hands. Are you for peace? I am, too, let's talk about flowers."

"They talk about doves and nobody knows a damn thing that's going on. You ask them what's going on in Congress, they don't know. All they know is peace. I think they're more interested in marching all together and singing folk songs and drinking hot chocolate."

Though Settle counted himself among this group of idealistic folk musicians, he didn't take himself too seriously, a trait that Shel appreciated.

They met when Settle was a frequent performer at the Bitter End on Bleecker Street. Shel, as he often did when he met a musician performing original songs that he liked, invited Settle to write songs with him. Shel's work ethic impressed Settle.

"If I had an idea and we were going to meet, I would give him what I had, which might be a verse or maybe a line or two for a chorus and just the beginnings of a tune," said Settle. "Usually Shel would have a complete song finished perfectly by the next day. He didn't put stuff aside and say, 'I'll get to that.' He would jump right on into it."

Another time, Mike told Shel he had an idea and gave him just one line that had popped into his head: "Ever since my masochistic baby left me I have nothing to hit but the wall." By the next time Settle saw him, Shel had written four or five verses and it turned into the song "Masochistic Baby."

"It was just amazing how many ways he was able to spin that out, verse after verse," said Settle.

Shel frequently suggested to musicians whose work he admired that they write a few songs together, although, when the tables were turned and someone approached Shel instead of vice versa, things sometimes turned out quite differently.

One evening Shel was hanging out at a Village café with a bunch of people, including Mike Settle, and a total stranger came up to the table to compliment Shel's work, adding that he'd love to write with him sometime. "Shel gives him his phone number and the guy walks off," Settle remembered. "I asked why he gave him his number, thinking it was kind of dicey."

Shel shrugged. "People do that all the time," he said. "They come up to me and they want to say they met me or hung out with me. I give them my phone number and nobody ever calls."

Shel was starting to write and copyright so many songs that he had to form a business to handle the licensing. After considering several different options, Shel christened his music company Evil Eye.

Evil Eye appealed to him for several reasons. First, he considered himself to be a modern-day Gypsy of sorts, and Evil Eye is one term for a Gypsy spell. Also, since his maternal grandmother was born in Hungary, where there has always been a sizable Gypsy community, it's possible he could have some Gypsy blood in him. Indeed, fast-forward a couple of decades, and the only time he changed a poem in one of his children's books after it was published was in a poem about Gypsies.

And sometimes he used the evil eye himself when he wanted to get his own way. He'd squint with one eye while making the other pop out like a bug eye that looked, well, evil.

"He always envisioned himself as a satyr or some kind of mythical being," said songwriter Chris Gantry. "He took what was a typical Chicago Jewish look and turned it into a mythical look. His clothes accentuated that look as well as shaving his head. He played on that look."

"He considered himself to be the evil eye who stares everybody down," said Judy Henske. "That was what Shel did, he terrified people. Everyone was afraid of him."

While some thought he cultivated this look specifically to intimidate people, Gantry said it was for another reason.

"He did it to cover up his insecurity and so he would have the kind of image where no one would dare question his self-esteem," said Gantry. "He was an odd-looking man. He knew he didn't look like Clark Gable or anyone like that, so he created an image that was very sexual because he was also very insecure around women. Of course, women loved the way he looked, and he always seemed to be involved with a woman you wouldn't expect him to be around."

In short, he had successfully used his sense of satire and irony to create an image that was the polar opposite of how he saw himself.

After spending the better part of two years recuperating from the car accident, Shel felt ready to travel again. But the aftereffects of the accident stayed with him, albeit in a curious way. Instead of going gangbusters and researching four travelogues a year for *Playboy,* he scaled down to doing only one or two a year. He still traveled as much as—or more than—he did previously, but he decided that the assignments bogged down his lifestyle too much. He wanted to see what it was like to start to live a totally footloose lifestyle, exploring new things, taking off and going where he wanted to on a whim, and answering to nobody—not even Hef—except his creative muse.

"I'm free to leave, go wherever I please, do whatever I want," he said. "I believe everyone should live like that. Don't be dependent on anyone else, man, woman, child or dog. I want to go everywhere, look at and listen to everything. You can go crazy with some of the wonderful stuff there is in life."

So unless he had a deadline that was etched in stone or he had promised a friend he would be at a particular place at a specific time, Shel extended that freedom by contacting friends only when he felt the urge, taking off the same moment when he decided he wanted to be somewhere else. He tended to be most accessible when he was immersing himself into a new artistic genre or style of music and wanted to learn everything he could about it. But the rest of the time, he instructed people to leave messages for him in New York or Chicago, developed the habit of showing up unannounced, and hoped that people would accept it. Those who did stayed in his life. Those who didn't fell by the wayside.

The surprising thing is that he actually detested the travel. "It's miserable. You're lonely, you spend all your time packing and unpacking and looking for friends and restaurants and bars," he said. "Then you take off and you have to look for new friends, new restaurants, and new bars. I'm not content when I'm traveling but I'm not content when I'm *not* traveling. So I guess I'll keep traveling."

Shel never set out to write or draw for children. It wasn't anywhere on his radar screen. To him, it was the opposite of what he was doing for

Playboy, and he initially thought his friend, children's book author Tomi Ungerer, was nuts for suggesting it.

Considering the impatience he occasionally displayed toward the children of his friends, he probably thought it was a joke when Ungerer first suggested that he write for children. At the same time, Shel made no secret of the contempt he felt for the majority of books written for children, both newly published and classics from decades earlier.

"If you want to write for kids you've got to start with *Charlotte's Web* and *Stewart Little,*" he said. "Those damn books are so bad they're beautiful. The condescension is not only thick enough to walk on but absolutely destructive. Hell, a kid's already scared of being small and insignificant. So what does E. B. White give them? A mouse who's afraid of being flushed down the toilet or rolled up in a window shade and a spider who's getting ready to die."

He didn't hold back when it came to *Alice's Adventures in Wonderland,* either, but his scorn went deeper than Lewis Carroll's classic story that—like the *ABZ* book—was really written for adults. Indeed, he seemed distressed at the then-burgeoning trend of looking back at the good old days with rosy nostalgia.

"I never met a kid who liked *Alice in Wonderland,* and yet we think back on it as a wonderful book," he said. "We think back on this jivey neverland childhood that never existed when we all sat around eating penny candy and reading *Alice in Wonderland.* Pretty soon they'll convince us that we went swimming in the old swimming hole. Growing up in Chicago, I never saw no swimming hole."

Ursula Nordstrom had been a formidable influence in the world of children's literature for more than two decades when she met Shel in the early 1960s. Nordstrom began her lengthy tenure at Harper & Brothers—which later became Harper & Row and finally HarperCollins—in the college textbook department in 1931. After five years, she switched to an assistant in the children's book department and then became the editorial director of the department, where she stayed until her retirement in 1979.

During that time, she worked with a roster of legendary authors including Laura Ingalls Wilder, Margaret Wise Brown, E. B. White, and Maurice Sendak. As an editor, Nordstrom's philosophy was to publish "good books for bad children," and she knew Shel would fit right in. Nordstrom had admired his cartoons in *Playboy,* and when Ungerer—one of her authors—told her he knew him, she campaigned for a meeting, because she knew a children's author when she saw one.

In January 1963, he published his first children's book with Nordstrom, *Lafcadio: The Lion Who Shot Back,* and it is the book he always said was his favorite. "It has more story in it," he said. "Maybe it's that it presents just one idea. I think that books, even for really little kids, can deal with more than one idea. A story could deal with more, even fifty, and so can the reader if the ideas are all laid out."

He was heartened by how kids reacted positively to *Lafcadio,* as he said in a radio interview with Studs Terkel, but admitted that the odds were against him for his first book given the market for children's books back then. "You have to keep their interest up," he said, describing the challenge of writing a book for children but that whose purchase depended upon the mother liking it, too. "Kids don't buy books, mothers buy kids' books, so if you give a mother something that she considers charming and ideally what kids want, she'll buy it." He knew that many of these mothers bought into the nostalgia-tinged rose-colored view of childhood that Shel considered to be poison, but in the end, he decided not to worry about it and just write for himself.

"There are a lot of middle-aged women writing children's books and a lot of middle-aged women buying them, so they are really writing for each other," he said. Back in the early '60s, there was a trend toward having the illustrations in children's books look like children drew them, which he viewed in the same negative light as Disney's three-fingered cartoon characters.

"Children's illustrators are trying to draw like kids because they think kids will like it, but the last thing a kid wants to see is a drawing where he thinks he could have done it," he said. "Kids want detail. I love Dr. Seuss and kids love Dr. Seuss because there are details. There are things happening in the drawings. If you can't draw any better than a kid, he doesn't want to see that."

After *Lafcadio,* Ursula asked him, "What else do you have?"

He responded by producing three different children's books, all of which would be published in 1964. While he considered Harper & Row to be his children's publisher and Simon & Schuster his adult publisher, Shel showed the storyboards for one of those books—*The Giving Tree*—to Simon & Schuster first, who turned it down.

Shel appealed to his friend William Cole, another editor at the company. "Look Shel, the trouble with this *Giving Tree* of yours is that it falls between two stools," Cole remembered telling him. "It's not a kid's book, too sad, and it isn't for adults, too simple."

"You're going to be very sorry," said Shel as he gathered up his materials and walked out the door. He then offered the book to Ursula Nordstrom, who eagerly accepted it.

But even as he was putting the finishing touches on *The Giving Tree,* he was already looking around for the next craft to lose himself in. "I was fed up with writing books a long time ago," he said at the end of 1963. "If you don't do it, it means you don't want to do it," he said.

He may have come across as smug, and even though years later he admitted to being insecure about his writing, like many men in their early thirties who'd had cantankerous relationships with their fathers, Shel felt that what he had accomplished so far was not enough. He needed to continue to produce more and more work and in new and different genres in order to hammer it home to his father: *I was right. You were wrong.* Of course, later on he would eventually learn that no matter how many books, cartoons, and songs he wrote, it would never be enough to overcome his insecurities.

But for now, the work kept him going; it kept him sane. He did reveal that he was working on a new children's book, but in a format that was new to him: a book of nonsense verse. The working title was *Uncle Shelby's Crazy Poems.*

At the time, the only collection of verse for children that remotely resembled what Shel had in mind was by Edward Lear, a British Victorian poet whose best-known work was *The Owl and the Pussycat.* Shel regarded Lear with the same gimlet eye he viewed most children's authors.

"He was full of shit," said Shel. "I think much better limericks are being written today than were being written by Lear, because Lear's last line was always the same as his second line," which, in Shel's eyes, committed the mortal sin of laziness. Yet Lear's work still inspired him in one way. "Lear's dirty limericks, of course, are the greatest of all, but we don't see much of them. I have something coming out with a lot of dirty limericks but I haven't used any dirty words. I've invented my own dirty words. They're not a substitute for the other words, but can be used any way you want them. It turns out twice as filthy."

It would take another decade until *Uncle Shelby's Crazy Poems,* otherwise known as *Where the Sidewalk Ends,* would be published.

4. *Different Dances*

By 1964, Shel had created a larger body of work than most people do in ten lifetimes, which included several records, numerous cartoons and travelogue features published in *Playboy* and other magazines, a variety of books for children and adults, and several collaborations in theater, music, and book publishing. His near-fatal car accident had not mellowed him out and made him more sanguine about life. Instead it made him even more determined to create as much in as many different venues as possible.

"I am a better cartoonist than anything else. I write pretty good, but I pride myself on cartooning," he said at the time. "And I can cartoon for awhile, but when I have had enough cartooning, I can lay back and do nothing. But if you can do something else, maybe you can write songs for a while. And then you get sick of writing songs."

And while he hated to continually explain his work and decipher the message behind each of his cartoons or songs, Shel had no qualms about spreading the gospel of his own personal philosophy.

"There's not one thing that is going to make people happy," he said. "Not me, and from what I've seen, not everybody else. People often ask, out of all the places in the world, where would you like to spend your life? *Nowhere!* I never want to stay in one place. I don't think one thing can make a man happy, one job or one town."

Of course, he did recognize there were benefits to settling down in one place and doing one thing. "I'd like to be happy with one thing, it would save a lot of energy," he noted. "I'd like to be happy with one woman. It would be easier and give me more time to work and time to relax. But I don't find that one town or one woman, or one job or one career makes me happy. What makes me happy is changing all the time."

And the more people he met, the better. Among them were some surprises.

Before he became known as Johnny Carson's sidekick on *The Tonight Show* in 1962, Ed McMahon was active as the host of a weekly horror movie series in Philadelphia in the mid-1950s. He bought the rights to a movie called *Daughter of Horror,* widely regarded as one of the more intelligent and artistic horror films of the time, which in turn led him to the Carson show. In keeping with his horror host role, McMahon appeared in full makeup to introduce the movie, but he was also a singer and later, after starting his *Tonight Show* gig, recorded several albums.

"In 1955, Ed McMahon was considered to be hip," said *Playboy* cartoonist Jay Lynch, who has the peculiar hobby of collecting different versions of the song "Somebody Else, Not Me," which Shel had included on *Hairy Jazz.* "When I mentioned my hobby to Shel, he not only told me that McMahon had also recorded it but said that he worked with him on that very album, *Ed McMahon Sings.*"

Then there was Burl Ives. "Shel gave me a whole bunch of songs and I recorded some of them," said the late singer. "One was 'When She Cries,' which I think is a remarkable song. I like his style and he's quite a fellow. He's a thinker. He comes in a different door from most songwriters." Other songs that Ives recorded by Shel include "Comin' After Jenny," and "Time," a song about growing old. ·

In 1964, Shel's output continued on fast-forward when his three children's books, and one for adults, were published.

Uncle Shelby's Zoo: Don't Bump the Glump and Other Fantasies came out first from Simon & Schuster, a collection of cartoons, most of which had previously appeared in *Playboy.* He undoubtedly took great pleasure in the fact that the parents shelling out money to buy the book—again, like the *ABZ Book,* he wrote *Uncle Shelby's Zoo* for adults, but it looked like it was for kids—would be outraged if they knew where the cartoons had originally been published. *A Giraffe and a Half* and *Who Wants a Cheap Rhinoceros?* followed.

But his biggest book to come out that year—indeed, a book that some would consider his most controversial work—was *The Giving Tree,* published in October. The first printing was a modest seven thousand copies.

Shel didn't set out to write *The Giving Tree* to send a message to society, a point he continually reiterated with many of the books, songs, and cartoons he would write in the future.

"It's about a boy and a tree," is how Shel described the book. "It has a pretty sad ending."

"It's just a relationship between two people; one gives and the other takes," he said. "I didn't start out to prove a message. It started out to be a good book for a kid. I imagine it reflects my ideas, but it is for children. I would like adults to buy it and read it, and I hope they can find enough in it."

In fact, given his disgust with the me-first attitude among the folksingers and other artists in the Village who were creating art as a form of self-analysis, it almost sounds like he wrote it as an experiment, a reaction to their own mushiness. While he clearly wanted to tell a story with universal implications, he also wanted to keep it deliberately murky.

"Non-specific is what everybody is digging today," he said. "And if you write a poem, I can't expect you to write about Shel Silverstein, can I? But if you write about jive-y mystical things I can say, 'Yeah, you're talking about me and my scene.' Just say something that nobody can understand and they'll really dig it now."

As the book caught on, the critics were fast and furious, and continued on through the height of the women's liberation movement ten years later.

Shel's friend and fellow cartoonist Jules Feiffer had a different, gentler take on the theme. "Women hate it because they think it's the exploitation of the mother tree giving everything and sacrificing everything," he said. "But it's clearly a little boy's fantasy of growing into manhood with the kind of love he never got and inventing it as a tree because Mom wasn't there to give it."

Every year, the *Chicago Tribune* ran a story profiling the city's most eligible bachelors, and Shel was a perennial favorite on the list. If any young marriage-minded Chicagoland women had Shel in their sights as a possibility, the update the paper published six months later did much to dash their hopes.

A reporter contacted him in 1964 for a follow-up, on the eve of his trip to the South Pacific. Were there any potential Mrs. Silversteins in his future? No, he answered unequivocally. "The closer you get to Tahiti, the further you get from marriage," he said.

"He always made it very clear that he had no intention of settling down, and he'd tell the girls not to get their hooks in him, because it wasn't going to work," said Dianne Chandler, the Playmate for September 1966, who became friends with Shel during the three-month-long photo shoot when she stayed in the Blue Room while he was living in the Mansion. "I think there were a lot of girls who really had stars in their eyes when they first met him. He was like a heat-seeking missile. When he was with you, he was *with* you, intensely concentrating on only you."

Chandler admits that she fell hard for Shel at first. But after a few encounters with him, she realized that he was not boyfriend material. "He's just here, he's having fun. In an hour from now he could be out of here," she explained.

Whenever she saw another girl get a little too clingy with him, Chandler knew what was coming. "He instantly saw the signs and would say something like, 'Well, let's see, where shall I put you on my list?' to let the girls know that they shouldn't expect anything from him.

"He always seemed to be on a quest, he knew his gift was magic, and he made no excuses for the way he acted," she added.

Though he eschewed fame, he wasn't above using his fame to his advantage when it came to attracting women. "They would squeal, 'Oh, it's Shel Silverstein!'" said Hillary Mapes, Jo Mapes's daughter. And he was off and running.

"He knew his way around a skirt," said Skip Williamson, a fellow cartoonist at *Playboy.*

Life at the Playboy Mansion was a kind of never-never land, and Shel fit right in. One day, writer Larry DuBois showed up at the Mansion for a two-hour interview with Hef and stayed for six months. "That's how that world worked," said DuBois. "When Shel showed up at the Chicago Mansion, he had no way of knowing whether he was going to be there for six hours or six weeks, because it all depended on how much fun he was having, what else was going on, and how he felt. And if Hef was comfortable having you around, he didn't care how long you were there."

Shel tended to view the Mansion antics as kind of a petri dish, a breeding ground he could use to generate ideas for his work.

"At the parties, Shel would always lurk in the background," said DuBois. "I'd see him just out of the corner of my eye, lurking on a couch somewhere, mostly watching. He did talk to people, but he wouldn't run across the room to say hello when someone walked in, he'd wait until you worked your way around to him. And he'd be dressed in the same clothes you saw him in ten nights ago."

Kerig Pope noted that Shel didn't talk to just anyone who wandered by. "He was automatically drawn to those people who had something to say. He was entertained by wit and brilliance. And if he encountered somebody—male or female—who was just kind of average, he wouldn't have any patience for them," said Pope.

When he did mingle at a party, he'd move from one group to another, sometimes rather quickly. When he had everything he could get from the group to fuel his creativity, he moved onto the next. Sometimes he would leave—either a cluster of people or the Mansion—in the middle of a sentence if he wasn't suitably engaged. "Shel was a tough customer, and he did not brook idiots lightly," said DuBois. "If he liked you and was intrigued by you, he was just the most engaging companion you could ever have. But, if you bored him or offended him, he could get rather chilly rather fast."

One of the things that would make him turn cool is if people started asking him boring questions about how he worked and where his ideas came from. "The temperature in the room would drop instantly," said DuBois. "That was just something you didn't discuss with Shel."

And when he had a sense that he had culled everything that he could from his time spent in a particular place, he never had any qualms about picking up and moving on.

"I remember one time when we were just sitting around the Chicago Mansion, and it was just time for Shel to move on," said DuBois. "I don't remember the context, but it was clear that he had done whatever he was going to do here and he literally just got up and put on his knapsack. I can still see him walking out of the ballroom. He said good-bye and went to New York and then God knows where else. I have no reason to believe that Shel ever owned a piece of luggage because whenever he left, he just had his knapsack."

Indeed, his needs were simple in terms of clothing. He traveled America in his jeans and his jeans jacket. He had duplicate wardrobes—the jeans, the tunics and caftans, and later, the pirate shirts—everywhere he went, and it was easy enough to pick up a few more if necessary. As long as he had his sketchbook and pens, he was all set.

"His rule was don't stay anyplace long enough for you to take root," said Dave Mapes. "His brain was almost always in motion and so was his body. Part of that was just the defensive side of Shel, he just didn't want to put down roots for whatever reason, or he couldn't put down roots, and that's why he would always remain in motion."

But despite his best intentions to remain emotionally unattached, it didn't always work. When he was at the Mansion, there were times when the If You Don't Swing, Don't Ring motto presented him with some hard life lessons.

Late one night, Shel was in the Red Room when he heard the sounds of passionate lovemaking coming through the wall, where a woman he was secretly in love with, but who had rejected him, was staying. "I remember lying there thinking, You better be able to take this, because this is a part of the dues. If you can't take it, go out where you're safe, where you'll never hear it, but you'll never have it, either."

The Mansion had one room called the breakfast room, where visitors and Bunnies wandered in to drink coffee or have breakfast or lunch. "It was the Mansion's version of a Starbucks," said DuBois. "You never knew who was going to show up, it was Jack Nicholson or Arnold Schwarzenegger." Shel would sit in the breakfast room and sometimes join the conversation—most of the time he was content just to listen—but his sketchpad was never far away. While he sat there, he'd doodle absentmindedly on his pad. DuBois always paid attention to Shel's doodles, and later on he would see that those drawings were the rough drafts of the illustrations that later filled *Where the Sidewalk Ends* and *A Light in the Attic*.

Because of his commitments to the magazine, Shel made it back to Chicago as often as possible. And now that money was not an issue, he began to help his parents out as much as he could. But the old hurts were there, as well as the tension between Shel and his father.

In an effort to make peace, Shel bought his father a brand-new reclining sofa to replace the decades-old couch with those horrible clear plastic slipcovers where Nathan sat to watch television. Like many immigrant parents, Nathan and Helen put up a fuss whenever their adult children spent money on them, and Nathan clearly resented Shel's success and the fact that his cartoons had paid for the couch. When the movers arrived to deliver the new couch and remove the old one, Shel's parents argued over it every step of the way in a routine worthy of classic Abbott and Costello. In the end, the new couch went back to the store and the old couch went back on its four floor protector disks along with the slipcovers, and the standoff between father and son was as strong as ever.

Now that he was traveling again, the relationship Shel had with his native city in his early thirties was as hostile as the relationship with his father.

"It's my home, and I get all excited about coming back, but then something happens," he said. "Chicago doesn't come through. It quits, at least when it comes to the things I care about." His major complaint was that the Chicago arts community in the early '60s was pretty much nonexistent, at least in his eyes. Of course, he was comparing it with the arts scene in New York, and any other city would come up short.

On the flip side, growing up in a city lacking in culture wasn't totally without its merits as Shel did realize that a blank slate was an advantage. "I haven't been subject to anyone else's ideas so I started out with what I had to say," he noted.

One reason Shel had soured on his hometown was because of the way an audience responded to his reaction to a performance he felt was below par.

"That which was good I felt very strong about, and that which I thought was bad I reacted against," he said. "So I booed, and the people sitting around me didn't take it well. Why are we so concerned about people's feelings? We forget that applause is supposed to mean a certain amount of appreciation and acceptance of the work. If the guy up there stinks, he stinks. He didn't make it exciting or connect with you and he should not be applauded. Yell like hell for what you like. And spit at what you don't like."

Shel began to encourage his friends to fully explore their own talents, perhaps not in as many directions as he did, but once somebody expressed interest in exploring another art form, Shel was right there. Jean Shepherd was one of the first. In early 1964, Shepherd mentioned to Shel that he'd like to write a book and have it published, but that he wasn't a writer, he was a comedian who primarily performed on radio. That's all it took.

"Shel kept talking about various other talent that he thought belonged in the magazine," said Hefner. "He kept talking about Jean, and he had been telling Jean to write, to put his material down on paper for *Playboy*. Jean had never written before and was reluctant to do it, but Shel sat down with a tape recorder and got him to tell some of his stories like he did on the air. They edited that material, and that's what began Jean Shepherd's writing career."

Though he enjoyed helping his friends explore new careers, Shel was still restless. He was looking for something new to explore, to immerse himself in, and he said that songwriting had little appeal for him anymore. "I'm sick of writing songs," he said. "It's possible that I might never write any more songs. It's also possible that in three months I could write another whole batch, but lately there has been no reason for me to write any songs."

The truth is he just didn't want to write folk songs anymore. Shel wanted to go to Nashville and write country music. After all, he had grown up listening to the *Grand Ole Opry* every Saturday night. But after his disgust over the folksinger scene, he was particularly drawn to the few people in country music he had met. "The people are real there," he said. "And they make no pretensions about the music."

So he set out on another path, using his *Playboy* reputation to make inroads into the country music world. In the beginning, some in Nashville were put off. Who was this Jew from Chicago who wants to write country music? But overall, they were intrigued.

Indeed, after dealing with the hypocrisy inherent to the folk scene, it was easy to see why country music appealed to him. "To me, country music was about telling it like it was, about being honest about your life in your music," said Kris Kristofferson. "Pop music was pretty bland, but country music was about cheating, drinking, going to jail. It was the white man's blues."

"I don't think his Jewishness was ever an issue in Nashville," said Melanie Howard, the widow of the songwriter Harlan Howard.

"He stood out, especially early on," said Bobby Bare. "People in Nashville were conservative, and Shel was kind of freaky looking."

But his ethnic background didn't seem to be a factor, and if it was, he let it slide off his back. Songwriter Chris Gantry met Shel back in 1967. "They thought he was odd looking and odd sounding, but then again all of us were from out of town," he said. "Shel was from Chicago, I was from New York, Kristofferson was from Brownsville, Texas. At the time, the business had the first influx of writers that came from a different part of the country instead of being home-grown, which was the traditional way."

Fred Foster, founder of the Monument Record Company, which had released albums by Roy Orbison and Dolly Parton, first met Shel at the Mansion in 1964. Foster was in Chicago to talk with Hef about producing a *Playboy* line of record albums, starting with one of Hef's protégés, Johnny Janis, a baritone crooner in the style of Frank Sinatra.

The introduction served Shel when he traveled to Nashville about a year later. Foster served as his mentor as Shel visited a dozen times over several months to grill him. It didn't take Foster long to anticipate Shel's frequent creative quirks. "In the middle of a conversation, he'd catch an idea out of thin air and just start writing," said Foster. "And then he'd disappear to finish it."

Another time, Foster noticed that Shel was staring at him peculiarly. "Uh-oh," thought Foster, "he's got a song in his head that's screaming to come out."

But instead of jumping up and starting to write ferociously in his sketchpad, he just kept staring. Foster was starting to worry. "He could be so explosive," he said.

Then Shel jumped out of his chair, screaming, "I got it! I got it!"

"What do you got?" asked Foster.

"The next chick I see who has double initials, I'm sending her to you, you'll make her a star, and we'll all be rich."

"What are you talking about?"

"I was just counting up all the double initial people around here," Shel replied in a matter-of-fact voice. "You go all the way back to Patti Page."

"And then he started rattling off the names of all the successful people I had worked with," Foster remembered. "Kris Kristofferson, Bob Becker, who worked in my publishing company. I published some of Harlan Howard's songs and did an album with him. Shel just kept going. Boudleaux Bryant, who with his wife Felice, wrote an astounding six thousand songs."

"That'll be failsafe," Shel told him. "Any chick I see who has double initials, she's a star. If she can get to you, she's a star."

Of course, Shel counted himself in that roster, too, given his double initials.

Because of his unique take on life—he probably appeared more real than anyone in Nashville—Shel seemed heartened at the warm reception he received.

"He was accepted here," said Foster. "He asked me one time, 'Can you imagine a Jew making it in Nashville?' I said, hell, yeah, who cares? You are what you are, and if you're likable and talented, you're going to make it. And he did.

"There were a few old-timers who never really got to know him and thought he was kind of bizarre," Foster added. "But the people in the Kristofferson genre and the younger producers like myself, we all adored him."

"He hung with people who were the vagabonds and tramps and misfits of Nashville," said Chris Gantry. "That's the only kind of people that he felt comfortable around."

While Shel wasn't recognized in Nashville as often as he was in New York or Chicago, there were times when someone would stop him on the

street or in a coffee shop and ask for an autograph. "He downplayed it," said Gantry. "He'd be very polite and sociable but try not to say anything that would make the conversation continue. He was very cool that way, he never called any attention to himself. And he didn't act like a star, either. He was more content just sitting back observing."

In 1965, Chess Records released Shel's album *I'm So Good That I Don't Have to Brag!* on the Cadet label. When his next record *Drain Your Brain* came out the following year, it was uniformly panned by critics. One critic for *The Los Angeles Times* wrote, "His cartoons in *Playboy* are funny. His songs aren't. And he can't sing, either."

But he *could* write songs. "He learned a lot about songwriting from me and I learned a lot about songwriting from him," said Chris Gantry. "We had a similar style. Our songs are like movies, you can see it unfold while you sing, and there's a lot of imagery in them. There's a beginning, a middle, and an ending. Our songs were very unlike the kind of songs that are being written now in Nashville, or basically anywhere."

However, what his new Nashville friends didn't know was that while Shel had a real love for country music, he viewed it in the same vein as his other artistic pursuits: as pure satire, writing songs where he was poking fun at the whole nature of country music, while being well aware that few people would get the joke.

"Shel's whole foray into country music began as a parody of country music," said Skip Williamson, a cartoonist at *Playboy*. "Shel's version of country, you know, isn't really country, it's a satire of country." However, once he got to know some of the musicians and songwriters and started writing with them and found it pretty easy to do, he took it more seriously and concentrated on honing his craft.

And he knew his voice was nothing to write home about. "Nobody gives me any static about my voice," Shel said. "They just aren't charmed by it. I don't see anyone running out and buying my records, but I like the way I sing."

"Ol' Shel has probably got the worst voice of anyone alive, but he's

also got the run of the Playboy mansion, and I'm not knocking anybody with a deal like that," joked Chet Atkins.

Bobby Bare told a funny story about one time when they were rehearsing at one of the usual low-budget motels where Shel stayed when he was in Nashville.

They had been going over stuff for a while, and finally Shel grabbed the guitar from Bare and started singing the song the way he thought it should be done. "He sang a couple of lines, and right away there was a pounding on the wall from the room next door," said Bare, "and a woman screamed 'Shut the fuck up!' I said, 'Shel, I've been sitting here singing for two or three hours and nothing happened. You open up your mouth once and that voice slashed through the wall and woke that woman up.'"

"I saw him once on the *Playboy After Hours* TV show when Hugh Hefner plunked a guitar in his hands, said 'Sing Shel' and then ran," said Ray Sawyer of Dr. Hook. "Shel sang in a voice that was like a whispered scream or someone getting his bollocks caught in barbed wire. He sang 'The Unicorn' and if I hadn't known how the schmucky thing went from the Irish Rovers' version, I wouldn't have known what Shel was trying to do. [Manager] Ronnie's [Haffkine] job as translator at times must have been close to deciphering the Rosetta Stone."

But that voice never staunched the flow of women to his bed.

"I'd pick his brain for tips on living cool," said Rik Elswit, also of Dr. Hook. "First and foremost, I had to know why women followed him around in packs. Shel was not handsome. Even in the artistic circles of the '60s, when sex was just an emphatic way of saying hello, he had vastly better luck than the rest of us. Maybe it was his eyes; they would twinkle and pierce simultaneously, giving you the impression that he knew something you didn't. For whatever reasons, women hit on him constantly, and hard. He made no promises or apologies. Yet, they'd all speak warmly of him afterward."

Kris Kristofferson tells of one of the countless times Shel was entertaining a woman in his room at the Ramada Inn. "He didn't want to turn the lights on, but he wanted a little light, so he called the front desk and asked if they could turn on the red message light on his phone," he said. "They turned it on, and he used it as his mood light."

If a girl just wanted to be friends instead of lovers, Shel was fine with that. "Shel just enjoyed their companionship if that was all they were willing to share with him," said Larry DuBois. "Shel was very sweet about that, he wasn't one of the assholes about girls."

He even had a framed needlepoint on his wall that read, *Shel Silverstein made me make this for him*. It was signed by a Playmate of the Year.

Dianne Chandler said that she and Shel remained friends after she moved out of the Mansion. "I wasn't his girlfriend, but whenever we'd go out, he'd treat me like a girlfriend, he'd put his arm around me or hug me, but he never tried to get intimate with me," she said. "We were really just good buddies, and I never knew him to really hit on anybody real hard. Everyone understood that Shel was like a butterfly, he never seemed to stick with one girlfriend for long. But, nobody got mad at him, because he was so sweet and upfront about it."

Chandler traveled for promotional gigs in the late 1960s for a few years after her centerfold first appeared, and she was always reluctant to travel to the Deep South.

"People there would ask me how I felt about working for that nigger-loving company, and I was appalled," she said.

But she needed the work, so she reluctantly went and would vent about it later with Shel. "He was the only person at *Playboy* I could really confide in without getting into trouble," she said. "He told me I had to be patient, and to look at the progress the company was making, but he would also say there was nothing I could do."

"You cannot single-handedly enlighten all the people in the South," he told her. "All you can do is set a good example."

And then he dropped a bomb.

"There are a lot of places in Chicago where I can't get an apartment because I'm a Jew," he said.

Though he lived at the Mansion most of the time, he rented a separate apartment nearby so he could have a private retreat. "Everybody was always after him to sing a song, tell a story, draw a cartoon," said Chandler, "and eventually the lack of privacy got to him, so he got a small place where he could be by himself and think and write. He once told me, 'Paradise is nice, but you can't get any work done there.'"

When he first looked for a rental, he couldn't rent in certain WASP-y neighborhoods, and had doors slammed in his face in places where he thought he was welcome. This despite the fact that he was well-known not only throughout the city but also across the country by this time.

When Shel was at the Mansion, he would still spend time with Hef, but as time went on, he went to fewer parties and nightly gatherings than before. If he wanted to leave Hef and *Playboy* behind for a while—as he had done with his other circles—he didn't want to let go entirely, since he owed a real debt to Hef for giving him his start. He held on, but just enough so that no one could ever question his integrity and commitment to Hef.

"It was almost as if Shel and Hef had a professional appreciation for one another, but it didn't go beyond that," said Chandler. "They both understood that if they became best buddies and went bowling together, it would diminish each of them in the other's eyes. They appreciated and admired one another, but Shel didn't want to let the bloom go off the rose, really. He didn't want to show his complete hand to Hef."

"I always felt Shel was holding something back, maybe because he had another outlet for it and he just didn't know where to put it yet," said Chandler. "He wasn't dissatisfied, but what he did was never enough. There was clearly something else that was more rewarding, but he didn't know what it was. I always thought that Shel was looking down the road or just over the next mountain to do something else."

In the late 1960s, tens of thousands of young people from all over the country began to gravitate to San Francisco—in particular, to the

Haight-Ashbury neighborhood—to partake of the counterculture move-ment of sex, drugs, and rock and roll, and Shel was among them. He had always made it a point to be where the hip, creative people were, and at that time the most happening place was San Francisco. The music pulled him in, as usual, as Janis Joplin, Jimi Hendrix, and the Jefferson Airplane were regular performers, and the people made him stay, especially the women. "He was very attracted to hippie chicks, and they were very at-tracted to him," said Hefner.

Shel initially stayed with friends in the city, but he soon discovered a unique community of houseboats across the bay in Sausalito, and de-cided to move there since San Francisco was beginning to feel a bit like the Mansion: too crowded and with too many people interrupting his work. He wanted to be in a place where he could sit outside and work or wander around on hours-long walks without having someone come up to him and start gushing about how much they loved his work.

First, he liked living near a large body of water. In Chicago, of course, Lake Michigan was never too far away. The great irony—keeping with his love of all things satirical—was that he became seasick at the drop of a hat. Because it was a bay, the water never got too rough, but whenever a storm went through that made the boats rock even a little, Shel would leave. "He was definitely a fair weather sailor," said Larry White.

He also liked funky buildings, and a houseboat fit the bill.

There was also guaranteed to be a steady stream of interesting people living nearby. The houseboat community was a mix of bohemian folks and wealthy people who saw it as an opportunity to live in a unique house right on the water. Activist Alan Watts, the painter known as Varda, actor Sterling Hayden, Janis Joplin, the Grateful Dead, comedian John Byner, and many other famous people lived nearby or were regular visitors. Shel met actor Rip Torn there, who was instrumental in having Shel score the music for Torn's 1972 movie about the country music industry, *Payday*.

Richardson Bay got its start in the 1950s when people without homes or much money converted wrecked World War II ships and barges into homes, either by fixing up the inside or by building a modified cabin on top. In the beginning, the houseboat community was essentially a community of squatters who had only salvage rights. "If you found an abandoned boat and fixed it up, everybody knew it was yours," said White. "The whole place was a bit like living in never-never land." And since Shel was a modern-day Peter Pan, the two fit together perfectly.

The community was self-sufficient, with community gardens and an organic septic system. The residents even created their own movie theater, with a screen on one boat and a projector on another and the movie would beam across the water. People could sit in their boats and watch movies at night.

The abandoned San Rafael ferry served as the path leading up to Shel's front door. It was in pretty ratty shape, with splintered boards all over the floors and walls, but it served as a literal barrier to the outside world, beyond which point was a magical place, a timeless world.

Shel's houseboat was built on an old World War II balloon barge. The boat was sixty-five feet long and eighteen feet wide, but with the extensions—including a large bedroom with the bed built on a platform that cantilevered out over the water—it stretched to almost eighty feet.

There were windows all around the boat, including some made of stained glass, and old worn oriental rugs covered the floor.

As was the case with his New York apartment, the houseboat primarily served as Shel's workspace, with numerous desks and tables scattered throughout surrounded by bookcases crammed with old books from floor to ceiling.

It was a place that made Shel's imagination run wild.

"Large windows wrapped around the bed so he could lay in bed, pull the curtains aside, and watch the moonlight dancing on the water," said White. Plus, he could listen to the late-night gatherings on the docks if he chose not to participate himself.

In the galley space—accessed by climbing down a ladder—was an old Franklin woodburning stove, and though Shel rarely cooked, he would invite friends over for coffee in the morning. In the galley there was a large window cantilevered out over the water just like his bed, and people would row right up to that window, and step into the boat to come in and have coffee with him. When they were ready to leave, they'd crawl out the window, get back into their rowboats, and paddle away.

Shel continued to serve as a surrogate uncle to some of his friends' kids, but in at least one instance, he was a bona fide father figure.

Jo Mapes knew it was time for her thirteen-year-old son to learn about the birds and the bees, but she believed it was a job for a man. In her mind, the only person who could do the job was Shel. "My mother respected him so much that she entrusted him with the task," said Dave. "While we talked, he stressed that just because I *could* make a baby didn't mean that I *should*. He was very much an advocate of taking responsibility for your own actions, and he really taught me about accountability."

Mapes was impressed that while Shel took his mother's request seriously, he also handled it with the seriousness it deserved. "It was a side of Shel I hadn't seen," he said. "It was a little bit more of his core, the real Shel without the big chuckle and his larger-than-life presence. And it was Shel speaking as Shel, not as a character in a song or a book."

At the same time, Shel couldn't resist introducing a wide-eyed teenage boy who had rivers of hormones coursing through his body to the possibilities of what the birds and the bees could present. Not too long after they had the Talk, Jo asked her son to deliver a Christmas present to Shel at the Mansion. The gift? A Christmas-themed fur-lined jock strap that Jo had made for Shel. "She bought a plain old high school jockstrap and lined it with fur," said Dave. She put brass bells on it and strategically positioned a sprig of mistletoe right on the waistband. "And I bicycled over, in the winter, to the Mansion. He let me in, and talk about heaven for a thirteen-year-old boy."

The Mapes family actually created a whole new circle for Shel because Jo Mapes eventually married Sam Hochman, who became one of Shel's lifelong friends. While he was still interested in pursuing as many new women as possible—and living at the Mansion, of course he had his pick—Shel also was strengthening what would turn into lifelong friendships. He simply wanted the familiar company around him at the same time his career was on fast-forward.

"Their marriage gave Shel two friendships in one," said Dave. "He had his friendship with Sam, and another with my Mom. Once Sam and Mom got together, that particular circle tightened for Shel."

Dave's sister Hillary remembers the version of the Talk that Shel delivered to her. "He was very opinionated about life," she said. "He sat down with me and said when I grew up, I shouldn't be like any of the other women. 'Don't ever grow up to be one of these stupid broads,' was the way he put it. He wanted me to be like my mother because she was a straight-shooting broad who didn't take any shit from anybody."

Like her brother, Hillary was touched by Shel's concern and his blunt advice. "He was bigger than life, but he was also hard to pin down," she said. "Once you thought you knew him, he would do something or act in a way to let you know that you really didn't know him."

Once, when Hillary was recovering from eye surgery, Shel visited every day to read to her. He wrote her a poem about the Zillary Bird, a play on her name, drew an accompanying picture, and gave it to her. She cherished it, but many years later the drawing was stolen.

Several years after the drawing went missing, Hillary ran into Shel at the Mansion and asked him to draw another one. "He never wanted anyone to know he was a nice guy, so he said, 'No way, forget it, I'm not doing it.'

"A month later, I saw him again and he handed me a drawing behind his back. He told me not to ever tell anybody that he had done this for me," she said, adding that the second drawing of the Zillary Bird was almost identical to the first one he had done years earlier, as was the poem.

"Shel really had a difficult time being intimate," Hillary said. "He handed me the poem behind his back because he didn't like the intimacy. For Shel to look me straight in the face and hand it to me would be an acknowledgement of something intimate between us, to admit he had feelings. And I knew he had them, but he wasn't good at showing them. So he'd get embarrassed and shut down."

In 1967, a little-known Canadian group of folksingers by way of Ireland would record a song Shel wrote back in 1962, which appeared on his album of that same year, *Inside Folk Songs*. It would propel both band and songwriter into the stratosphere, at least for a little while.

The Irish Rovers were a little-known touring band of folksingers who, like a thousand other bands at the time, were trying to become a little more known. They had already recorded a live album for the Decca label that didn't go anywhere, but since they had booked a gig on the *Smothers Brothers* TV show, their rep at the record company arranged for the band of five Irishmen to record another album while they were in Los Angeles. The studio brought on professional musicians for the session, which included an unknown singer and guitarist named Glen Campbell, who had cut a song called "Gentle on My Mind" the previous day.

The Rovers had been primarily performing for children, and a song that always delighted the kids was a fable Shel had written about Noah's ark called "The Unicorn." The group decided to include it on their second album and chose it for the title, even though the other songs on the album were old Irish ballads and folk songs.

"The Unicorn" single hit the top of the charts in the spring when it was first released and stayed there through the rest of the summer. Shel had written his first number one song.

In 1968, it had been four years since *The Giving Tree* had been published to wide acclaim and criticism, and Ursula Nordstrom's impatience was starting to show because it didn't look like Shel was going to deliver another children's book any time soon. The sales department and executives at Harper & Row were pressuring her for another book by Shel that would fill the company's coffers and build on his growing name recognition.

Occasionally, whenever he was in New York, Shel would drop by the offices for a visit, but Nordstrom knew that if she put any pressure on him, she didn't know when she'd see him again.

After *The Giving Tree* came out, he loosely promised her that his next book would be ready in, say, three or four years, but 1968 came and went, and Shel mentioned nothing about a firm deadline.

Nordstrom's frustration with him rubbed her the wrong way in her deadline-oriented world. In a letter she wrote in 1968 in response to a phone call she had received from Shel out of the blue, Nordstrom wrote in her typical charm-mixed-with-drama style, "You are a rotten no-goodnik to disappear for such long periods of time. Not even a postcard, you rat."

In reply, he updated her about the status of the children's poems for his expected next book—tentatively titled *Uncle Shelby's Crazy Poems*—and mentioned meeting Maurice Sendak, another author in her stable, on Fire Island. Shel suggested hiring the author of *Where the Wild Things Are* to illustrate his book. She told him that Sendak didn't normally collaborate with others, but that *Crazy Poems* might be the exception. In any case, she was encouraging Shel to get on with his work and send her whatever he could as soon as possible, citing an upcoming sales conference where next season's books are presented to sales reps and others in the marketing department so they could start selling to their accounts.

The two of them were having lunch together, and Nordstrom told Shel she was feeling a little blue. She asked how he learned to be so comfortable with himself, and if he was in therapy.

"No therapy!" he said loudly in the quiet restaurant. "Why should I? If I were hung up on goats, why I would just find myself the sweetest prettiest cleanest goat in the world, that's what I'd do."

Nordstrom quickly changed the subject.

He worked on what he wanted to work on in his own time. But the concept of *Sidewalk* had been taking root in his brain for many years, since the early '60s at least. In the days when he was trying to cultivate his *Playboy* image, out of necessity, it seems, he didn't talk about what he was working on for children, and he let few people from one of his worlds cross over into another.

His buddy Ron Haffkine was one of the privileged few. He dropped by Shel's Greenwich Village apartment to pick him up to go out to dinner. Shel let him in, but told him to wait while he finished up his work.

"As I sat on the couch waiting, I observed something about him that I have seen many times, but the impact of that first time I have never forgotten. As he worked, hunched over his desk, his long bony fingers drew and redrew each character as he giggled to himself like a child," said Haffkine. "There would be quiet for a while, then a burst of laughter. It was as though he were enjoying something that someone else had created especially for him."

On February 24, 1969, Johnny Cash first sang "A Boy Named Sue" in public at his San Quentin Prison concert, which was being recorded for an album to be released in the spring. At his performance, Cash was reading the words more than he was singing them. "The lyrics were so new to me that I had to sing them off a sheet of paper on a music stand, but they were exactly right for the moment," said Cash. "They lightened the mood in what was otherwise a very heavy show. In fact, the laughter just about tore the roof off."

When the time came to choose the songs for the *Live at San Quentin* album, Cash suggested "Sue." His producer and manager didn't agree, because it was a novelty song, not a country song, and they thought he'd lose some of his country fans.

But then Cash told them that "A Boy Named Sue" had been written by the same man who wrote "The Unicorn," and they put it on the album.

When the song came out a few months later, it hit number one on the

Billboard country charts for five weeks and spent three weeks at number two on the pop charts.

Shel supposedly wrote the song after hearing Jean Shepherd complain about his name, because he was often teased as a child for having a girl's name. Shep turned his experiences into rich farce on his radio show, among them a teacher in elementary school who always spelled his name Gene, and once when he was automatically put into a gym class for girls because of his name. "I fist-fought my way through every grade in school," said Shepherd. "How do you think I got so aggressive? So wiry?"

While the exact inspiration for the song remains undocumented, Jean's protests were custom-made for Shel's innate ability to take a unique aspect of a person's life and turn it into a song. In any case, Shel won his first Grammy the following year for "A Boy Named Sue," named as best country song.

The powers-that-be at RCA saw the value in riding on the coattails of Cash's album, and Shel's next album, *A Boy Named Sue and Other Country Songs,* was released in May of 1969. However, the album sold poorly, which could be variously attributed to (a) Shel's ethnic background, (b) his lack of national name recognition despite Cash's number-one rendition of "A Boy Named Sue," (c) his raspy voice, or (d) all of the above. But to Shel, it didn't matter; he was already on to the next thing by the time the album was released.

Despite his increasing fame, Shel was still open to listening to the work of unknown songwriters. Jef Jaisun was a songwriter living in San Francisco with a few novelty tunes he wanted to record and produce. He knew Shel lived just across the bay, and he wanted to try them out on him first, especially since "A Boy Named Sue" was all over the radio that summer. He convinced a friend of a friend to provide an introduction, and he visited Shel on his houseboat, guitar in tow.

"It felt a bit like going to the top of the mountain to talk to the guru," Jaisun said.

Shel told him that he'd take a listen and Jeff played the two songs he had prepared. Shel liked the songs but said that both were a little too long. "When you do a comedy, make it short and get off," Shel told him.

Jaisun took his advice and completely sliced the middle verse out of "It's Ragtime," the song on the B side of the record he released in the fall of 1969. The A side was "Friendly Neighborhood Narco Agent," which became the top song of 1975 on the Dr. Demento weekly radio show.

As the world was beating a path to his door in the wake of his song-writing success, Shel was in retreat, and for good reason. Nineteen seventy was about to bring him the biggest surprise of his life so far.

5. *Drain My Brain*

The pace of life on the West Coast suited Shel, and as the '70s began, he spent the majority of his time living in California.

In 1970, it wasn't entirely clear that the Summer of Love had completely ended, so while some who had committed their lives to saving the world and ending the Vietnam War through peace, love, and flower power were still hanging on, many others had left it behind and were clearly looking to see what was next. Then, as now, California was the place where many trends got their start before eventually becoming part of mainstream America, and some of the possibilities in the experimental stage included organic food, disco spreading beyond the walls of local gay discotheques, communal living, and the back-to-the-land movement. Those who didn't want to leave San Francisco but who favored living in a cooperative neighborhood with like-minded people had begun to flock to the small houseboat communities in the bay.

Larry White was a photographer who lived in a nearby houseboat on San Francisco Bay and served as the caretaker for some of the other boats in the community. John Kendall was a graduate student who had just arrived from New Hampshire to attend school, and like most students, he was broke and looking for a place to stay. They had met in the city, and White invited him out to Richardson Bay to stay for the winter because he needed another person to help him houseboat-sit for one of his clients. White asked Kendall if he was handy with tools.

The cantilevered window in the galley of Shel's houseboat turned out to be a huge design flaw because it was built too close to the surface of the water. Whenever more than a few people were visiting, the boat sank down a few inches, and water poured in through the window.

Though Shel loved his houseboat, he knew that it needed some work and he wasn't the one to do it. "Shel was not handy," said White. "He wasn't good with a hammer and pliers and didn't know how to put things together. While he was a visionary in his work, he was not a practical person and he didn't know how to fix his boat."

Nashville producer Fred Foster remembered that the first time he met Shel at the Mansion it was clear the place was filled with men who were less than handy around the house. Then again, with a staff numbering over a hundred, twenty-four-hour room service, and more nubile young girls gathered in one place than they knew what to do with, knowing how to handle a hammer and nails wasn't usually the first priority.

"They were talking about this expensive pool table that they couldn't use because the felt was warped, and they didn't know what to do," said Foster. "Hef and all the big shots at the magazine were gathered around the table, examining it at every angle and wringing their hands while Shel stood by watching this, utterly fascinated. I told them it's sitting by the swimming pool, for God's sake, with all this humidity the felt is curling up. Put a heat lamp over the thing and it will straighten out. They did, it worked, and they couldn't get over it. I think I even got a note from Hef."

Shel knew that while he needed to find a couple of people to work on his boat, he didn't want to tell them outright that he wanted them to completely overhaul the boat. After all, even though the '60s were over in the rest of the country, people in San Francisco were still living like it was the Summer of Love, and he knew it would be hard to find people who wanted to work.

Kendall remembered the way he and White got suckered into doing the work.

"Guys," said Shel, "I've got this opportunity to go somewhere for the winter, but I'm really torn between staying here and freezing my ass off on my boat or going to the Mansion, where it's a lot warmer and with much better visuals."

"Once he got us to agree to stay on his boat, he slipped in the killer," said Kendall.

"Make sure it's safe, and it would be great if you could do some scraping every so often," he said on his way out the door. Kendall wasn't opposed to doing a little work, but he was shocked at the condition of the boat.

"Once we got down there, I saw it was an absolute mess," said Kendall. "The hull was all rusted and we had to get down there with scrapers and steel brushes. We spent the entire winter cleaning the hull while thinking of Shel in the Mansion with all the Bunnies." But they never considered abandoning the job. Besides, Kendall was fascinated with Shel's work, and he thought that living on his houseboat for even a few months would provide him with a little bit of a window into Shel's brain.

While many would hesitate at offering someone they had just met the opportunity to spend the winter in their home, by this time Shel had honed his instincts about human nature to the extent that he could size up a person in a few seconds. Shel knew people so well that he was able to capture the universal foibles of humans in a few choice words or well-aimed brushstrokes. While he always lived and traveled alone, he was smart enough to realize that he needed people to help him with the stuff in the background so he could live his life the way he wanted.

"When you saw the places where he lived and how he put himself together, he did so very well, but in order to pull it off he needed people around him who could do it for him," said White. "He really had to be able to trust in people to make sure that things were done right for him, and he did."

White also saw how clearly Shel's child's-eye view of the world extended to his art. "It was obvious in his work," he said. "If he didn't have a purity of thought and if there wasn't a certain amount of naïveté in his personality, his work never would have come out of him so effortlessly, or looking the way it did."

Serving as caretakers-in-residence on Shel's boat meant there were occasional surprises. "Every now and then there would be a little knock at the door, and the voice on the other side would ask if Shel was there," said Kendall. "When we opened the door, more often than not a beautiful girl would be standing there." The exchange usually sounded something like this:

"I was just in the area and thought I'd stop by and say hi to Shel," she'd say.

"And who are you?" the two twenty-something men would ask while they tried not to drool.

"I'm Miss January."

But there were surprises inside as well. Along with thousands of books lining the shelves around the room were hundreds of puppets and dolls, perched right in front of the books, as if they were watching over the room and offering a benevolent blessing. Many of them were hand-carved Asian puppets Shel had picked up on his travels.

"He did love puppets," said White, adding that Shel never did anything with them in terms of his art. "I think he was attracted to their interpretive nature and the fact that they were pieces of art. And he loved that they were unusual, one-of-a-kind things."

Tucked in with the puppets was another, more disturbing find. Kendall told of pulling out books to read or picking up one of the puppets to examine it more closely, and more often than not, hiding behind the book or puppet would be a nitroglycerine tablet. In addition to being a powerful explosive, nitroglycerine is a frequently prescribed medication that can ease the symptoms of angina, pain in the upper body that comes when the heart isn't receiving adequate oxygen. Angina is usually caused by arteries that are gradually narrowing, and slipping a small nitroglycerine tablet under the tongue will widen the arteries and increase the flow of blood to the heart, thus relieving the symptoms.

It's likely that Shel was first diagnosed with angina and a chronic heart condition in the wake of his car accident, because the army would not have drafted him otherwise. It's also probable that besides having bad childhood experiences with doctors, the diagnosis made him swear off doctors forever and was instrumental behind his decision not to drink heavily or do drugs for most of his life. His was probably the most unusual request that some of the drug dealers in the '60s and '70s received in their businesses: "A hundred tabs of nitro, and hurry!"

When Kendall mentioned the stashes to White, he said that Shel kept them around just in case he started to have chest pains.

"I had an idea that something was going on, but we never talked about it," he said. "Shel was definitely a man's man. He didn't want to show any sort of weakness at all, and his energy was so enormously high. He wanted people to feel at ease while he was around and he didn't want them to start treating him differently, so he would never mention anything like that."

If he did, the other houseboat residents may have wanted to hold a party or an awareness-raising fund-raiser, and that was the last thing he would have wanted. But the Richardson Bay community regularly welcomed any excuse to throw a party or fund-raiser.

Larry Moyer, a good friend of Shel's and the photographer for his *Playboy* travelogues, also lived in the houseboat community.

One time Moyer had a fund-raiser on his boat to raise money so he could take his sick cat to the vet. "So many people showed up that the boat sank," Kendall remembered. "People just kept coming and the boat got lower and lower and finally the water started to come in the door. He didn't think too much about it, and we took all the electrical equipment out but more people came and the damn boat sank. So Moyer said maybe it was time to get off the boat, and some stepped onto the dock and others started to bail it out and little by little, it came back up. It was a pretty strange time."

White stayed for a full year on Shel's houseboat, and Kendall stayed for the winter and in the spring he moved to another houseboat nearby. When he was back for a short visit, Shel looked over some of the drawings and photographs Kendall had created over the winter.

"He complimented me on my work and told me to stay with it, to stay creative," said Kendall.

"Don't get a bullshit job you hate," were Shel's parting words. "Do something you love, time will pass, and you'll have fun."

Kendall followed Shel's advice: Today he's a marine artist back in New Hampshire who still works in the sepia pen-and-ink wash technique he first experimented with while living on Shel's boat. Some of Shel's other friends were starting to follow his advice, even borrowing a page or two from Shel's rulebook by branching out into other areas of creativity. For one, Kris Kristofferson decided to try his hand at acting in movies after writing two hit songs: "Me & Bobby McGee," released three months after Janis Joplin's death, was a Billboard number one hit in March 1971; and "Sunday Morning Coming Down," sung by Johnny Cash, was voted 1970's Song of the Year by the Country Music Association.

While Shel regularly encouraged his friends, Kristofferson's announcement caught him by surprise. "He couldn't figure out for the life of him why someone who had the talent and opportunity for songwriting would want to go out to Hollywood and be famous in movies," said Pat Dailey, a musician in Key West who met Shel in 1984. "He thought being a writer was the best job in the world."

But Shel continued to crank out so many good songs that they were beginning to pile up. "He had nowhere to go with them," said Bob Gibson. "Nobody in Nashville was recording that kind of stuff." He was still writing country songs that had a bit of a wild, offbeat quality to them, but there was a whole other kind of song he was writing that he didn't even dare to present to country producers. He needed to find a band that would interpret them the way he envisioned them when they first popped out of his head and onto paper.

In 1970, Shel was hanging out 150 miles up the coast in Mendocino because Bob Gibson had recently moved there. Gibson was still performing and writing folk songs and hadn't had much success, and he was in a serious funk over it. Shel was always quick to drop everything and get on a plane whenever an old friend needed help.

"I'd been doing the same set of songs for several years, and I wasn't writing or learning," said Gibson. "Shel was very helpful in jarring me out of this, he'd come up there and we'd write songs."

When she was growing up, Meridian Green, Bob Gibson's daughter, had known Shel as one of her father's closest friends, but overall Gibson tended to keep his family life very separate from his professional life, and Green never once called his father's friend Uncle Shel. While he was in Mendocino, he ran into Green and they went out to a restaurant, where Shel made a pass at her.

"I was eighteen at the time, and my romantic ideal looked more like Prince Valiant than some bald-headed guy," she said. "It was probably a mark of mutual respect that he waited until I was of age, because there were certainly other men in my father's life who didn't have the grace to wait until I was legal."

It was around this time in 1970 when Shel recorded a demo session for an album he planned to call *Fuck 'Em,* after the first song on the record. The session included his crudest and most raucous songs, and though it would have no trouble being released today, back then he must have done it as a joke, although later in the decade he would insist on pushing the envelope again with *Different Dances,* a graphic book for adults that HarperCollins published only because he threatened to take his children's book franchise elsewhere if they turned it down.

Shel's lyrics in the early '70s did not particularly endear him to the growing movement of women who had adopted the slogan "A woman needs a man like a fish needs a bicycle" as their national creed, and no doubt the songs on *Fuck 'Em* would have caused many parents to have second thoughts about buying his children's books if they knew he'd written songs like "Julie's Working," about a prostitute and "I Love My Right Hand," no explanation necessary.

The record was never released, and aside from making a few copies to pass out to friends, few people would have suspected that the author of *The Giving Tree* had written such extreme adult-themed material.

Or that he would become a father. After all, he was known not to be overly fond of children. But on June 30, 1970, he did just that.

Shoshanna Jordan Hastings was born to Susan Taylor Hastings, a twenty-six-year-old woman whom Shel had met at the Mansion. After he had settled in Sausalito she followed him out there, and when he found out she was pregnant with his child, he installed her in an apartment nearby and visited on a regular basis.

Shel, of course, wasn't the perfect father or companion, for that matter: He still traveled at the drop of a hat and rabidly pursued new women wherever he went. But while he performed his Uncle Shelby *shtick* with the kids of his friends and got a great reception, he realized early on that it didn't get very far with his own child.

Maybe it was finally time to do another children's book, to finish working on his book of crazy poems. That way, after it was published, perhaps he'd know more about how to be a father.

As Shel became more involved in the music industry, his contributions to *Playboy* began to dry up. From 1967 through 1971, he'd contributed only seven features and none at all in 1972.

"His main connection with *Playboy* was with Hefner," said songwriter Drew Reid. "And as Hefner removed himself more from the day-to-day hands-on stuff, I think that was why he pulled back from contributing to the magazine."

He was still actively looking for a band to interpret his non-country songs, and he had started to think about putting it together himself. One day in Mendocino, he floated an idea by Lenny Laks, proprietor of the Uncommon Good coffeehouse, a popular local hangout. Laks and Shel had done some songwriting together, and Shel came in to talk to him about an idea.

"Shel starts talking in his usual raspy rapid-fire voice, 'Here's what I want to do. I'm moving to Woodstock, New York. I'm going to start a band but I'm not going to be in the band. But I'm going to write all the songs, and I want you to come with me to be the singer.'

"I sat there thinking for a while then said, let me get this straight," Laks remembered. "You're going to start a band that you are not going to be in. And they're going to sing songs, some of which you haven't written yet. Then you're going to move three thousand miles away. And you want me to come with you based on this information?"

"Exactly!" said Shel.

Laks turned him down and Shel continued on his quest. When Shel decided to do something, he never let anything interfere with his ability to get it done, and he believed that others could accomplish the same things if only they made up their minds to do it. It wouldn't be the first time he became frustrated when his friends didn't share his optimism.

"He did get very upset with me at one time," said Jeannie Seely, a top country music singer in the '70s and a longstanding performer at the Grand Ole Opry. "Shel and Owen Bradley pitched the song 'One's on the Way' to me. I told them I thought it was very well written, but not one that I would be comfortable singing, because I was fighting for the rights of women to have legal affordable birth control so that we had more of a choice in our lifestyles," she said. "I didn't think I could sell the song since I couldn't even picture myself in that situation. Me and my method acting. I find the song amusing now, but at the time I felt very strongly about my convictions, even though I could have used that hit record!"

He went to Loretta Lynn next, and even though she had her doubts about Shel's choice of songs, after Seely turned it down, Lynn recorded "One's on the Way" in 1972 and it hit number one on the Billboard country chart. After this success, Shel wrote another song, this time specifically for her, but Lynn turned it down.

"When Shel wrote 'Hey Loretta,' I didn't like it because I don't care for songs about myself," she said. "He heard that I wasn't going to do it and flew in from Alaska. We finally put it on an album, but the disc jockeys demanded that we also make it a single. I got to like it—especially when it got to be Number One."

In December of 1972, with his career going on all cylinders, Shel's world suddenly screeched to a halt when his father died at the age of eighty-two.

Nathan's death would affect him for the rest of his life. One day in 1981, Shel was writing songs with his friend Drew Reid, who mentioned that he was having a tough time lately because his father died a year earlier, and they were very close. "I don't know how I'm going to get over it," he told Shel.

"Shel looked at me and said, 'Drew, you're not supposed to get over it. My father died nine years ago, and I think of him every day. That's what you're supposed to do. My father influenced me and I think of him every day and I love him as much as the day he died.' Then he said it again, 'You're *not* supposed to get over it.'"

He'd always done what he wanted for his entire life, and sometimes deliberately did something because he knew it would rile up his father. But now, knowing that Nathan was gone and that he was last in line, he ramped it up even more. With his father's death a reality, it underscored the importance of following his own calling no matter what. He simply didn't want to do what he didn't want to do.

He was still spending a lot of time in Sausalito to be near his daughter, but he had also been exploring Key West, Florida, for a couple of years and meeting new friends to hang out with. With the "you could be dead tomorrow" mantra playing over and over in his mind in the wake of Nathan's death, Shel decided to buy a house and add another home base he could fly to on the spur of the moment, though he would eventually turn it into the place where he'd spend the majority of his time in later years.

Key West appealed to Shel for a number of reasons; primary among them was its free-wheeling devil-may-care attitude.

"In Key West in the early seventies, one of the main pot dealers in town was the fire chief," said Drew Reid, who moved there in 1973. "Sometimes the shrimpers would bring in shrimp, and sometimes they'd bring in bales of pot, and it didn't matter, and the cops used to sell dime bags of pot out of their cop cars. It was totally insane.

"Shel liked Key West because people wouldn't bug him," he added. "Whenever people came up to him, he was usually very gracious, but it would interrupt his concentration because he never stopped thinking."

"He was always very much into the metaphysics of an area," said Skip Williamson. "The Florida Keys have that kind of exoticness that really appealed to his artistic sensibilities because people think it's full of pirates and Caribbean voodoo queens. It just seemed to be a natural place for him to live."

Shel lived at 618 William Street on Solaris Hill, which at sixteen feet above sea level, is the highest point in Key West. He lived around the corner from an old cemetery, and on his morning walks, he'd often wander through the place where the sailors from the USS *Maine* that blew up in Havana Harbor in 1898—sparking the beginning of the Spanish-American War—were buried.

Like his other homes, Shel set up his small house to be a working studio, where some days the only thing visible on the horizontal surfaces throughout the place were countless sheets of long blank unlined paper with drawings and fragments of songs and poems scrawled every which way, always writing in big block letters, a habit he picked up in Nashville.

"If you're in a recording studio and you really need to communicate something to the people on the other side of the glass, you write it out with a Sharpie pen in big block capital letters and hold it up," said Reid. "I never saw him write a word that wasn't in block capital letters."

He recalled Shel's lifelong habit of misspelled words. "His mind was going ninety miles an hour, he wasn't going to stop and look something up in a dictionary," said Reid. "Whatever was going on in his brain at that time was what was going down on the paper. He wasn't stopping for anything and he wasn't thinking about anything else."

He noted that Shel was so focused and disciplined when he was working that nothing could interrupt his concentration. Key West is a very small island, and in the '70s only prop planes could land at the airport. They'd fly at treetop level heading into the airport. "No matter where you were in Key West, depending on the direction of the wind that day, you could practically see the whites of the pilot's eyes," he said. "We'd be sitting in Shel's backyard and he'd be writing something down when an airplane would go over. I'd scream, 'Here they come!' and he wouldn't even look up. It never bothered him at all."

In the early '70s, Dr. Hook and the Medicine Show was a hard-living, rough-and-tumble band of unknown musicians playing hard-edged rock and roll with occasional country and folk overtones. They had been kicking around the New York metropolitan area and the South for a few years and were biding their time while their erstwhile manager shopped their demos around to various record companies.

The manager was just about to give up when he met Ron Haffkine, a director and producer and a friend of Shel's since the Village beatnik days of the late 1950s.

Haffkine and Shel were working on the music for a movie called *Who is Harry Kellerman and Why is He Saying All Those Terrible Things About Me?* with Dustin Hoffman slated to star. Shel was writing the musical score and Haffkine was serving as music director; another of Shel's longtime buddies, Herb Gardner, wrote the screenplay. Ulu Grosbard, the film's director, had told Haffkine to start scouting for a band. The financial backers for the film wanted a big act to perform the songs, a band like Simon and Garfunkel, but neither Haffkine nor Shel thought they were right for the music.

Haffkine was running out of time when he ran into Dr. Hook's manager, who happened to have the demos with him, but added he was about to dump them. Ron asked for a listen. "As soon as I heard Dennis's voice, I knew they were the guys to do Shel's songs for *Kellerman*," he said.

Haffkine gave the band a few songs to try out, and Shel headed out to New Jersey to see them perform. "It was a really sleazy bar," said Shel. "There was a revolving red light for psychedelic schmaltz and a fairly naked go-go chick shaking her ass around to 'Last Morning,' which was a personal, sensitive song I wrote for the movie. Even in that atmosphere, they brought it off."

Grosbard and the backers approved of Dr. Hook—which included Ray Sawyer on guitar and vocals, Dennis Locorriere on vocals, guitar and bass, George Cummings on steel guitar, Bill Francis on keyboard and vocals, and Jay David on vocals and drums—and production on the movie commenced. The movie was released in 1971, with Shel making a cameo appearance as a singer with the band. *Kellerman* bombed at the box office, but Dr. Hook got a record deal with CBS/Columbia and Shel found a band to handle his more unconventional songs, "Looking for Pussy" among them.

After recording most of their first album, with all but one of the songs written by Shel, the band moved to San Francisco. They were still looking for a single for the album when Shel played a little ditty he had just written. Their first album, *Dr. Hook & the Medicine Show,* came out in 1971, and that last-minute single, "Sylvia's Mother"—a tearjerker about a guy in a phone booth calling to talk to his ex-girlfriend but her mother won't let him speak to her and tells him Sylvia is marrying someone else—initially sank without a trace.

Instead of releasing a second single from the album and hoping for better luck, the label decided to try "Sylvia's Mother" once more. When the single was released for the second time in July 1972, the planets aligned and the song hit number one.

Like virtually all of Shel's songs and cartoons, "Sylvia's Mother" was based on a true story, though in the song he changed her last name. "It happened pretty much the way it was in the song," he said. "I called Sylvia and her mother said, 'She can't talk to you.' I said, 'Why not?' She said Sylvia was packing and she was leaving to get married, which was a big surprise to me. The guy was in Mexico and he was a bullfighter and a painter. At the time I thought that was like being a combination brain surgeon and encyclopedia salesman. Her mother finally let me talk to her, but her last words were, 'Shel, don't spoil it.'

"For about ten seconds I had this ego charge, as if I could have spoiled it," he said. "But I couldn't have spoiled it with a sledgehammer."

"I imagine I'm seventeen years old again and running out of coins in a phone booth and having my girlfriend's mother telling me that she's getting married to somebody else," said Dennis Locorriere. "Shel's songs unfold as you sing them and they've made me so much more of a singer."

With the success of "Sylvia's Mother," Dr. Hook began a heavy touring schedule, and occasionally Shel would tag along. Mike Mulvaney was the stage manager at the Exit Inn in Nashville when the band played there. Though his usual duties were to make sure the stage was set up properly and handle the lighting, with Dr. Hook, Mulvaney also had to give them stage calls every five minutes until show time.

"They knew exactly when the marijuana would hit," said Mulvaney. "I would go into the green room and tell them they had ten minutes to go. I swear I got a contact high just from sticking my head in the door. I don't think they played straight for the entire three-show run."

While Shel spent time backstage with the band, once they started playing, he'd sit at a table near the stage by himself. Sometimes people in the audience would talk to him and they'd exchange a few words, but other times he'd excuse himself and either head backstage to watch the show from the wings or get onstage to join the band.

Occasionally, Ray or Dennis would alert the audience that Shel was in the audience and as part of his job, Mulvaney would shine a spotlight on him. "He would kind of wave, but depending on his mood he could be a little standoffish. Other times he was very friendly," he said.

The shows were totally unscripted. "I never knew where they were going next," said Mulvaney. "One night Shel would get up and do a couple of numbers with them, but the next night, nothing." And when Cummings wasn't playing guitar, he wanted the spotlight on him as he acted out certain songs onstage, "Get My Rocks Off" among them. "He would get up on the front of the stage and squat down and pretend he was masturbating," said Mulvaney. "And of course, at that point, he wanted the spotlight right on his crotch."

Mulvaney said he spoke with Shel backstage about songwriting. In addition to working at the Exit Inn, he was on staff as a songwriter for Billy Davis, the songwriter who wrote "I'd Like to Buy the World a Coke," and Shel knew Davis from the records he did for Cadet, an offshoot of Chess Records. Mulvaney had followed and studied Shel's songwriting technique for years. After Dr. Hook's first show at the Exit Inn, Mulvaney was so inspired by Shel that he went home and wrote a song about Shel that he gave to him after the last show.

"He read it and started laughing," he said. "He couldn't believe that somebody had written a song like that about him."

Even though he spent only three nights talking casual chitchat with Shel, as Mulvaney watched him interact with people and the band, he was able to sense what made him tick. "He was sociable only to the point that he needed to be sociable to recharge his batteries," he said. "And once they were recharged, he was off. I always had the feeling that his brain raced around like a roulette wheel and where the ball stops is where you work. If the ball stopped on music, he would write some lyrics. If it stopped on children, he'd write a poem and draw a cartoon."

Later on, Shel performed at the Exit Inn as part of a roster of different acts. That night the audience was unusually rowdy and disruptive toward the performers. A few acts went on before him, but nobody could get the audience to quiet down. His friend songwriter Chris Gantry watched.

"When Shel got onstage, he just stood at the microphone and stared at the audience and didn't say a word," he said. "He stayed like that for about ten minutes, an eternity in a nightclub. Finally, everyone realized he was staring at them and they all shut up. He cleared his throat and started to speak."

"Well, my children," he began, "are you ready for your daddy to tell you a story now? Are you going to be good boys and girls?"

"You could have heard a pin drop," said Gantry. "Shel launched into his song, 'Santa Claus and Jesus,' where the two disagreed about the true meaning of Christmas. By the middle of his performance, he had the audience eating out of his hand. For his second number, he sang one of his most vulgar songs, and the audience went wild."

Gantry said this was standard procedure for Shel, and attributed it to the fact that he just didn't like to sing in public. People would bug him to sing, all right then, he'll *sing*. "He then pulled out the bawdiest, filthiest song he could to shock them," he said. "Their jaws dropped open, and then he'd do a second number that was twice as bad."

It's assumed that these people didn't ask him to sing in public again.

After the success of "Sylvia's Mother," Dr. Hook went back into the studio to record their next album, *Sloppy Seconds,* and Shel wrote all the songs. The first single, "Carry Me, Carrie," bombed like "Sylvia's Mother" did the first time around, but instead of rereleasing it, the next single was "Cover of the *Rolling Stone*," a song about the members of a rock band who have everything they could have dreamed of—sex, drugs, money—but what they want most of all is to have their picture on the cover of *Rolling Stone* magazine.

Shel wrote the song in his usual seat-of-the-pants style. "Shel called us up at four in the morning from a phone booth," said Ray Sawyer. "He had a guitar in there with him and he said, 'Listen, I've just written a song and I want you to take it down before I forget it.' I don't know why he didn't have a pen and paper with him, but you don't ask Shel things like that. I took the song down in an old address book and it was 'The Cover of the *Rolling Stone.*'" The song reached number two on the Billboard pop charts in 1973.

At other times, when he didn't want to write down a song and wasn't near a phone, he just started recording on his cassette player to capture the song as it came pouring out of him. The trouble arose later when he sent it off to the members of Dr. Hook and they tried to make out the words behind Shel's gravelly voice.

"Shel used to send us tapes," said Sawyer. "Shel singing on an album is one thing, but with Shel singing on the fly, you have to really use your imagination. He would send a demo with just his voice and whatever's going on in the background wherever he decided to make the tape: on the beach, in an airplane, or with chicks at a party. People say he ain't singing, but now, after a period of two years or so, I say that the motherfucker can sing, he's saying a whole lot more than people can grasp."

Shel enjoyed touring with Dr. Hook and writing their songs, and he had always been exceedingly generous about sharing writing credits with his collaborators, even if they contributed only a line or two. Once the band became internationally known, however, they started to get greedy, demanding more money for gigs, larger royalty percentages, and began fighting among themselves over how much each was contributing to songs, to performances, to the band's general success. And to Shel, greed and money had nothing to do with the creative process. After all, this was a man who didn't cash his royalty checks from his children's books for years. Instead, he would stuff them in a drawer and forget about them. After a few years, they piled up and because they were so large, they threw off the accounting systems at Harper, so eventually the publisher forced him to cash them.

Rik Elswit, who joined the band after the first album came out, witnessed this firsthand. "We were sitting around Columbia's Folsom Street studio in San Francisco, arguing loudly for our respective percentages of a song we'd just finished, when Shel came through the door. He stopped, looked us over, and scowled.

" 'What are you guys doing?' he asked. 'You can't quantify magic. How can you possibly figure out what the most important parts of a song are? Art is magic and magic doesn't work like that. Do you really want to live your life as if this is the last good idea you'll ever have?'

"He told us that anyone who wrote with him got equal credit, even if they only contributed one line or one idea," said Elswit. "That way, his collaborators went away happy and more than willing to write with him again, and he never had to fight over percentages again."

"A lot of people have a lot of trouble when two people collaborate," said Shel. "The question that often comes up is, Who did what? Did you write three lines or the chorus? And that causes a lot of pain."

Shel's role model in collaboration was Bob Gibson. When Gibson's publisher sent a contract for "The First Battalion," the first song they wrote together, the royalties were split between them equally. Shel protested, thinking he didn't write half the song. But when Gibson pressed him, he couldn't determine how much he did write, and his friend ended up teaching him an important lesson: Since it was futile to figure out who did what, all cowriters are equal because the song would have turned out differently—or not completed at all—if one person hadn't been there.

"The song would not exist without them," said Shel. He constantly stressed this philosophy to his Nashville cowriters, but it either fell on deaf ears when they dealt with other people, or with surprise, admiration and gratitude when Shel bestowed it on an unsuspecting collaborator. Indeed, in the future, Shel was known to drop friendships with people to whom it was clear they were in it for the money and not the sheer joy of writing songs.

Take Ten   **by Silverstein**

SILVERSTEIN

"... and then we all went home and put
on our fathers' old uniforms."

LEFT: Shel's cartoons in *Pacific Stars and Stripes*
helped boost the morale of soldiers during the
Korean War. © 1956, 2006 *Stars and Stripes*

BELOW: After his first cartoon appeared in
Playboy, Shel began to travel around the world
on assignment for the magazine. Here he is in
Yokohama, Japan, after traveling there on the
U.S.S. President Wilson.
© 1956, 2006 *Stars and Stripes*

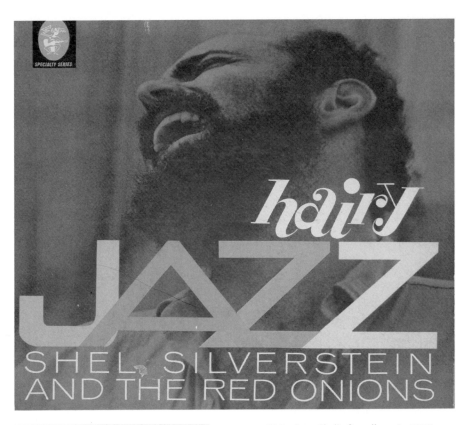

SPECIALTY SERIES

hairy
JAZZ
SHEL SILVERSTEIN
AND THE RED ONIONS

ABOVE: *Hairy Jazz*: Shel's first album in 1959 on Elektra. "The sessions were fast, furious, and great fun," said producer and label founder Jac Holzman. AUTHOR'S COLLECTION

LEFT: The program from *Look Charlie*, the musical-cum-variety show that Shel staged with his good friend, radio personality Jean Shepherd, at New York's Orpheum Theatre in 1959. AUTHOR'S COLLECTION

OPPOSITE TOP: The Serendipity Singers' version of Shel's song "Plastic" was issued as a promotional single at the 1966 National Plastics Exposition. CHEMICAL HERITAGE FOUNDATION IMAGE ARCHIVES

OPPOSITE BOTTOM: Shel in the studio with Waylon Jennings and movie director Tony Richardson, recording the soundtrack for the 1970 movie *Ned Kelly*. PHOTOFEST

Get in the mood for the
'66 PLASTICS SHOW

while enjoying this
recording of the
new song
PLASTIC
by the Serendipity Singers

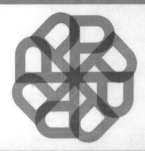

VISIT THE
MONSANTO
plastic performance
CENTER

BOOTH 2339
NATIONAL PLASTICS EXPOSITION
JUNE 6-10
NEW YORK COLISEUM

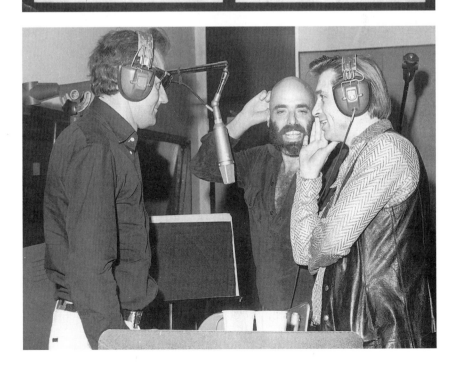

TOP: Promotional photo of Shel and Dustin Hoffman from *Who is Harry Kellerman and Why is He Saying All Those Terrible Things About Me?* (1971) PHOTOFEST

BOTTOM: A bewigged Shel with Dustin Hoffman and two unidentified women during a break in the production of *Who is Harry Kellerman and Why is He Saying All Those Terrible Things About Me?* PHOTOFEST

TOP: Shel and Dustin Hoffman during another break in moviemaking with two unidentified women. PHOTOFEST

BOTTOM: Shel's houseboat in Sausalito, as drawn by John Kendall, who stayed there in the early 1970s when Shel was out of town.

JOHN KENDALL, WWW.JAKENDALL.COM

TOP: Shel with fellow *Playboy* cartoonist Skip Williamson in 1977. "Shel had a love-hate relationship with almost everything," said Williamson of his close friend. "It was the nature of his personality to be outraged, but at the same time, to be fused by it." SKIP WILLIAMSON, WWW.SKIPWILLIAMSON.COM

BOTTOM: Shel didn't like having his picture taken, but songwriting partner and friend Mickey James managed to snap this photo on the porch of Shel's Key West house. MICKEY JAMES

TOP: Shel's cottage on Martha's Vineyard was the smallest of all his homes.

HELEN SCARBOROUGH

BOTTOM: Shel working on the porch at his Martha's Vineyard home.

HELEN SCARBOROUGH

BELOW: *Old Dogs* was the last project Shel worked on before his death, gathering his friends together to make a CD about the joys and perils of growing old. (Top row: Bobby Bare, Mel Tillis, Jerry Reed. Bottom row: Shel and Waylon Jennings.) AUTHOR'S COLLECTION

BELOW: A publicity shot for *Where the Sidewalk Ends* taken in Ringwood State Park, New Jersey. PHOTOFEST

He also realized that magic didn't strike on every effort, and he continually raised the bar with his friends and collaborators to help them be more than they thought they could. One afternoon, Shel asked Gibson if he wanted to write some songs. Bob said, Sure, let's write a song. Shel then replied, "We're not writing one song, we're writing two. You can write just one song, but it may not be very good."

Later on, he revealed why he and Gibson remained friends for so many years. "There are certain people that I admire greatly, but I could never collaborate with them because of their attitude," said Shel. "You can't be too worried about whether the song expresses all your feelings, you just have to let it go. He just gave me what he had, and I didn't mess with it. I gave him what I had and he didn't fuck with it. It was just fun. He sure wasn't gonna put up with any problems and I sure wasn't gonna do anything that was painful. The whole idea for all of us was avoiding pain at every turn."

As Shel saw it, the members of Dr. Hook were getting way too big for their britches, and he didn't want to have anything to do with it.

"Fame didn't mean anything to Shel," said Larry DuBois. "He had spent decades around famous people and he wasn't intimidated at all. He didn't go out of his way to be polite to famous people and he'd nick you no matter who you were if he thought you deserved it."

While others flocked to celebrities because of their fame, if they didn't have talent or a unique perspective of some kind, Shel kept his distance.

"What really drew Shel to someone was talent and the fun from being around people who talked about things that really interested him," added DuBois.

But despite any antagonism he felt toward the man, sometimes he'd just look around for Hef. To the general public, Hugh Hefner might not seem like the most exciting person in the world, and many undoubtedly were left scratching their heads over what drew all those chicks to that guy with the pajamas and the pipe.

"One thing that people don't realize about Hef is when he's on camera doing a TV interview, he's very straight and serious," said DuBois. "But when he's with his pals, he's very funny, he's very sharp, and that's what drew Hef and Shel together. If they were sitting with other people and they were both on, the repartee between them was intense and funny and electric. Shel really enjoyed Hef because they were two old pals who could really bust each other's chops."

But life at the Mansion did have its downside, as seen in a June 28, 1972, interoffice memo to clarify the damage from the time the Rolling Stones spent a few days at the Mansion, and Shel's beloved Red Room was trashed.

"The Red and Blue Room fixtures were damaged and both glass bulb protectors had to be replaced. The white rug in the bathroom was burnt along with the toilet seat, two bath mats and four towels. Chair, couch and bedspread are stained, requiring replacement and/or reupholstering."

Occasionally, Shel would tag along with Hef on promotions for the magazine and afterward, he'd wander off. He was in Champaign, Illinois, with Hefner for the unveiling of a plastic sculpture of Barbi Benton, Hef's main squeeze at the time. Fred Koller, a local singer-songwriter, was outside sitting on his porch singing and playing the guitar to practice for a gig that night when Shel walked by. He came onto the porch and started singing along. Koller had grown up in Homewood outside of Chicago, the same town where the Sylvia of "Sylvia's Mother" had lived. They struck up a friendship and wrote numerous songs together over the next several years, including "Happy Caucasian," "Goodnight Little Houseplant," and "Yes Mister Rogers."

Koller traveled to Shel's houseboat about once a year for a marathon songwriting session. They typically went on a two-week bender, cranking out anywhere from twenty to forty completed songs during that time.

"Everything that Shel said got turned into a song twenty-four hours a day," said Koller. "We were constantly writing. He was definitely a lyricist and really strong on plotting out songs, twisting and turning it and then bringing it back around again. That was probably his biggest strength."

During Koller's 1973 visit, in between writing songs, Shel was also organizing the poems and illustrations for *Where the Sidewalk Ends*. "He had poems and drawings for that book scattered everywhere," he said. "He was always in the middle of a million projects and he taught a class at San Quentin Prison for maybe a week or two. We'd spend hours each day driving around San Francisco and Santa Cruz to stop in junk and craft stores. He liked to buy figurines and weird folk art from South America."

Of course, there were the old bookstores, and since Koller also collected books, Shel had a comrade in arms. "We'd spend three or four hours every day in a bookstore and he just filled boxes with books," said Koller, who noted that Shel had a collector's keen eye. "The houseboat was filled with old Big Little books and Oz books, but there were many books by early illustrators where he was trying to get all their work to complete his collection."

He would do the same thing whenever he discovered a new author whose work he liked. "He didn't carry around books to read," said Koller. "But whenever he'd read a short story by an author he never heard of, he'd search for everything that person ever wrote. He always had a very strong sense of the history behind the art, and he could quote Johnny Mercer songs day in and day out."

In 1973, dismayed by the selfishness and antics of the members of Dr. Hook, Shel turned his musical energies once more to Nashville, where he met a man who would become a lifelong friend, a great influence on his own work, and someone with whom he would share an eerily similar tragedy.

Bobby Bare met Shel when he was looking for a songwriter to write an album where all the songs were centered around one uniting theme, in other words, a concept album. Back then, concept albums were unheard of in country music.

"I wanted some great songwriter like Harlan Howard or somebody to write me an album, and nobody could do it," said Bare. He met Shel at a party in Nashville one Saturday night, told him what he was looking for, and Shel said he would think about it. He was going back to Chicago the next day.

On Monday, Shel called Bare and said he had written all the songs for an album he called *Lullabys, Legends and Lies.* Bare was flabbergasted, so he asked when he could hear it and Shel told him he could be there in a few hours.

"We listened to the songs and they were very visual and clever," said Bare, who immediately went into the studio and sat down with a guitar and a mike and recorded demos for a few songs, including "Marie Laveau," "The Winner," and "Rosalie's Good Eats Café."

"The presence of Shel was palpable," said Lloyd Green, a Nashville steel guitar legend. "He influenced the way we cut those tunes, and he had a lot of input with Bare. He was a force, and a charismatic figure to be reckoned with."

"It was so different than what I had ever done before," said Bare, "and if it wasn't for a few chance meetings and pass-alongs of the demos, the double album never would have been released, it was so radical for the time."

The album was a roaring success, spending thirty weeks on the Billboard country charts in 1973. "Marie Laveau" hit number one and "Daddy, What If" peaked at number two. But more important, the two men had so much fun making the record that they ended up collaborating on many more records through the next twenty-five years.

Lullabys sold so well that RCA released two more Bobby Bare albums with Shel's songs. *Singin' in the Kitchen* came out in 1974 and *Hard Time Hungrys* was released in 1975. While neither album approached the heights of *Lullabys,* Bare and Shel became fast friends, talking several times a day on the phone and visiting each other whenever possible. That friendship would serve as a balm when Susan Hastings, Shoshanna's mother, died on June 29, 1975.

They never married, of course, and never lived together, but Shel had been a good father in his own way, and since his daughter's birth, he felt obligated to take care of Hastings even though she was just another one of his many girlfriends. He would still jump on a plane at a moment's notice, minutes after deciding he needed to be somewhere and he needed to be there as soon as possible, but he provided for Hastings nevertheless. And he still cared for her, even if she had never totally accepted the way he lived his life.

"I know that her death was a big loss," said Hillary Mapes. "It was a big hit for him. And it was an invasion, an intrusion to say something to him about it. You weren't going to write Shel a condolence letter."

Susan's parents, Curt and Meg Marshall, lived in Baltimore where Hastings had grown up, and they took Shoshanna in. There was never any question of Shel becoming a full-time parent. It just wasn't in the cards.

"I don't think he would've made an especially good full-time father," said Skip Williamson, who had a daughter the same age as Shoshanna. "Shel was an independent guy, so sometimes when she was with him, he had problems dealing with the demands of a child. She knew how to 'work her Daddy,' and Shel didn't like being worked."

Once, when Shoshanna was visiting him, she lost a tooth, and she put it under her pillow in exchange for the customary quarter. Because Shel believed in not sugarcoating the truth to kids—he detested the traditional childhood legends of Santa Claus and the tooth fairy—and so when Shoshanna woke the next morning and saw no coin under her pillow, she started to scream. Shel immediately began to have second thoughts.

"What am I doing, all she wanted was a lousy quarter," he later said. So he grabbed a fistful of coins from his spare change jar and tossed them on Shoshanna's bed. "Faced with a screaming six-year-old, for my own comfort I continue the legend of the tooth fairy," he said.

Shel wasn't about to give up totally on Dr. Hook, but he wanted to rein them in a bit by hiring them as musicians on his next album, *Freakin' at the Freakers Ball.* They were sharing the bill with the highly respected traditional jazz band the Turk Murphy Band. Murphy is the father of the traditional jazz movement in this country that began in the post-Depression years. The band spent time both on the road traveling across the country to expose people to this new style of music, and were also based in clubs in New York and San Francisco at one time. Shel had met Turk when the band had played in New York, and since he was still a big fan of the Dixieland-style jazz that he had grown up with, he decided to have a little fun. He booked time at a studio in San Francisco and asked Turk to join him at a party and to bring along his band members, who had no idea what they were in for. Ron Haffkine served as producer and musical director at the recording session.

Leon Oakley played the cornet in Turk's band, and some of the songs on the album—including "Masochistic Baby" and "I Saw Polly in a Porno with a Pony"—would have shocked Turk's fans. "They were used to the traditional jazz tunes and barroom ballads we normally played," said Oakley.

Despite the dubious choice of material and dramatic change of venue for the band, Oakley said they enjoyed the experience. "It was a fun experience for Turk and the rest of us, if a bit of a departure," he said. And some of the work created by the other musicians who were all playing on separate tracks fell by the wayside, probably because they took another song on the album, "I Got Stoned and I Missed It," too literally. "When they mixed the results, many musicians who were over the edge of musical sanity were left on the editing room floor," he noted.

One of the songs on the album was "Don't Give a Dose to the One You Love Most." In 1972, Shel was friendly with a Sausalito pharmacist who was on a town committee to distribute information to counter a VD epidemic that was raging at the time. The pharmacist asked Shel if he could write a song.

Once he remembered seeing posters in Haight-Ashbury a few years earlier that trumpeted DON'T GIVE A DOSE TO THE ONE YOU LOVE MOST, Shel had his song.

The song was later used on a one-hour special TV documentary called *VD Blues,* produced by PBS in the fall of 1972. Shel offered the song to Dr. Hook, but they decided against recording it. "We had enough problems with people thinking us a bunch of degenerates," said Dennis Locorriere. "We didn't want them thinking we'd gotten VD as well."

After *Freakers Ball* wrapped, Shel started to think about his next record. "Next time, I'll probably do a very gentle album," he said. "I run into difficulty because people want to find a nice clean handle for everyone, and you can't do that for any creative person. Nobody has only one side. You want people to allow for all of you."

As it turned out, his next album, *Crouchin' on the Outside,* which came out a year after *Freakers Ball,* was a double-album reissue of *Drain My Brain* and *I'm So Good That I Don't Have to Brag!* His next original album, *Songs and Stories,* wouldn't appear until 1978, and it was anything but gentle. It was a precursor to his future spoken recordings of his children's poetry books where he rarely sang and instead whispered, yelled, ranted, and raved his way through the poems.

In addition to the aspiring songwriters who still approached Shel in droves, occasionally a musician with a few more notches on his belt would also seek out his advice. In 1974, Bob Dylan, who Shel had met at the Gate of Horn some fifteen years earlier, visited Shel on his houseboat to play a few songs he was considering for his next album.

They sat on the deck of the San Rafael ferry, and Shel listened while Bob played a few tunes. He asked for Shel's thoughts about a few lyrics where he was stuck, whether he couldn't find the exact word he wanted to use or puzzled over a couple different endings. Shel offered his ideas, suggested a few changes, and sent Dylan away with his blessing. Dylan was heartened that an old acquaintance, whom he thought was still bitter over his eclipse of Shel's best friend Bob Gibson, was so open and forthcoming with his expertise.

The album turned out to be *Blood on the Tracks,* and when it was released in January of 1975, it was hailed as Dylan's best, containing such classics as "Tangled Up in Blue," "Shelter from the Storm," and "Simple Twist of Fate."

In 1974 alone, *The Giving Tree* sold a hundred thousand copies. Sales of the book had been essentially doubling every year in the decade since its publication. Shel had effectively removed himself from the book; after all, he only looked forward, never back, since he couldn't learn anything new from something he had already done.

In 1974, he was finalizing the poems and drawings that had taken root over a decade earlier as *Uncle Shelby's Crazy Poems,* but would now be published as *Where the Sidewalk Ends.* Ursula Nordstrom, his long-suffering editor at Harper & Row, was thrilled. However, because it wasn't a short book with a simple storyline like *The Giving Tree* or *A Giraffe and a Half* but a collection of unrelated poems, Shel was constantly tinkering with the poems and drawings in the book. And because this was the one part of the work that he absolutely detested—making the poems and illustrations ready for the printer was the opposite of his typical spontaneous creativity—it took a lot for him to commit to finish the book.

"I think in those days it was much more a gentleman's agreement that you will deliver when it's ready and we will publish you," said Joan Robins, who worked with Shel on publicity for *Where the Sidewalk Ends.* Besides, his children's books generated so much revenue for the company that all they could do was sit on their hands. However, once the book was in the catalog and sales reps were already talking up the book to their accounts, there was no turning back.

Nordstrom loudly bemoaned Shel's efforts to get the book ready, complaining his revisions involved "thousands of pieces of paper and millions of changes."

All of Nordstrom's relationships with her authors were friendly but also somewhat contentious, according to Robins, because she never hesitated to speak her mind. "While she had her periods when she was on the outs with Shel, she couldn't help but be somewhat in awe of him," said Robins, noting that Nordstrom was actually sometimes afraid of him because he could be pretty harsh to her at times. "In the end, they always got along because he had a great respect for her and her kind of genius."

There was an incident where the two locked horns for days during the production of *Sidewalk*. Shel insisted that a poem go in the book while Ursula was horrified at the prospect of children being exposed to it. Robins remembered it well, and she sided with Nordstrom.

"The poem was called 'Headstand,' about some kids playing in the sand who are burying everything they can find," she said. "The drawing showed a man standing on his head and all you saw of him was his torso and his legs, his head was buried in the sand.

"They were always fighting about that poem," said Robins. "The more Ursula said she couldn't stand it, the more Shel said he wanted it in the book." In the end, Nordstrom won, but when production was under way for his later collections, *A Light in the Attic* and *Falling Up,* he again insisted on including "Headstand" in the book and the same scenario replayed itself this time with Robins as his editor, replacing Nordstrom who had retired.

"He wanted it in the book and he knew I didn't like it," said Robins. "It just horrified me and he couldn't understand why, but he did have a real feeling for anybody who had a very strong emotional reaction to his work. He was after people's emotional feelings rather than their intellectual analysis."

In the end, "Headstand" was never published, in part because he wanted to respect Nordstrom's opinions, even after her death.

One of the more intriguing aspects of his children's poems was that if he decided that something in a poem wasn't working, instead of tinkering with a word or phrase, he'd crumple up the paper and start over.

"His writing had to be spontaneous," said Robins. "If I suggested that he change the poem in some way, even one word, and he agreed, he'd simply put it aside and come up with another version of it. But he would not correct it, he'd never change it, instead he came up with a new version of the poem so that it was totally spontaneous. When he wrote, his words had to tumble all over the place or else it wasn't right for him."

He also made a fine distinction between the work he did for *Playboy* and his children's books. "To him, they were worlds apart," said Robins. "He never referred to the children's books as cartoons. Instead, they were illustrations or drawings. Cartoons were what he did for *Playboy*.

"A cartoon is basically a one-liner," said Robins. "The drawings in his books were not, they had a lot more depth."

Where the Sidewalk Ends was published in November 1974, and would eventually turn out to be one of the best-selling children's books ever, but it was immediately banned in a number of school libraries across the country because some parents thought that the poems would lead children to disobey their parents and teachers. Shel largely ignored his critics and was incredulous when he heard that his book had been banned, but there was one poem that he did change after *Sidewalk* was published.

After the book had been out for a few months, Joan Robins received a letter from a Gypsy man who wrote an impassioned letter to protest "The Gypsies Are Coming," a poem based on an Old World myth about Gypsies who buy non-Gypsy children to use for labor or to sell later on. Robins forwarded the letter to Shel, who responded that he would change *Gypsies* to *Googies* in subsequent printings of the book because he didn't intend it to be offensive.

"He used to say he was part Gypsy," said Robins. "He always thought his temperament was a result of that, which is why he agreed to change the poem."

In 1975, Ursula Nordstrom must have been beside herself with joy when Shel told her he had another book on the way less than a year after *Sidewalk* was published. He was finishing up work on *The Missing Piece*—originally called *The Missing Link*—and because it only encompassed one idea instead of the hundreds of different ideas in *Sidewalk,* Shel was right on schedule.

"He recited the whole thing to me and at that time I thought it was very, very good, in fact, terrific," she wrote. "I hope he hasn't messed it up—and I am pretty sure he hasn't. At any rate, I am hoping it can be a fall 1976 book and if it is as close to final form as he said over the phone, it can be." In fact, it turned out it was published early, in May of 1976, to Nordstrom's great delight.

Harper & Row was celebrating the return of one of their best cash cows just as Shel announced that he would do no more interviews with the media, though he never did too many to begin with, since he considered them a waste of his time, time that would be better spent working. Joan Robins, working in the publicity department at the time, arranged the notorious 1975 *Publishers Weekly* interview in which he uttered his parting words:

"So I'll keep on communicating, but only my way. Lots of things I won't do. I won't go on television because who am I talking to? Johnny Carson? The camera? Twenty million people I can't see? Uh-uh. And I won't give any more interviews."

"That was the one aspect of fame that irritated him the most," said Skip Williamson. "He was regularly invited to be a guest on *The Tonight Show,* but he didn't like the lack of intimacy about it, the lack of personal touch."

"Shel didn't like interviews," said Robins. "He was gun-shy about them."

But when it came to public speaking, at least at the time, he was open to it, only very nervous, depending on who was sitting in the audience.

Shortly after *Sidewalk* came out, Robins booked him to speak at a librarians' convention in Chicago. "He was very worried," she said, and he asked her to go with him.

Why was he nervous about facing a bunch of librarians?

"He had an enormous respect for them and didn't want to do anything that might offend them," she said. "He also didn't like to perform. He tended to be shy with groups of people he didn't know well, and this was a different world. And he knew they were important and wanted to make a good impression on them. In his other worlds he could be a little bit rough, and he didn't want to risk it here."

Once he got up to speak before the group, after an initial case of nerves, Shel calmed down and eased into it. And even when a member of the audience—who just happened to be a high school teacher who was also a nun—asked him the kind of message-behind-the-story question that he hated about *The Giving Tree,* he answered it graciously.

"What did you mean to say?" she asked.

"It's about two beings," Shel replied. "One who likes to give, and another who likes to take." All she said was, "Oh."

6. *Underwater Land*

In May of 1976, *The Missing Piece* was published, Shel's first children's book after *Where the Sidewalk Ends,* which had firmly cemented Shel's reputation as a children's author, though to him it was still only one of numerous outlets for his creative passions.

The book was highly anticipated by both publisher and public. However, parents who bought *Sidewalk* by the armful and were expecting a similar story, were confused by *The Missing Piece.* It's the story of a circle with a wedge-shaped chunk missing, which spends its days in search of the piece. When it finds the wedge, they fit together perfectly, but the circle feels disillusioned because with the wedge in place it's traveling too fast and is therefore missing lots of sights along the way. "I could have ended the book there," he said, referring to the point in the story where the piece found the wedge. "But instead it goes off singing, it's still looking for the missing piece. That's the madness of the book, the disturbing part of it."

As before, criticism from both professional reviewers and readers didn't matter to Shel. It was simply a story that popped into his head and therefore needed to be told, and whatever message people thought he was sending had nothing to do with him and everything to do with their own perspectives on life. And besides, he was too busy exploring.

One time, Shel decided he wanted to study Russian. "That lasted about a weekend," said Fred Koller. "If he wanted to do something it had to happen in a hurry. The same thing happened when he decided to learn a new instrument." Another time, he wanted to buy a camper because he couldn't figure out where he wanted to live. He looked around, but by the time he found something he liked, he had changed his mind and decided he wanted to go to Martha's Vineyard and buy a place there. And so he did.

He bought a cottage in the Oak Bluffs section of the Vineyard in a small private community known as the Camp Meeting Association. The campground got its start in 1835 when a group of Methodist ministers came to the island for their annual conference and needed a place to stay. In the beginning, they'd just pitch tents, but within a couple of decades they started to build permanent wooden cottages on the tent platforms on tiny lots, and soon hundreds of cottages built in the fairy-tale Carpenter Gothic style with gingerbread trim and sharply peaked roofs were dotting the campground.

Today, like then, most of the residents stayed just for the summer. Shel's cottage fit his criteria: it was small, near water, architecturally unique, had an interesting history, and was squished in close to its neighbors. And it had a front porch where he could sit and play guitar or doodle on his sketchpad while he watched people pass by. The one exception was that the cottage was so small that he couldn't keep many books there.

But that didn't matter, because wherever he was at any given time was where he absolutely needed to be. As Shel was getting a little older—he was closing in on fifty—he wanted to have familiar faces around him more, so whenever he got an urge to see an old pal, it didn't matter if they were in the same time zone or halfway around the world, he asked them to come to meet him, and the sooner the better. And he'd foot the bill.

Occasionally, he had a hard time figuring out where he wanted to go next. In that case, the decision was made for reasons that would appear totally frivolous to others but made perfect sense to him.

"He didn't really know where he lived," said William Price Fox, who first met Shel in the Village in the 1950s. Fox witnessed the process Shel went through when he wanted to go somewhere but wasn't sure where to head, and it involved countless phone calls. "Who was in Manhattan? How much mail did he have in Key West? What was the weather like in Chicago? Had the workers stopped working on his houseboat in Sausalito?" said Fox, running down the litany. "Finally he called a girlfriend in Nashville and asked if she could call Stewart's Cafe to see what was on the dinner menu. Ham, collards and cornbread, she told him. He thought about it. Then she added, 'And they've got banana pudding.'

" 'Tell them to hold a couple orders for me, okay?'

"She laughed, 'I already did.' "

As usual, pudding was the tie-breaker.

Sometimes, however, his traveling was dictated by an emergency. In the late fall of 1976, as Shel was starting to come to terms with the death of Susan Hastings, he received some bad news from one of his closest friends, Bobby Bare. Bare's daughter Cari, who sang on Bare's album *Singin' in the Kitchen* and appears on the album cover, died suddenly at the age of fifteen, supposedly from a botched abortion.

"My sister died when I was nine and she was fifteen," said Bobby Bare Jr. "She woke up Thanksgiving Eve having a baby. Nobody in the house knew she was pregnant. You've got a fifteen-year-old having a baby, and within two or three weeks she dies. That's a bunch of darkness to take on."

Shel comforted Bare the best he could, and the two friends grew even closer. Neither knew it would only be a few short years in the future when Bare would have to console Shel for a similar tragedy in his own life.

In the spring of 1977, Shel spent a few weeks with his old friend William Price Fox in Columbia, South Carolina. Fox, an English professor at the University of South Carolina, wanted to convert a few short stories from his book *Southern Fried,* a collection of humorous tales of people living in the South in the years after World War II, into a musical that would then be presented with student and nonacademic actors at the Town Theatre.

Fox was working with Franklin Ashley, a fellow professor now at the College of Charleston, who contributed a few of his own songs to the project. "Bill started talking about Shel's songs and he played some for me," said Ashley. Fox called Shel and asked him to come down, and because Shel hadn't written a musical before he jumped at the chance.

"We used some of his old songs and he wrote a couple of new ones that we fit into the story," said Ashley. The cast was composed only of African Americans. "It was not only the first all-black musical the Town Theater had ever done, it was also one of the first times that blacks had ever been on the stage.

"That added an extra dollop to the whole project, too," said Ashley. "Here we were, three white guys working for this entire black cast. But you know they liked the stuff, and they thought he was a blast."

And instead of drawing up a contract and charging an outrageous fee, Shel and Fox did the deal with a handshake, and Shel charged only a dollar for the right to use his songs in the musical.

When Hef bought the Playboy Mansion West in the exclusive Los Angeles neighborhood of Holmby Hills in the early '70s, he spent a few years shuttling between the two Mansions, but by 1974 he had moved out West full-time. The magazine's corporate office was still in Chicago, but in Shel's eyes, Hef's decision to relinquish much of the control to the executives who were essentially running the company by this time was enough. The atmosphere at the magazine went from that of a free-wheeling nonstop party to a buttoned-up conservatively run typical American corporation. In 1975, the Chicago Mansion was essentially vacated. Between December 1973 and January 1978, Shel contributed no work to *Playboy*. Though both Hef and several editors continually asked Shel for more cartoons and stories, or to revise the ones he had submitted years earlier, Shel felt that Hef had sold out and had let down all those who were with him from the early days.

Skip Williamson, a fellow cartoonist at *Playboy* who eventually became art director at the magazine, had crossed paths with Shel several times over the years, but they didn't become friends until 1976. Like other cartoonists at the magazine, Williamson had long been intimidated by Shel because of his history and because his relationship with Hef went way back. Understandably, it sometimes took a while for a cartoonist to work up the nerve to introduce himself to the magazine's star.

The day came when he got his chance. Williamson was in the Chicago office when Shel was there, and he introduced himself by showing Shel his sketchbook. Shel liked what he saw, and they became fast friends. At the time Shel happened to be looking for another cartoonist to bounce ideas off of, so the timing was fortuitous. Shel was privately struggling with some graphic adult cartoons he was working on for his 1979 book *Different Dances.*

"He was having cartoonist's block and had sequestered himself in order to work on it," Williamson said. "The first thing he said to me was that he was having trouble with the book and he asked me to take a look at it. I told him what I thought, we knocked around some ideas, and soon I was going up to see him every day."

The two cartoonists would sit and draw together in silence for a while before getting sidetracked into philosophical discussions about what constituted art and what didn't. "Shel believed that if you did a drawing and whited it out and redrew it to change something, it was cheating," said Williamson. "But then he'd do a drawing and cut pieces of it apart and rearrange them, and that was okay. We'd talk about that kind of stuff and sometimes Bob Gibson would come by and they'd start singing and writing songs, and reminiscing about the old days. It wasn't always easy and it took a while, but he was able to knock out the book once he had the energy of another artist working in the room there with him," he added.

While Shel was struggling with his work, Williamson would often join him on his hours-long rambling walks through the city. "We'd go into a storefront where a little old Italian guy sold violins and other instruments and Shel would walk out with five banjos," he said. "Five minutes later, we'd be in a restaurant and Shel would be off in his own universe scribbling down notes on his cocktail napkin. Most of the time, he'd just crank it out, but with this book he was having trouble, he was just stymied on it."

Perhaps it was because it had been years since he had contributed regularly to *Playboy*. He was mad at Hef for closing the Chicago Mansion, for ceding control of the magazine to the executive suite, for taking the company public—something that Hef would later regret as well—and the cartoons he was working on for the book were too similar to the stuff he used to crank out for *Playboy*, and he needed these drawings to be something entirely different.

Or it could have been that he was working on a project that he wasn't sure would ever see the light of day. He was planning to use *Different Dances* as a chip in a high-stakes poker game with Harper & Row to see how much they really wanted him. Of course, he didn't care about the money and could always find another publisher for his children's books, but the proof was in *Different Dances*. Would Harper & Row agree to publish it?

When Shel began to confide in Williamson, he revealed that he did the children's books with great reluctance. "He told me, 'Skip, just write children's books, it's *easy*.' He told me it was the easiest thing he did," said Williamson. "Initially, I figured he was just talking about artistic energy, and if you get into *any* project, whether it's writing songs or children's books or comic strips or stories, the energy of the project takes on a life of its own and it creates itself."

But after spending some time with Shel and learning a little about what made him tick, Williamson realized if something was easy for Shel to do and it didn't challenge him or give him a chance to learn anything new, the work would become extraordinarily difficult. And indeed, this was one reason why he became blocked while working on *Different Dances*.

"He was a very kind of project-oriented guy," said Williamson. "I think he was greatly relieved when he moved from one different kind of project to another *different* kind of project. He decided, 'Time to do an album!' so that's what happened. Then it was, 'Gotta do a children's book!' or 'I wanna draw some cartoons!' He'd move from one project to the next, and if he got tired of everything, he'd go hang out with Willie Nelson for a while."

His quirks amused Williamson. "He was a purist, and he'd get upset about crazy stuff," he said. "When the remake of the movie *The Postman Always Rings Twice* came out, he was outraged. Shel said, 'How could they do that? It's one of the greatest movie classics ever.' I told him it couldn't have been all bad if the screenplay was written by David Mamet, to which he replied, 'Who the fuck is David Mamet?'"

Of course, he would find out soon enough.

He didn't like to take public transportation, and he didn't like to take cabs if he didn't have to—shades of the aftermath of his 1959 car accident—so on their walks, they'd often end up at Melvin B's, an outdoor café in Shel's old neighborhood, and he was a bit nostalgic about the place. It was also close to the *Playboy* offices. But Shel may have kept going back because the café's motto matched his own: "There are no rules."

Williamson said Shel once told him a funny story about the time he realized how other people might perceive him.

"When you're walking down the street did you ever see someone coming toward you, and you get a vibe that you better cross the street because you don't want to cross paths with this person?" asked Shel.

"Of course," said Williamson.

Shel continued. "I was coming out of a restaurant the other day and I look up and coming into the restaurant as I was leaving was this guy who just scared the shit out of me." He paused for a few seconds, before he said, "Then I realized it was a mirror."

"Fashion didn't mean too much to him, and he was very conscious of being a bohemian character," said Williamson. "He dressed in real baggy clothes, whatever was comfortable, and half the time he would wear a

Greek seaman's hat. He was always amazed by people and their different styles and how they presented themselves physically. He really enjoyed observing all manner of bizarre styles. We'd sit in the café and he'd watch the parade go by and doodle on cocktail napkins."

Thanks to Williamson, Shel was able to produce enough work on *Different Dances* that he could present it to Harper & Row. While he knew the publisher valued his work, given the millions of dollars his books generated for the company, he wanted to find out exactly how badly they wanted to keep him on board. So he took a few storyboards for the book over to the publisher, and as he showed them the different images he discussed the premise of the book.

"He pitched it as *The Adventures of a Boy and His Penis*," was how one editor put it. "They were mostly single-page drawings, and some of them were fairly pornographic."

As the editors looked on in silence—a few with abject horror on their faces—he flipped through the storyboards and laid out the terms.

"Okay, this is my next book, and you have to take it exactly as it is, there can't be any changes," he told them. "Oh, and you don't get the other book that goes with it—my next children's book called *A Light in the Attic*—unless you do *Different Dances*."

His demands were met with more silence.

"I've had all these best-selling books for Harper and Row, and they told me I could do anything I wanted to do and they'd publish it," was how Shel explained it to Williamson. "This book will *not* make a profit for me," he continued, "but I've already made enough money for them, so they can justify doing this one for me."

A tug-of-war immediately broke out between the corporate and editorial offices of Harper & Row, even though they all knew how much money Shel's children's books generated for the company. Once *Sidewalk* was published, it dwarfed everything else in the children's department, and the publisher didn't want him to jump ship for another company.

Today Jonathan Dolger is a literary agent, but back in the late '70s he was an editor in the adult trade division of Harper & Row when Shel came in with *Different Dances*. "The executives told me, 'We don't want to do this, tell him not to do it,'" said Dolger, who was very enthusiastic about the book and also saw how much money the company would lose if Shel walked out the door.

"This book was very important to him," said Dolger. "His whole life was this book, but at the time Harper was run by a bunch of uptight Wall Street WASPs who thought it was just too much." But Shel was enormously profitable to Harper and so they agreed to publish *Different Dances* on the condition that he deliver his next children's book, which would be *A Light in the Attic,* within two years.

He agreed, and the company conceived of *Different Dances* as a very high-priced oversized hardcover book with a small printing with no advertising, hoping that nobody would notice it.

"When you have an author like Shel who wants to do something out of his usual genre, you don't want to let him leave over something like this if you can help it," said Dolger. "This was not like publishing Henry Miller, but it was very clear that Harper didn't want to jeopardize the ongoing relationship with Shel over this one title."

"Everyone was very worried that *Dances* would put off his children's book followers, parents and teachers," said Joan Robins. "Shel didn't want to offend anybody, he just didn't want people to be prejudiced against him just because he had this whole other world going on."

Dolger had inadvertently developed a reputation for dealing with difficult authors, and so when Harper agreed to Shel's shotgun terms, he took over supervising production on *Dances*. Even though Shel was thrilled that *Dances* would be published, he still hemmed and hawed about committing to a firm deadline, because that would mean he was answering to the suits, not to himself and his creative process.

So he did what he needed to do in order to get the job done: he moved into the conference room a few floors up from the editorial offices at Harper & Row and worked on laying out *Different Dances* until it was done. "He was there more than anyone else who worked in the office," said Dolger. "He really camped out." Even though it was an adult book, most of the production work was done by the children's department. The conference room was near the adult department, but the juvenile offices were in a different part of the building and accessible only by elevator. It was physically very hard for the people working in the children's department to keep going back and forth from their offices up to the conference room, but they did so because of the unspoken thought: "We'll humor this guy now, because the next book he does is the one we really want."

Even though it was Shel's least favorite part of the process of putting out a book, once he began to work, he put the blinders on and plowed through until he was done. Dolger didn't check in on Shel's progress much in the first few weeks, primarily because there was no space to spare in the room. "He used huge boards to lay out the pages, and you couldn't really move them around," he said. "When I did go in there, I couldn't breathe." But he did spend more time with Shel toward the end of production.

"I was there more to make sure there was not going to be any controversy than to contribute anything conceptually or editorially," Dolger explained, though he wasn't sure if there were any cartoons or scenes that the higher-ups were going to demand be cut from the book. "There were so many versions of so many things that Shel was directing in his head that who would remember if anything was taken out at the end? We published the book, but he was his own publisher in that sense. Everything was subject to his approval."

When the book came out in 1979 it sold poorly, to no one's surprise. The publicity department did nothing to call attention to it, and the sales department made certain that the book could not be sold in the ultraconservative Bible Belt due to its risqué content. The November 1, 1979, *Library Journal* review described the book as such: "A familiar Silverstein theme, destructive exploitation in the name of Love, gets extended treatment here, and parenting takes some sour and cynical swipes."

As was the case with the record albums he made in the '60s, it's possible that the majority of the copies were bought up by professional and aspiring cartoonists who studied Shel's work for the sheer craft and his ability to convey a wide range of emotions with just a few strokes of the pen.

But not all cartoonists were enamored of his work. Shel once spotted cartoonist Robert Crumb at a party and walked over to introduce himself. He told Crumb he was pleased to meet him and he liked his art. According to Williamson, Crumb pointedly ignored him, which hurt Shel very much.

However Crumb wasn't rejecting Shel or his work, but *Playboy*. "At the time, the magazine was trying to woo him to do some work for the magazine, and Crumb was getting great pleasure out of telling them no," said Williamson. "He thought Shel had been sent in as a shill, but Shel took it as personal criticism from another artist. It was really just a big misunderstanding, and it was the only time I'd ever seen him disturbed by any kind of criticism for what he did."

It was yet another reason why Shel had grown tired of the magazine. *Playboy* was only a small part of what he did, and for one of his peers to assume he was acting on behalf of the magazine, especially when he was so fed up with it, must have infuriated him. Things came to a head in 1977 when Hef's daughter Christie came to work for the company. Barely two years old when her parents split up, she stayed in touch with her father throughout her childhood and after earning a degree in English from Brandeis University, Christie started working at her father's magazine empire, which they both viewed as a temporary move. But her arrival coincided with a general housecleaning in the wake of the first financial losses reported by Playboy Enterprises, and Hef started to give her more responsibilities. She would go on to create a more professional and corporate atmosphere at the company until becoming firmly entrenched with her appointment as president in the spring of 1982 when she was only twenty-nine.

"Shel felt it was the end of an era, and it was," said Williamson. "After Christie took the helm, she cleaned house of a lot of the people he had worked with. Christie started running it like a business, but it took all the fun out of the place."

Despite this, Hef was still after Shel to start contributing to the magazine again. "Hef was bugging him, readers were bugging him, but he wasn't the least bit interested," said Kerig Pope. "Hef had a lot of unpublished manuscripts that Shel had done for *Playboy* over the years, but they needed to be refined in order to be published and Shel just didn't want to do it."

Once he had a firm commitment from Harper & Row to publish *Different Dances,* Shel figured he could just spin off some of the segments in the book and sell them to the magazine, and that worked for a while. But because he was so dismayed with what Hef had done to the company, as well as having to deal with editors whose primary concern was the bottom line, he decided to have some fun while also underscoring his importance to the magazine.

He began to negotiate with the editors for the rights to publish his work, asking for outrageous amounts just to prove he could get it. "Not many people know that Shel was really good at business negotiations," said Williamson. "He offered the editors his work but asked for ungodly amounts of money. He held their feet to the fire and they would play hardball, but he'd always get the money. The editors were always pissed off when he left, vowing that he'd never work for the magazine again, which, of course, was stupid."

Shelling out more money didn't exactly work as an incentive for him to stick to the deadline they had given him. On the contrary, he still pushed the deadlines to the limit to see how much he could get away with before they threw up their hands and said no more. But he knew they wouldn't do that, or else they'd incur Hef's wrath and then *they'd* be out of a job.

Instead of creating new work from scratch, Shel decided to take a look at the manuscripts that Hef had been holding on to for years to see if there were any he could dash off a few quick cartoons for, and to tweak some of the text. After all, Hef gave him his start, it wouldn't take long, and he had been working on a few other pieces as well. Maybe those would work.

But it didn't. In fact, the block he had faced when he was working on *Different Dances* returned, and it got worse. "He had what amounted to an artist's block," said Pope. "He could write, but he couldn't draw. He could draw *cartoons,* but he felt that these pieces were a little too serious for cartoons."

That's because the pieces that blocked him weren't meant to be funny and included "The Devil and Billie Markham" and "Rosalie's Good Eats Café." The latter is a story about the characters who hang out at a café, many with serious drug problems and others who are alcoholics. Even though he regularly satirized addicts and alcoholics in his songs, this was something different.

One day, Pope was called into the editor's office, which usually meant something was wrong. "Shel was there. He pointed at me mockingly and called me a son of a bitch. 'You're the guy who knew I couldn't draw these things,' he said. Based on what he was sending me, I figured that Shel just wasn't capable of drawing cartoons as seriously as he wanted to. I thought at that point, he was just nervous about it."

Pope decided to pair him up with Brad Holland, an illustrator whose style was very serious and very surreal. A self-taught artist, Holland illustrated the cover of Billy Joel's 1986 album *The Bridge.* He and Shel hit it off from the start.

"Brad did magnificent illustrations, like someone shooting a game of pool with a person curled up as a fetal shape," said Pope. "Those were the kind of serious ideas that Shel couldn't and didn't want to draw."

But there was still the issue of Shel's inaccessibility. "There was simply no way to get hold of Shel," said Pope. Between his numerous addresses and his habit of heading to the airport moments after he decided he needed to be somewhere else and *now,* no one ever knew where he was at any given time. And getting him on the phone was a problem because he didn't have answering machines hooked up at his various homes.

"He was an absolute perfectionist," said Pope. "He would do things over and over and over because he wanted it just so." Bumping up against a magazine's strict deadline, as well as collaborating with Holland so he could finish the illustrations, Pope reached for the Maalox more times than he bothered to count.

Once, with a deadline pressing down, Pope was so desperate to find Shel that he called his mother to see if she knew where he was. Helen Silverstein, in her early eighties, was still living in Chicago and Shel visited her regularly. In fact, she was one of only a handful of people who always knew the whereabouts of her son. She did and told Pope where to find him. When Shel found out, he yelled at him for calling Helen. "He didn't want people to know where he was, and he pretty much wanted everybody to stay out of his family business," said Pope. "But his mom was the only person who knew where the hell he was. I thought it was hilarious."

On another occasion, Pope was down to the wire on a deadline and he just *had* to find Shel, but all his attempts so far had proved futile. "After looking for him in all his usual hideouts, I gave up. Of course, I then bumped into him in a used bookstore a few blocks away from the office," he said.

"You'd never think about looking in your own backyard," said Shel with a big grin.

"We both laughed because it was a game," said Pope, "and it was a game he liked to play, and he played a lot. Let's face it, he could afford to."

Shel contributed six works to the magazine each year during 1979 and 1980, but by 1981 the thrill had worn off again. After having only one piece published in 1981 and 1982, he didn't have another piece appear in *Playboy* until January of 1989.

"Shel was never really interested in doing the cartoons as a regular thing," said Pope. "Of course, *Playboy* would have kept running his work if he kept doing them, but it bored him after a while and he got into something else."

That *something else* was theater. And he found out "who the fuck" David Mamet was.

Meanwhile, out in Sausalito in 1978, things were starting to get ugly, and Shel didn't want to be anywhere near it. He *hated* conflict.

That was when the first shot was fired in what became known as the houseboat wars of the mid-'70s. As housing prices in the Bay Area began to rise, more people moved into the houseboat community, and the local waste treatment facilities became overwhelmed, which led some houseboat dwellers to discharge their waste directly into the bay. The state created an agency assigned to prepare a long-term plan for the community and regulate future development.

The agency determined that in order for the houseboats to stay, residents would be required to bring their homes up to code, connect to the city sewer system, and permanently berth at a dock. Needless to say, the new regulations bore little resemblance to the haphazard arrangements that had developed organically when people first moved onto the docks twenty years earlier. Some of the houseboat owners complied, others didn't, and the sheriffs and police went in after them.

Shel didn't want anything to do with it, and that was the beginning of the end of his houseboat residence. "I was a little surprised that he didn't get a little bit more involved, but I think all the battles and protests erased some of the charm for him and he didn't come around quite as often anymore," said Larry White, who describes the community today as similar to a trailer park. "Everybody's tied up side by side by side. The waterfront was developed and his boat was moved to another, sanitized dock. It just doesn't have the charm that it used to."

Although Shel didn't sell his houseboat, he began to spend less time in Sausalito, and eventually stopped going there altogether.

Despite bedding hundreds, perhaps thousands of women through the years, Shel was still mystified by the ways of women, and it took very little to gain his rapt attention. Ellen Dominique dated Shel on and off in the '70s and '80s, and she was surprised at the little things that fascinated him.

She was visiting him at his apartment one evening when she decided to touch up her fingernail polish. "I put on a head wrap, whipped out the nail polish, and got to work," she said. "It just blew him away. He asked what I was doing, and I said my nails needed a little touch-up. Most men would leave the room. Shel didn't; he just stayed behind and stared."

It's likely that Dominique's mundane activity inspired Shel to write the song "Paintin' Her Fingernails," which appeared in the February 1980 issue of *Playboy*. She thought that he was so intrigued because while he absolutely adored women, he didn't like to keep them around long enough for him to be privy to such girly activities.

"He didn't have women around him unless it was on his terms," she said. "He thought they were a lot of trouble with all the commitment, crying, and hanging on."

At the same time, he still loved going out with new women and finding out all about a new person. "He was fascinated by people," said Dominique. "When I was with him, he made me feel like I was the only one in the room, and it's hard to find a man that does that for a woman."

Because she knew how Shel was—and that she wouldn't be enough for him—Dominique would occasionally fix him up with her girlfriends, though they usually went out only a couple of times. "They didn't last long," she said. "They couldn't keep up with him."

More likely is that as he got older, he was less likely to spend time with women who didn't meet his requirement that a woman be smart and possess some degree of intellectual curiosity. "She had to be brilliant," said Dominique. "She had to be very smart, very articulate, and very fast, because Shel didn't like to have any slow people around him. Whenever I finished a conversation with Shel, I always remembered everything he said and went over it in my mind over and over, simply because he was so brilliant and because of the observations he'd always make about people."

"Shel had a love–hate relationship with almost everything," said Skip

Williamson. "It was the nature of his personality to be outraged, but at the same time, to be fused by it. He always liked to comment on life in general, no matter what it was. It wasn't technically an argument, but you had to have a certain level of intellect, otherwise you'd piss him off."

One time Dominique set him up with a woman she readily describes as a bimbo. "She was very beautiful and very loose," she said. "I thought he might like it and take advantage of her, but they didn't hit it off and she didn't hang around."

Dominique describes the extent of their relationship as very mental and very physical. "That's all he wanted," she said. "He didn't want women calling up the next day to cry about their problems, and in that way he was selfish. At the same time, he was also straightforward about what he *did* want."

"You're here now so let's have fun, and then next week we can do it again and it'll be all fresh and new," he told her once.

But at the same time, there was a part of Shel that didn't believe that she'd be back the next week.

"Shel never assumed that a girl would take up with him just like that," said Larry DuBois. "He wasn't like a Warren Beatty who just took it for granted that the girls would go for him. In fact, Shel often told me, 'Every time I see a girl start to take off her clothes, I always think it's too good to be true.'

"He always said it in this sincere, angelic little boy voice straight out of the fifties, and every time he said it I laughed."

When 1979 rolled around, Shel decided it was time to do another album, which became *The Great Conch Train Robbery*. He had written a lot of songs about the people he knew in Key West and Nashville, and he thought it was time to put some of them on an album. *Songs & Stories* had come out the previous year, but it contained "songs" that Shel recited more than sang, similar to his CDs where he recited his children's poems with vocal inflections that had a range of several octaves.

He still scribbled down his ideas and lyrics in his sketchpad and on scraps of paper, tablecloths, even his own arms, but Shel had become a little more cautious when it came to writing down his lyrics intact. Somewhere along the line, Shel began to worry that another songwriter would come upon one of his scraps of paper and claim it as his own. While no one could steal Shel's drawings or illustrations—they were too instantly recognizable as his own—they could in fact "borrow" his words, even though the case could be argued that a song written by Shel would be just as easy to recognize.

As a result, he had stopped writing down his lyrics, and when it came time to pick the songs for *The Great Conch Train Robbery*, it added a bit of a challenge to producer Michael Melford's job.

"I met him in his hotel room and he asked me to help him choose the songs," said Melford. "He said it was difficult because he had hundreds of songs. I asked if he had lead sheets or lyrics for any of them, and he told me they were all in his head, nothing was written down. This was the first time I had encountered this, and he said he didn't want anybody to steal them. Until a song was recorded—by him or anyone else—he wouldn't write anything down."

Shel played over a hundred songs for Melford over the next couple of nights. "I sat there with a notepad and wrote down the titles of the songs, or a couple of words about what the song was about because he didn't even have lists of songs to give to me," he said. "They were all in his head. I think he didn't write down his songs because he wanted to be careful about keeping certain things private."

Dan Mobley, a singer-songwriter who collaborated with Shel, said there was another reason. "Shel believed that until a song was recorded, it didn't exist," said Mobley. "We'd get together and write a song and record it as soon as possible, even if it was only the two of us playing guitar and singing on his cassette recorder."

Shel believed that if the words were written down, it was still too easy

to forget how the melody goes, how one lick punctuates a particular line, and so on.

"Unless it's recorded," Shel told Mobley, "how is anyone going to know about it?"

But the sad fact is that there are countless tapes floating around his friends' houses—most probably even destroyed by now—that contain songs that Shel wrote that no one knows about specifically because he *didn't* write them down and register them for copyright. BMI, a central registry where songwriters can copyright their songs to guard against theft, lists just over eight hundred songs by Shel that were registered. He may have completed hundreds more over his lifetime.

In any case, Melford said that one reason why Shel decided to make *The Great Conch Train Robbery* was because he had a lot of songs he had written that he decided he wasn't going to give to anybody else. "Bobby Bare, Johnny Cash, and other singers were always looking for songs from him, and he'd give them a few because he made a lot of money writing songs for them. But the songs on *Conch Train* were songs he was saving for himself, they were more personal to him."

Some people thought that one of the songs on the album—"Rough on the Living" which describes how Nashville treats dead country singers better than those who are alive and kicking—was about Elvis Presley, but Shel wrote it about Lester Flatt, a pioneer bluegrass singer and guitarist. When Flatt died on May 11, 1979, Shel had already booked the studio time for *Conch Train*. Nashville had largely forgotten the accomplished musician in favor of the new country music that was starting to be written at the time. It was a testament again to Shel's talent that he was able to essentially write the song overnight and record it the next day.

Another song Shel insisted on recording never made it to the album. "You're a Cunt, Not a Honky Tonk Angel" was an answer song to the Kitty Wells hit "It Wasn't God Who Made Honky Tonk Angels." Her song, in turn, was an answer song to Hank Thompson's 1952 number one hit "Wild Side of Life," but Shel put an additional twist on his song by setting it to the same melody as Thompson's song.

"He insisted on recording the song and I did everything I could to persuade him not to do it," said Melford. "He wanted to record it even if it didn't end up on the album." Which, of course, it didn't. But after 1970's *Fuck 'Em,* Shel was used to recording songs he knew would never make it to a pressed album; he merely wanted to do it for pure shock value.

Shel had a reputation for being opinionated, not only about life but especially about his work, so he sometimes found it difficult to accept guidance from Melford.

"He was very headstrong," said Melford. "He had certain ideas about how he wanted to do things, and the biggest problem I had was working with him on the vocals. He resisted at first, but then he decided to cooperate and follow my suggestions." Indeed, of all of Shel's albums, on *Conch Train* he sounds more like he's singing instead of rasping or croaking, as is the case on his other albums.

Melford was amazed at Shel's boundless energy. "He seemed to never sleep," he said. "We would record all day, then he'd go out in the evening to various clubs and hang out with friends and listen to the performers, then he'd go back to his room and he'd write until late at night. *Then* he'd meet friends for breakfast at six in the morning."

While Shel was very outgoing and gregarious, Melford sensed that he was basically a shy person who was rather insecure about his work. More than any one incident, Melford said he picked up on it from the relationship they had as artist and producer. "It's a relationship of trust, because when they go into the recording studio all artists have insecurities, and they look to the producer to give them some guidance as to when something is good and when it's not," he said. "He did that with me despite all the bravado and bluster he had on the surface. Underneath, there was substantial self-doubt. But he overcame his anxiety and had a lot of courage to go out and try a lot of different things."

The Great Conch Train Robbery had additional significance for Shel. He wrote the title song for Sarah Spencer, who drove the real conch train in Key West, a tourist attraction that takes sightseers on a tour around the island to show various historical sites. In the song, Shel described the train as being "like some weird ride from Disneyland, it drove the tourists round and round." Sarah was in her early twenties while Shel was pushing fifty when they met.

In 1980 after disco died and before the techno-slick punk big-hair trends of the '80s dawned, Spencer was still a hippie with a peace sign tattooed on her wrist. Sarah and Shel grew close, and she was a woman who could deal with his unchanging, unyielding ways. So they spent time together whenever he was in Key West.

A few years later, they would grow even closer than either could have imagined. But first, Shel had to deal with the biggest tragedy of his life.

7. *The Lifeboat Is Sinking*

Shel's attitude toward children was starting to soften, mostly because he was starting to spend more time with his daughter.

She would stay with him for a few weeks in the summer and on week-long school vacations during the year, and he essentially supported her year-round. His relationship with Shoshanna began to blossom. He started to run some of his ideas by her and show her some of his cartoons and drawings, and she'd give him feedback.

Perhaps this unexpected collaborative work with his daughter helped to stoke his desire to write plays and work in the theater to a larger extent than he would have otherwise. Even though he continued to write songs with other songwriters on a regular basis and often camped out in the studio during recording sessions, he still created his stories and cartoons by himself. Seeing his words literally come alive on stage was a whole new experience for him. Yet, as was the case with all his work, he was primarily creating for himself without a thought if there would be an audience for it.

"I don't think he wrote most of the plays really caring if they were performed," said Karen Kohlhaas, a founder of Chicago's Atlantic Theatre, who first met Shel in 1985 when she was a theater student in New York. "Just like all his work, he wrote it for himself first."

"His writing grew by being involved in the theater largely because there was so much support for him there," said Lynne McCalford, who worked with Shel when his one-act plays were first produced at New York's Ensemble Studio Theatre in the early '80s while she was an intern there. He felt very nurtured there, which is probably a big reason why he threw himself into the theater: it not only nurtured and sheltered him, but it also provided him with a venue where he could grow his writing in ways that were impossible in his other fields.

But he didn't start thinking of himself as a playwright just because that was where he was directing his energies. Instead, he continued as before, thinking of himself as a writer who just happened to ply his craft in a number of different arenas. "He was like an actor who is doing a lot of serious roles and suddenly starts to do comedy," said McCalford. "You don't think of it as separate, like over here I'm a serious actor and over there I'm a comic actor. It's just another dimension of the craft and you feel like you're able to do it all."

Perhaps that's why he felt so drawn to the theater, because it's one of the few arts where it's impossible to fake it. He'd seen it countless times before, in music, at *Playboy,* and in children's books: whenever someone hits it big, there's an overwhelming tendency to let things slide, to let the success and fame do most of the heavy lifting, cranking out just enough every year to make the corporate executives and the bottom line happy.

Also, in a studio theater setting, where the emphasis is on talented beginners, Shel was surrounded by people who viewed their art in the same way that he did: with a wide-eyed innocence and a hunger for taking what they've learned and applying it to their craft.

Of course, being associated with a famous cartoonist and children's author didn't exactly hurt the theater. Most of the people who came through the doors and worked on the stage at the theater were not famous when they first showed up. "Studio theaters normally get unknowns whether they're writers, actors, or directors," said McCalford. "When they become famous, then you can't find them because they end up in Los Angeles and in a whole different world. Shel provided an interesting twist on the norm, since everyone already knew who he was." Of course, what goes unsaid is that the majority of celebrities would rarely admit so publicly that they need to hone their craft in an environment prone to leaks to the media from fellow students. Shel, of course, couldn't care less about that sort of thing; he was interested only in learning something new.

After rehearsals were over for the day, however, Shel still preferred to spend the evening with one or two people instead of a group.

"He was not one to say, 'Let's go out with six other people,'" said Mc-Calford. "He could work very well with people when he was working on a play, but afterwards he always wanted to go off one-on-one. He was much better divulging his thoughts to one person who he felt was really listening instead of trying to get the attention of everyone in the group."

"All my work has been done alone," he said. "You draw alone. You write alone. You compose music alone. But theater is a collaborative art and it takes a different personality. You must relate to other people. You get the joys you get from being in a relationship, and also the pain. It's like asking, 'Is it better to live with someone or to live alone?' The answer is that it's just different."

At the same time, he didn't like having people over to his house unless they were working on a project together, and it had to be either outside on the porch or in the backyard. "He always liked being outside and didn't like to have people in his house," said Dan Mobley. "He clearly viewed it as an invasion of his private space. Shel wasn't the most domestic person and rarely cleaned his house, but he didn't want a cleaning lady in his house for three hours. So instead, he hired three cleaning ladies to be there for one hour and then get the hell out."

It was his friend, playwright Herb Gardner, who first encouraged Shel to start writing plays. He'd come up with ideas for different one-act plays as readily as ideas for songs and cartoons popped into his head. The only thing is because he had never worked in the medium before, instead of writing them down he blurted them out whenever he was with Gardner. Finally, Gardner told him to stop.

"Herb said, 'You've got to stop telling me the ideas because you're not writing them,'" said Shel. "I realized I had to shut up and start writing. You can't keep saying you're moving to the country and not do it. After a while, your friends stop throwing you going-away parties."

"He had flamboyancies in his life that people were aware of, but in his own way, Shel was a very understated man," said McCalford. "He was very happy when he first had success with the off-Broadway genre and even more so when it continued."

In fact, it never really ended. From 1981, when his first play *The Lady or the Tiger Show,* was produced, up until his death, he never strayed from writing for the theater, as he had strayed from his other creative pursuits. His plays were produced in theaters in both New York and Chicago.

The Lady or the Tiger Show was the first play Shel wrote that was performed off-Broadway, and is still regarded in many theatrical circles as his best work. It's staged as a television game show where the contestant, Lamar Darfield, has to choose between two doors: Behind one sits Florence Haskins, the woman whom Lamar has secretly loved since high school, while behind the other is a snarling man-eating tiger who will make an appetizer out of him in small order. His odds are even for picking either, of course, and the situation quickly turns into a morality play where he asks how badly he wants her after all. A supporting cast of characters includes a rabidly enthusiastic game show host, a priest, and a greedy producer. In a way, Shel was remarkably prescient in writing *The Lady or the Tiger Show* in 1981, since it echoes the reality shows that would come to permeate the culture two decades later.

Of course, once Shel learned something new and felt he had a handle on it, he was eager to show his friends how to do it, too. "Shel taught me how to write for the theater by showing me how he wrote his plays," said Chris Gantry, who had previously written songs with Shel.

One day, Gantry bumped into Shel on Duval Street in Key West, and because he knew Shel was getting a lot of attention for his short plays in New York at the time, he asked him for some advice about playwriting. "I told him that I didn't know how to get started and asked how he did it," said Gantry. Shades of collaborative songwriting déjà vu followed when Shel told him to bring a pad and a pen to his house the next morning.

When Gantry showed up, Shel told him to sit down and grab his pen. "Do exactly what I tell you to do," he said, blurting out the rest. "When I tell you to go, start writing with no preconceived notions about what your play is about. I'm going to time you and give you a little more than an hour. The first thing that comes into your mind is the title of the play. Then you'll write about a man and a woman, use *M* for man and *W* for woman. Start writing free-form, free association and don't take your pen off the page. The key is not thinking about it. If you get to a place where you don't know what to say, and the first thing that comes into your head is 'I have a carrot and stick up my ass,' then you write that down, that's your line."

Gantry followed Shel's advice, and was pleasantly surprised when the words just flowed out of him, just they did when he wrote songs with Shel.

"At the end of an hour, I'd written a play," he said. "I asked if he wanted to hear it and he said he didn't care about the play, he just wanted to show me the form and how to do it."

Gantry repeated the process the next day, this time without Shel. At the end of an hour, he had another play. He was still amazed and continued to do the same thing every morning until he had written about a hundred plays. He submitted the first five he had written to the Tennessee Williams Playwriting Contest and won, which was a total fluke because no one had previously submitted short one-act plays to the contest; the long form was the norm. "It blew Shel's mind and affected him a bit, because I told him he should enter the contest next year," said Gantry. "But he said he was afraid that he might put his plays in and lose."

Of course, a brand-new creative arena also presented Shel with a whole new crop of women to pursue, whether they were rank beginners or longtime professionals.

And as usual, not every woman could deal with Shel's lifestyle. Actress Deborah Reagan, who played the lead in *The Lady or the Tiger Show,* dated Shel for a while, and it soon became clear that she wanted more from him than he could give. In this case, however, he couldn't just get on a plane and leave a disgruntled woman behind or duck into an alley as he had done in the late 1950s. He had to continue to work with Reagan.

"I don't think she was able to cope with what a relationship with Shel entailed," said McCalford. "He was never able to settle down, he really believed it would ruin the relationship. His issue about marriage was that he didn't like what it turned into. Marriage was a committed relationship, and he thought the relationship was clouded by the day-to-day routine."

And it obviously lost its spontaneity, which was something that Shel lived for. For instance, he had the uncanny habit of running into friends in the most out-of-the-way and unlikely venues. Shel had met so many people over the years in so many different places that it wasn't unusual for him to run into them again in diners and clubs that were off the beaten path, or down a dark alley.

"I never knew where I was going to run into him," said Joe Sun, who had met and worked with Shel in Key West. "One night, I was walking down a dark alley in Nashville down by Elliston Place, and here comes Shel heading toward me. I asked him where he was going and he said he was just out on the town checking things out."

When these accidental meetings did occur, Shel was often by himself. Though he attended lots of gatherings with lots of people, he rarely ran with a pack, preferring instead to travel solo to where he wanted to go without worrying about having to entertain someone who was tagging along. It also allowed him to take off and hop on a plane if he felt like it.

His spontaneity was such that sometimes it wasn't even a matter of setting a songwriting date for the following morning; occasionally he insisted on doing it on the spur of the moment. One morning in 1981, when Shoshanna was visiting Shel in Nashville, they were having breakfast in a coffee shop when singer Mac Davis stopped by their table. He told Shel that he had always been a big fan and wanted to write a song with him someday. Shel said he'd like that.

Davis said he'd give him a call, but Shel said, "Let's do it now." Davis didn't want to interrupt his time with his daughter, but Shel insisted and he sat down and they wrote two songs at the table. One of the songs was "Pour Me Another Tequila, Sheila." Davis ended up recording the song, as well as Bobby Bare.

While Shel still liked to write songs with other songwriters, he increasingly wanted to keep his cards close to his chest and instead of writing together, he'd look to his peers for their opinions of songs he'd already written.

"I never cowrote with him," said songwriter Drew Reid. "He had already written some songs and was reworking them and tweaking them and trying out different verses and I'd go over to his house in Key West and he'd bounce it all off me. He'd ask what I thought, was that a good progression and is that phrase any good? And I would suggest various chord changes or maybe rearrange it a bit."

Since Shel had taught himself how to play guitar, and wrote most of his songs in the basic I-IV-V chord progression that is the standard of most pop songs, he sometimes got stuck when he wanted something different. "Sometimes he knew the kind of sound that he wanted, but didn't know how it translated to a particular chord," said Reid. If he couldn't do it, Shel would ask Reid what he was hearing by singing a few notes of the melody. "I'd run through a couple of chords and when I hit it, he'd stop me and say 'That's it, that one right there.' So I'd tell him, 'Hell, Shel, you want a D minor 7,' and he'd say, 'What the hell are you talking about?'" But in the end, he got the sound he wanted and that's all that mattered.

Because he was tweaking songs with Reid and not writing them, which required him to concentrate for long periods of time, Shel's attention span could be even more scattered. His sessions with Reid coincided with the time when he was finalizing the poems and illustrations for the mammoth production session for *A Light in the Attic.*

"His house was just a working studio, with all of his projects and works-in-progress all over the place, massive piles of stuff everywhere," said Reid. "He had pages of the book laid out on the floor in rows, and he'd take a break from our work and walk up and down the rows as he put this book together in his mind. He'd pick up one page and put it over there, then pick up another page and put it over *there.*"

And sometimes he'd get the urge to run back to the guest house on his property where he had a studio for the painting and sculpture he dabbled in.

"Sometimes he'd take a break from what we were doing, say, 'I'll be right back,' and run out the door," said Reid. "And he'd go over and slap some clay or paint on something for twenty minutes and then come back.

"Some people are real spiritual about creating things, but Shel wasn't," he said. "He was very matter-of-fact about it: This is what I do, I get up in the morning and away I go. At the same time, he was very focused and disciplined in his way. Whenever he told me to show up at his house at nine in the morning and we'll go for two or three hours, that's exactly what we did. It wasn't like I got there and he said let's watch the butterflies fly around the backyard or let's get a fish sandwich. When I got there it was all business. He was very relaxed, very cordial, but we got right down to work. And he worked like that seven days a week, 365 days a year."

"He was always right in the moment," said Reid. "If we were sitting at a café and he wanted to show me something he'd pull out five cocktail napkins and they'd go blowing down the street and we'd have to run after them. One time, he was at a club where I was playing, and I remember looking at him when I was in the middle of a song and something came to him and he pulled out his pen and wrote on his wrist."

Even though he never went anywhere without his sketchbook, sometimes he needed to write it down so quickly that he didn't want to waste any time opening the pad.

"He didn't have time, he wanted to get it right down," said Reid. "That's the way those guys are. Mickey Newbury, who was a friend of Shel's, had a great story about what it's like to be a songwriter. He said, 'Man, if you're a songwriter, and you're riding on a Greyhound bus in the middle of the Mojave Desert when a song comes to you, you stop the bus and get out and write it.'"

Shel's drug of choice was espresso. Reid said that one reason why Shel was always ready to go by the time he arrived for their 9 A.M. sessions was that he'd already had a couple of cups. "He was ready to go," he said.

On occasion, Shel would pretend he drank something harder than espresso, like the days in the Village when he'd nurse a glass of wine the entire night, depending on the kind of people he was with. One time, he was in Nashville cutting some demos with a full band of studio musicians, and Shel had a pint of peach brandy that was about half-full hanging out of his back pocket. When someone made a comment about it with surprise because Shel was never known to drink, Shel said he wasn't drinking. He bought it and poured half of it out so the pickers would *think* he was drinking; he thought they'd relate to him more.

While he often tried out new material on adults, it was primarily to gauge the reaction and volume of laughter. With his kids' books, he knew he needed more detailed feedback and more than just his daughter's reactions to determine whether a particular poem would end up in *A Light in the Attic*. And so, he'd head for the most public gathering spot around, usually a playground. And while some kids would take one look at the bald-headed full-bearded man dressed in a pirate shirt, running shorts, and a grungy leather jacket and stay far away, others were drawn to him.

"He not only wore strange clothes, but he wore them for great lengths of time, so they really did get very grotty-looking," said Kerig Pope. "And while many around him were sometimes tempted to say, 'Hey, Shel, we know you can afford to go buy a new leather jacket,' no one dared to say anything."

He was the last holdout from the beatnik days of 1950s Greenwich Village. "That's where the clothing and his style came from," said Pope. "He never lost it and actually remained true to it, even when everyone else changed around him. It was a calling for him."

The kids who weren't scared off at the playground sat in rapt wonder, listening to Shel toss out a few poems the same way he tried out songs on-stage at the Exit Inn. And when he was in his market research mode, he'd head to the nearest playground no matter where he was: New York, Key West, or on the road. He even held court when he spent three weeks in Columbia, South Carolina, to work on *Southern Fried*.

"The kids came and gathered and stayed while Shel told them stories and gave them money to buy more peanuts for the pigeons," said William Price Fox. "When he had a quorum, he'd rear back and in a voice that sounded as if it were being squeezed through gravel and tin cans, he'd sing, 'Help! I'm being swallowed by a boa constrictor.' I saw Shel do this over and over again and I've never seen kids so completely happy and alive."

Shel also relied on other sounding boards in the form of friends, their children, and other writers.

"He'd send out a set of poems and ask them to choose their favorites," said Joan Robins. "He never asked about what they *didn't* like, he only wanted to hear about their favorites. He was very particular about that because he wanted to hear which of the poems really spoke to people, and that's how he decided which poems were going to make the cut."

Once his research was completed, the easy part was over. It was time to buckle down on production for his next two children's books. *The Missing Piece Meets the Big O*, published in May 1981, is the sequel to *The Missing Piece*. It's the story of a wedge-shaped character looking for a companion, which after a series of hits and misses, arrives in the form of a circle with a chunk missing, which happens to be the exact size of the wedge. It works for a while, but the wedge grows and eventually learns how to get along on its own, after encountering the "Big O," a circle that needs nothing. Interestingly, the publisher lists the book for grades eight and up, but a *School Library Journal* reviewer recommended the story as being appropriate for college students and those in the process of getting divorced, but not for young children. *A Light in the Attic,* which came out in October of the same year, was billed as the successor to *Where the Sidewalk Ends.* Shel was so pleased with the work Joan Robins had done on *Different Dances* that he asked her to become his editor, since Ursula Nordstrom had retired in 1979. Another editor, Robert Warren, came on board to help out as well.

Harper must have thought it was a windfall since Shel was going to have two books come out in the same year, but Warren says it worked out because Shel just happened to have the sequel to *The Missing Piece* ready at that point. "Shel would work on things constantly, and there were tons of poems and drawings and different manuscripts that he'd go back and forth with whenever the spirit moved him," said Warren.

Jim Skofield had been an editorial assistant in the children's department at Harper & Row for about a year and a half when Shel moved into the conference room to work on *Attic,* just as he had done for *Different Dances.* With the production and editorial staff tied up helping Shel, somebody was needed to go out and run errands for Shel, show finished layouts to the editorial director, and get copies made of his layouts. In other words, a glorified gofer.

"I was on Shel Patrol," said Skofield, "and my main purpose was to do whatever was necessary to accommodate his mood swings in regard to the layout of the book." Occasionally, being on Shel Patrol also involved running to the local sushi restaurant to bring in sushi for Shel, which he loved.

Shel did everything by hand, with pen and ink. Computer programs for the kind of work he was doing were nonexistent, and even if today's top-of-the-line graphics software existed back then, it's doubtful he would have used it. He wanted to *feel* the work as the pen moved across the paper. Every horizontal surface in the conference room and most of the wall space was covered with countless scraps of paper, not only with the drawings and poems for the book but notes Shel made to himself, doodles, and takeout menus. The final drawings were reproduced on very glossy white fine paper and put through a machine to coat it with a thin layer of wax, making it easy to move the drawings around on oversized Masonite boards so Shel could play around with the placement.

Once Shel was happy with the layout, Skofield took the board to a nearby print shop to be photostated. When Shel approved the photostat, it would go to the printer.

Most children's book authors would consider the photostat to be the last word, but Shel didn't work that way. "He was an absolute perfectionist," said Skofield. "He cared enormously about the page layout. It was not enough for him to have a drawing reproduced to scale and a couple of other sizes for comparison. Shel not only wanted it at hundred percent scale, but also at ninety-seven percent and ninety-six percent, and he'd be able to tell the difference. Then he would decide it was too large and he'd want to try eighty-seven percent. Then he would go back to the ninety-six percent and say 'It's still a wee bit too large, let's take it back to ninety-five percent.'"

Skofield also made a number of mock-up pages so Shel could experiment with the order in which the poems appeared in the book. But nothing was ever set in stone until the last possible moment. "Even when he said he was happy with it, he usually would end up changing it many times," Skofield noted.

Shel's right-hand man during these marathon sessions was Kim Llewellyn, who had been working at Harper for six months when Shel decided to hire her to be his assistant. Indeed, on *Attic,* she was credited with the book and cover design.

"Kim was very involved in selecting the quality of paper that was used and the binding and all of the mechanics of making the actual book because she knew how much Shel loved books," said Warren. "He was absolutely fascinated with books and having a huge collection of books. He loved the feel of a book, the weight, the smell, everything. A book to him was something that he was creating but it was also something that he just loved as an object, which is why he was so meticulous about how it looked and how it felt."

He camped out in the conference room for a total of two months. Some days he would come in and work all day, others he'd work four or five hours, and sometimes he'd show up late in the afternoon and work through the night. Llewellyn was always by his side.

Skofield said that he came in with both rough and finished sketches. "He'd sometimes make several different drawings for one poem and then choose between them," he said. "And if he was unhappy with the way something looked, he'd redraw the entire thing instead of whiting out the section he didn't like."

The other editors would be running errands, offering comments or talking quietly, but as often as possible, they'd stand back over Shel's shoulder and watch him work.

"He was very, very focused," said Warren. "It was fascinating to watch him draw because he would start by putting his pen in the middle of the page and start drawing, but the picture would emerge from the center and spiral outward."

Joan Robins concurs. "His technique of drawing was very odd. Shel would start out with a couple of lines right in the middle of the page and the drawing would kind of pop out of it," she said. "He didn't set out with an idea of what he was going to draw, like, 'I'm going to draw a man, or a flower or whatever.' His pencil hit the page and the drawing came out of it."

Unlike many artists and writers, Shel actually preferred to have people around when he was working. "Even though he liked to work quietly, Shel liked having people around him," said Robins.

But there was another reason why he wanted to have people around him in the conference room. "He liked to think of Harper as his home, but I also think he felt it was his jail to some extent because he could only work on one thing when production was under way for the books," said Robins. And sometimes he took it out on his "jailers." "He'd question the production editor about something and anyone who just happened to be there, but that was what he wanted, and since he was a best-selling author he got it."

His editors were known to grumble, "Shel's in-house," and everyone knew what that meant, even editors who weren't working with him, since his production took the time and resources of other editors away from their own projects.

"Every editor bitches about his authors, including Shel Silverstein, but not any more than any other writer," said Skofield. "Everyone knew that one of the reasons that they continued to have a job at Harper's was because Shel Silverstein brought in a significant amount of money to the company."

Skofield added that while he didn't get into any in-depth conversations with Shel, he believes that Shel wouldn't have been an easy individual to get to know. "Because of his intensity and his constant focus, he really reminded me of a hermit, or a monk," said Skofield, and not just because of his ability to concentrate. "Along with the dark beard, the dark eyes, and the shaved head, Shel always wore the same thing: a tunic that was usually hanging out of his pants. He had that air of someone who is so caught up in what he was doing that he didn't have time or attention to care about how he looked."

A Light in the Attic was published in October 1981, and though it would go on to spend 182 weeks on *The New York Times* best-seller list, a record for the longest tenure on the list at the time, like *Where The Sidewalk Ends,* it generated criticism among parents, teachers, and the media.

"His books were very controversial because they were so different from anything else that was published for children at the time," said Robins.

"These books appealed to the valiant side of the children and there is something slightly provocative about the poems." Her favorite review of *A Light in the Attic* was by the conservative columnist George Will, who described the book as "A good antidote to a headache." In addition, the book would be banned twelve years later at the Fruitland Park Elementary School library in Lake County, Florida, after a parent complained about the poem "Little Abigail and the Beautiful Pony," where the title character tells her parents she'll die if they refuse to buy her a pony. They don't, and she does, which prompted school authorities to agree with the aggrieved parent.

For his part, Shel still continued to ignore his critics. "I think if you're a creative person, you should just go about your business, do your work and not care about how it's received. Not that I don't care about success. I do, but only because it lets me do what I want. I was always prepared for success but that means that I have to be prepared for failure too."

In his children's books, Shel liked to create elaborate autographs, often making pictures and personalizing them to the recipient. He didn't participate in official book signings at bookstores; instead he'd graciously grant a child or adult's impromptu request.

"Whenever you wanted an autograph from him it was always more than an autograph," said Dan Waisman, who owned a bookstore in Madison, Wisconsin. "It was always a cartoon using the first letter of whoever's name he was autographing. To my knowledge, he would not just scribble out an autograph. It was a ten-minute operation."

Helen Scarborough, who met Shel on the Vineyard with her husband in 1980 when they moved to the community full-time, said that his autograph process was extremely detailed. She bought his books for her grandchildren and gave them to him to sign, and she'd watch while he personalized them both according to the book and the child in what usually turned into a ten-minute operation for each signature.

"He would make a picture of a Giving Tree and then incorporate the child's name into the illustration," she said. It wasn't unusual for people to drop books off at his house with the name of the recipient, and they'd pick up the book a few days later.

Over the years, Shel had gradually started to pull back from attending the huge lavish parties at the Playboy Mansion West, preferring instead to spend his time in smaller, more intimate gatherings. "In the eighties, Shel was more likely to hang around the Mansion when there weren't a whole bunch of people around," said Larry DuBois. "I'd mostly see him when it was just a few of Hef's good friends getting together. He liked to sit in the breakfast room at the Mansion West, which was called the Mediterranean Room, where he'd be strumming his guitar or doodling on a sketchpad."

The Mediterranean Room was also where Larry DuBois saw him for the first time after his daughter died.

On April 24, 1982, Shoshanna died very unexpectedly of a brain aneurysm at her grandparents' house in Baltimore. She was only eleven years old. "It was the single most devastating event of his life, and I don't think he ever really recovered from it," said Hefner.

"It killed the man," said Chris Gantry. "He really loved that little girl. He went into shock. If you live in fantasyland in your head for the majority of your life, which is where Shel lived, then all of a sudden you get the harsh three-dimensional reality of the real deal, well, it was a rude awakening for him."

"Shel was never one to talk openly about himself, and after Shoshanna died, he absolutely shut down," said Hillary Mapes. "Once I told him how sorry I was, and he just kind of disappeared into himself for a moment. He just couldn't deal with it. The whole idea that Shel had a child was fascinating because Shel was absolutely anti-marriage, and against having children, but this just killed him."

Shortly after his daughter died, Shel headed out to the Mansion West. DuBois sat with him in the Mediterranean Room and just listened to him talk. "What I heard was utter devastation," he said. "I can still see

Shel sitting at that table just absolutely destroyed by the death of that girl. I don't remember the words that he said, but, oh God, was he hurting."

Joan Robins remembered when Shel called to tell her the news. "He said, 'I'm just calling to tell you I'm all right,' and that was all he said," she said. "He just wanted to reassure me that he wasn't considering suicide. He adored that little girl, she was a beautiful child. It was such a shock."

He decided that the best thing to do was to simply pour himself into his work, but there was no way he could think about doing another children's book; the pain was still too fresh. While the time lag between *Where the Sidewalk Ends* and *Attic* was seven years, his next full-length book of children's poetry, *Falling Up,* would not appear for fifteen years. If he had been considering it, Shoshanna's death all but squelched the idea. *Who Wants a Cheap Rhinoceros?* originally published in 1964, was revised and republished in January 1983, but it had been already scheduled when Shoshanna died.

Aside from turning away from children's books, Shoshanna's death did not affect his work at all, said his friends. Because he didn't drink or do drugs, the only thing he could do was throw himself into his work even more, in particular, the theater. His friends believed that the collaborative nature of writing plays and then staging them served to keep him from succumbing to the deep grief he felt.

"The theater work got him through a very dark period in his life," said Lynne McCalford.

"Nothing ever affected Shel's work, it was his undying passion," said Gantry. "It was the one thing he could do that could give him relief and a sense of control in his life that he may not have felt he had at the time. Shoshanna's death was so difficult for him that he became even more absorbed in his work as a way to cope, but he never talked about it in detail with anyone."

No one, except for his close friend Bobby Bare, who knew exactly what Shel was going through, since his young daughter had suddenly died several years earlier.

"The experience really bonded them," said Fred Koller. "It was just a terrible couple of years."

The following year, he finally answered his question "Who the fuck is David Mamet?" In fact, the celebrated playwright would turn out to be one of Shel's closest friends for the rest of his life. They met when Greg Mosher and Art Wolff were directing a trio of one-act plays at the Goodman Theater in Chicago. Mamet wrote one play, Shel penned another, while theater heavyweight Elaine May wrote the third.

Mamet was seventeen years younger than Shel, and remembered thinking of Shel as a "demigod" when he was growing up in Chicago. When they first met, Mamet had created quite a body of work himself: His plays *Sexual Perversity in Chicago* and *American Buffalo* had opened to rave reviews in the mid-'70s. He had written the screenplays for the 1981 film *The Postman Always Rings Twice* and *The Verdict,* which came out the following year.

"We high school kids would see him on State Parkway and say, 'Do you know who that is?' And we all knew who it was," said Mamet.

Mamet remained in awe all during the limited one-month run. "We went out to some fish place and closed the joint," he said. "In the dawn, Shel and I walked up and down North Michigan, walking the other back to his hotel, and quoting Kipling to each other."

They had a lot in common. "Shel was good at picking up on the idiosyncrasies of daily life, what people do and say and act like most of the time," said McCalford. "He had great insight and was able to portray it accurately, often in a dark way. That's what he found funny, and he was able to convey it on stage."

He also had a habit of writing a series of plays around one theme and one simple prop that connected them all. Shel set one group of plays in a bathroom and called it the Bathroom Plays. There were also the Box Plays, the Bag Plays, the Bedroom Plays, and the Sign Plays. They were initially presented at Ensemble Studio Theatre in workshops or as part of the theater's annual one-act play marathon held each fall.

Sometimes he compressed the idea, writing one play as a sequence of sketches where all they have in common is the same prop. *The Crate* revolves around a battered wooden crate that was dragged in off the street. Shel relished the idea of creating something from an object so utilitarian and basic. Another play, *Talk,* was part of the collection of plays titled "Happy Endings." The plot involves a man and a woman in bed and he is trying to get her to do something she has mixed feelings about, but *talk* is substituted for *have sex* throughout the play. The result are some pretty funny protestations from her that she's not the kind of girl who usually *talks* on the first date, and what would her mother think if she could see her daughter *talking*.

"It was a game for myself," he said. "The idea of limitation pushed me on. If someone had said I could have any facilities—we'll build you anything—I can't think what I would've wanted. I don't want to show the sinking of the *Lusitania*. But I liked the idea of using a box and making something good out of it."

There's a common thread that runs through almost all his plays, no matter how side-splittingly funny they are. "He sets up all the sides of an issue and he goes all the way with both sides," said Kohlhaas. "He doesn't criticize or offer an opinion. There's an element in almost all of them in which someone is being asked to answer for their actions, like someone's contesting the actions of another person. They're challenging them on it."

He also recycled some material from his earlier work, as one of the sketches featured a panhandler on Tin Pan Alley attempting to auction off a "sure hit songwriter's pen," a concept that first appeared as a song by the same name on Bobby Bare's *Lullabys, Legends and Lies,* and later on Shel's 1978 album *Songs & Stories.*

Shel's plays were not commercial, and they were never produced on Broadway; off-Broadway was the closest he got. The dark humor that was

Shel's stock in trade was not built for Broadway, and he liked it better that way, since no matter which field he had pursued, he never aimed for the top. In fact, he rarely aimed at all, though if he had wanted his work to be more commercially viable, he could have equaled the success of *Sidewalk* and *Attic* in his other genres as well. But he didn't want to do that.

To him, the runaway success of his children's books was nothing more than a fluke. And at this point, his emotions were still too raw to pursue another book for children.

But then something happened in his life to change all that.

In between his excursions to New York and Chicago to work on new plays, in the aftermath of Shoshanna's death, he preferred to stick around Key West.

"Shel really lay real low for a while in the Keys and he lost a lot of weight," said Drew Reid, who noted that Key West appealed to him because to him, now, it represented his own history, where he consciously chose to put down roots. "It was really the first place where he had settled down. And everybody mostly left him alone."

While he would be gracious to tourists who sought him out for an autograph, he was never comfortable with the attention. And when it came from locals, particularly musicians who thought he could help them get somewhere because of his fame, he bristled.

"There were always people who wanted to take advantage of him," said Reid. "Some thought he was going to make them a star, and they got bummed out when it didn't happen." As before, Shel reacted in the same way whenever someone wanted to latch their star to his: He quietly withdrew from them. "They thought I was in the star-making business," he told Reid. Though he usually reacted in this way with people who weren't already a close acquaintance, he would also pull back if a friend asked too directly for his help. Shel liked it to be his own idea to help out a buddy.

He also liked Key West because he felt he was living in a community of artists and writers, though not all of them accepted him.

"Some of the heavyweights in Key West, like Tennessee Williams, really didn't accept him," said Chris Gantry. "They looked at him as a cartoonist and a lightweight, and they never took the time to see the depth in Shel's work, the messages, the lessons, the insights in his poems and stories."

Shel continued to write songs by himself and to seek out new collaborators. Though he preferred to hang out in the dive joints of Key West, he still made forays into the touristy places like Sloppy Joe's, a restaurant and music club that featured top bands and was a favorite hangout of Ernest Hemingway in the 1930s. Pat Dailey, a musician based in Put-In-Bay, Ohio, an island community on Lake Erie, which is commonly called the Key West of the North, spent winters in Key West performing at the various clubs in the area.

At the end of one of Dailey's shows in the winter of 1984, Shel went backstage to see if he wanted to write some songs together. Dailey couldn't believe that "*the* Shel Silverstein," as he put it, offered to write with him, and told him so. Shel, of course, had no patience with Dailey's attitude. "If you're going to be that way, then we can't work together," he remembered Shel scolding him. "He couldn't abide that kind of adulation. To him the work was the work. You just did it. He'd always ask, 'What are you writing?' and he'd know if I wasn't working, if I was giving him excuses."

But there was another reason why Shel was rooted to Key West. On November 10, 1983, Shel became a father for the second time, this time to a son, Matthew. The mother was Sarah Spencer, the woman who drove the conch train and inspired his song "The Great Conch Train Robbery."

His friends offered up a variety of explanations: perhaps he was unconsciously responding to the loss of his daughter, maybe he was more aware of his own mortality, he had gotten older, he wanted a second chance to right the wrongs he felt he had committed the first time around.

Or maybe, simply, it just happened. And because Shel felt he was given a second chance, he decided he would fully dedicate himself to his son. One thing was certain: he figured he might as well do everything he could to buckle down and take care of his health.

"He took extremely good care of himself, every morning it was yoga, breakfast, and walking," said Pat Dailey. He still hadn't seen a doctor since 1960. He was also a bit of a hypochondriac. "One time when we were in New Orleans, Shel got a rash of red dots on his forearms, and he couldn't figure out why," said Dailey. "We were walking through the French Quarter and there was a drunk in the gutter all sprawled out. Shel's first reaction was to notice the guy didn't have any red dots on his forearms. He said, 'Look how lucky that guy is.'"

In any case, if he felt guilty because he hadn't spent enough time with Shoshanna and her mother, he wasn't going to make the same mistake the second time around.

"He was very close to Matthew and his mother, and he took very good care of her," said Lynne McCalford. "He supported her through school so she could get her teaching degree, and he bought her a house. I remember him saying that she deserved it because she was a good mother to his son. And Shel had a wonderful relationship with her because she knew what he was like, that he was never going to settle down."

8. *The Empty Room*

For the first time in his adult life, Shel was retreating from his globe-trotting ways. Now that he had established comfortable homes in Key West, New York, and Martha's Vineyard—and had a young son of his own—he was beginning to stay put instead of jumping on a plane minutes after deciding he wanted to be somewhere else.

He'd occasionally head to Chicago to be with his mother, whose health was deteriorating. Shel needed to make the difficult decision to put his mother in a nursing home, and he agonized over it.

Drew Reid marveled at the changes in him when he saw Shel playing with a baby on the beach. "He was singing all those stupid little songs and cooing, and I had no idea what was going on, I'd never seen him act like this before," he said. "Later on, I asked whose kid was he playing with, and Shel answered, 'That's my kid, do you think I'd put up with this for anybody else?' "

Besides amazing his friends, the time he spent playing with Matthew finally did what nothing else could: it rekindled Shel's desire to do another children's book. But he didn't want to repeat what he had already done, like *Sidewalk* or *Attic*, rather, he wanted to create something that was totally new for him but which harked back to olden times with a rich sense of history.

"Playing with Matthew as a baby gave him the idea to do a book that would appeal to really young children instead of the eight- or nine-year-olds he had aimed for in the past," said Joan Robins. "He was thinking of something specifically for little children and how they interact and grow, and that's how he came up with the idea for *Runny Babbit*."

Shel had always loved spoonerisms, where the first letter of one word is swapped with the first letter of the word that follows. Spoonerisms were named after the Reverend William Archibald Spooner (1844–1930), a dean and president at New College in Oxford, England. He was a well-educated man, as well as being an Anglican priest, but found that when he became excited or agitated while giving a lecture or a sermon, he would swap the consonants of his words, causing parishioners and students to laugh at inappropriate times. Some mishaps attributed to him include "You have hissed my mystery lecture," "Our Lord is a shoving leopard," and "Three cheers for our queer old dean."

Some observers said that his tongue couldn't keep up with his brain, which undoubtedly endeared him to Shel, who had always had trouble keeping his hand and pen ahead of his brain. With Matthew, Shel was also observing for the first time how children learn to talk, and spoonerisms must have elicited peals of giggles from father and son alike. He already knew how children flocked to his books because of their humor and subversive nature, and he believed that writing a book using spoonerisms throughout would help cultivate a lifelong love of reading among children as well.

"It went on forever, not just because Shel was Shel, but also because he was trying to address common problems that children had when learning to read," said Robins. In addition to the switched-out letters, there were phonetic problems as well, and everything had to rhyme.

Most important, it was the first book since *Lafcadio* was published in 1963 that had a running story line with a group of characters that interacted with each other.

Just as he wouldn't be rushed by his work or struggling to meet a deadline, once the idea for a book of spoonerisms had won him over, he needed to explore it on his own terms and in his own time. He first told Robins about his idea in 1985, but she knew better than to do more than to occasionally ask him how it was going.

Helen and Henry Scarborough lived in the same campground in Martha's Vineyard where Shel had his cottage. Henry was the unofficial electrician for the campground and whenever Shel had a problem, he'd go down and fix it. They struck up a friendship that included Helen, and the three were soon having dinner together on a regular basis where she fixed gazpacho or paella, since those were his favorite dishes.

He lived much the same way on the Vineyard as he did in Key West, only the Vineyard was much quieter—especially in the winter—and Shel regarded it as even more of a retreat away from the world.

But he still followed the same routine as he did in Florida, New York, or Chicago: He worked, played music, and walked everywhere he went, sometimes for hours. He also made new friends, and with them he began to do something he had never done before: confide in them.

"He had a very sensitive side," Helen Scarborough remembered. "We had a lot of private talks and it really upset him when he had to put his mother in a nursing home. I was doing hospice work at the time so I explained to him how everyone comes to the end of the line and sometimes you just do what you have to do."

He also frequently invited Matt and his mother, Sarah, up to the Vineyard to spend a couple of weeks; sometimes they came together, sometimes Matt would come by himself.

Scarborough would sometimes watch Shel and Matt play together. "I never saw him act like a father with Matt, it was more a case of one human being interacting with another, like 'Here's someone else I can discover things with.' But he was fascinated by how a child's mind works even though I think that Matthew got on his nerves as much as he amused him because after all, he wasn't the kind of man who liked to have people around him all the time."

Larry White felt that once Matt was born Shel did change, but in a subtle way. "He was always kind of childlike in his own way," he said. "Shel had an innocence and naïveté that allowed his imagination to do the work he did. Many people would say that he wasn't a realist, and in that sense they were right. He was more of an idealist. He didn't suddenly become the ultimate father figure, but I think that it really grounded him in many ways."

Collaborating with other songwriters was something he had done his entire life to ground himself, a habit he continued. After all these years, he still was surprised at what adding another mind to the mix could do.

He met Mickey and Sharon James in Key West in the winter of 1987. They were a husband-and-wife team of performers and songwriters who frequently traveled to Key West to entertain in the busy tourist season. When Mickey spotted him on the street, he introduced himself as a fan and suggested they try collaborating on a few songs. Shel was noncommittal—after all, he didn't know who this guy was—but James told him the name of the club where he was playing. A few nights later, he saw Shel standing in the crowd.

After the show, Shel caught up with him and told him to be at his house at eight o'clock the following morning to write. James showed up at the prescribed hour and when Shel opened the door he looked at his watch. "You knocked on the door at exactly eight," he said. "I'm very suspicious about people who are right on time," he told him. James thought he blew it and turned to leave, but Shel pulled him inside. Later, after he had spent time with Shel, he realized it was one of many tests he used to scope out people.

"He tended to play with people until he got to know them," said James. Shel was pretty ruthless on him the first time they worked together, asking him why he chose a certain word or phrase, and James found it difficult to work with him at first.

"I'm fairly domineering in my cowriting relationships, but I knew from the start not to do that with Shel," he said. "He was not a man you could push around. It was very hard to write with him at first because of everything he had done, but I kept quiet and accepted most of his ideas and suggestions. Unlike a lot of other songwriters, he was very, very fair. Shel's vision of the cowriting process was that whoever started the song ultimately had the say about where that song went."

They began to write together on a regular basis, and the collaboration evolved into a friendship with Mickey and his wife. But still, the work always came first. "Shel was a driven writer. He wrote all day, *every* day, and often all night, too. It was his whole life," said Mickey. "Sometimes he'd call me at midnight when he was writing a song and wanted to run something by me. We'd talk for fifteen minutes and then he'd hang up to work on the song."

Shel was typically very strict when it came to the structure of a song. "He always thought that the second verse should either move the story forward, regress into the past, or expand," said James. "He was very academic about his songwriting, but he was entirely self-taught. He just knew what worked for him and what didn't. I didn't know any of those things, but he was absolutely right."

Shel also had enough experience to realize when something wasn't going to work.

"The songs didn't always turn out great, but a lot of them did," said James. "Sometimes he had the wrong beat, and sometimes he took songs in the wrong direction. He had amazing insights into what people wanted to hear."

But he never took it personally. When something wasn't working and he knew it, instead of agonizing over the blood he had spilled in the process like many writers, he just crumpled up the paper and started over.

"His brain was sometimes scrambled because he ingested so much information and he lost track of where it had come from," said James. One morning when they were writing together, he asked Mickey and Sharon for their opinion of a particular line: "One less bell to answer, one less egg to fry."

Sharon broke the news that The Fifth Dimension had already used the line in their song "One Less Bell to Answer," which was a hit in the early '70s.

Shel shrugged, tore the sheet of paper off the pad, and then looked at them. "Okay, what's next?"

James wasn't surprised. "He was always reading hundreds of short stories, and as a result, he had all of this stuff rolling around in his head, countless ideas and devices he could then use in his songwriting."

Occasionally he would become impatient with Mickey when they were writing together. Either James would hit a block and he'd stare at Shel or stare at a tree, waiting for inspiration to strike, or he said something that was pretty pedestrian. Or he committed the unforgivable sin of using a cliché.

In any case, Shel would announce that the session was over and Mickey would be dismissed. "It was like being sent home to do my assignment," he said, "and that's just what I did. If we had already scheduled another session, I better make damn sure I had a couple of verses ready, or he'd be angry. This was not a game to him. This was life."

And no clichés whatsoever. Clichés were poison to Shel, unless it was a play on a cliché.

Mickey once gave Shel one of his own songs to critique. "It had three verses and a chorus, the standard format," he said. "The next day he called and he added eighteen verses and took it in a whole different direction."

Shel was writing with other songwriters in Key West as well, and he met them the same way he checked out Mickey James: by standing in the shadows of the clubs and watching while they performed their original material.

Dan Mobley, a long-standing singer-songwriter in Key West, was performing at the Hog's Breath Saloon when Shel first approached him. "He leaned across the fence and asked me if I wrote the song I had just fin-ished singing," said Mobley. "When I told him I did, he invited me to come to his house. I didn't really know who he was. I recognized him, but I didn't know he wrote songs, too."

The first song they wrote together was "Dopeheads on Mopeds." In Key West, the primary mode of transportation is by scooter. "I just hap-pened to mention to him about how so many tourists drink a couple of hundred beers or smoke a few joints and then go out and rent a moped," said Mobley. "I called them dopeheads on mopeds, and Shel was off and running. He came back with the lyrics the next day." Mobley often per-forms the song, but he also recorded "Dopeheads on Mopeds" on *Key Changes,* a CD he produced himself, containing songs he wrote with Shel.

More often, their songwriting sessions followed the same give-and-take pattern Shel had experienced with other songwriters, although there were times when he would spring fully forth with the song close to complete if Mobley gave him a particularly compelling title. "But mostly he wanted me to provide the music with a melody line and the chords and every-thing so he could make something out of that," he said.

Shel had no use for intricate melodies or complicated chord progres-sions. Once, Mobley had written a beautiful melody on his guitar and he was refining it because it was a bit tricky. "I was very proud of it, so I played it for Shel," he said, fully expecting him to compliment the melody.

"But he told me that he couldn't do anything with it because he wasn't used to working with music that complex," said Mobley. As was the case with most of his songs since he wrote his first song with Bob Gibson, Shel based most of his songs on the basic chord I-IV-V progression.

Mobley thought about songs like "A Boy Named Sue" and "The Cover of the Rolling Stone," and realized that this was the foundation for the ma-jority of Shel's songs. He was a little disappointed, but he played the melody once more for Shel, recording it in his boom box in case he wanted to hear it again.

A week later, Shel called Dan and told him to come over because he had something he wanted him to listen to. Shel started singing a song that he had set to Dan's complicated melody. "It was so beautiful, I just cried," said Mobley. "And then I looked up and he had a tear in his eye. I *never* saw him cry, but I think it was because he saw that I was so happy."

Though Shel might spend part of every day with his songwriting collaborators for weeks on end, they usually fell out of touch at the end of the season when each went their separate ways, Shel to the Vineyard and the performers to other tourist hot spots. Sometimes Shel would call out of the blue to see how they were doing. The whereabouts of much of the work that Shel created with his cowriters is unknown, unless either he or the cowriter took the initiative to register the song with BMI or another song copyright service.

"A year would go by, but his first question was always 'What are you writing?'" said James. "I suspect that was the first thing he asked a lot of his writer friends. If he respected your writing, he wanted to know that you were still writing. Whenever I told him that I hadn't written for a while he would sound disappointed in me but he never chastised me for it. He really believed that the only way to be a writer was to do it all the time."

James once gained an important insight into the way Shel's mind worked. "I went to his house for a session and he had just finished writing 'The Devil and Billy Markham' and sent it off to *Playboy,* so I congratulated him and said he must feel really great!"

"No, I feel really shitty," he said. "It's over."

James said that one statement revealed how vital the actual process of creating was to him. "I feel the best when I finish a project," he said. "I have something that I can turn into money or make somebody laugh or show people how clever I am. Shel wasn't like that, he was totally into the process, and he was very sad when it was over."

In 1988, Ursula Nordstrom, Shel's first editor at HarperCollins, died. And although Shel hadn't worked directly with her for over a decade since *Sidewalk,* he viewed it as the end of an era. She was the first of many of his longtime friends who would die in the next decade.

Even though he hadn't written a new children's book for Harper since *A Light in the Attic* in 1981, interest in Shel and his books continued to be strong. People and businesses would regularly contact HarperCollins with requests to license the art and poems in Shel's books, not only to reprint his work but to use his work to promote one of their products. Robert Warren, his editor, took these phone calls, and if they were legitimate requests, he'd track Shel down and ask what he wanted to do. Because many of the proposals revolved around people who wanted to cash in on his fame, Shel turned most of them down.

"I remember one time there was a manufacturer of hardwood floors that wanted to use *The Giving Tree* to promote one of their products," said Warren. "Shel thought it was a crazy scheme and we had a good laugh over it. He was a curious celebrity because he really sought to stay out of the limelight."

In past years, Shel would have gone ballistic. Now, he just shrugged it off. It's easy to imagine that he would have written a song about the absurdity of the idea of branding a line of wood flooring after *The Giving Tree,* but there was always the danger that people would think he was looking to capitalize off his phenomenal success as a children's author, and that, in turn, would bring him unwanted attention and put him back in the spotlight. He didn't want another "Boy Named Sue." Now that he was close to sixty years old, he wanted to just be able to create and live quietly without having his life put under a microscope.

Despite his disappointment with Mickey James, over the years Shel was easier on his friends who didn't—or chose not to—respond to his encouragements and admonishments that they were wasting their talents; in many cases, he didn't bring it up at all. And he admitted that the damage others had inflicted on him over the years "was nothing compared with what I did to myself and do to myself daily." As he began to ease up with his creative friends, he cut himself a little more slack, as well.

His friendships with old and new friends started to deepen during this period. He would frequently call a friend and invite them to come visit him wherever he happened to be. And he started to open up in ways that his buddies were very surprised to hear coming from him.

"Despite his success and his fame, we spent a lot of time talking about the insecurities of writing, and the constant battle in your head," said Pat Dailey.

Shel started to talk with his friends about how he wrestled to keep from falling into depression and apathy. Even though his public face was happy-go-lucky and funny and cheery, close friends describe another side that surfaced more frequently as he grew older: He was a deeply serious man on a spiritual quest who was trying to reach some kind of truth, and to feel good and enjoy himself at the same time, but sometimes he really struggled to keep his head above water. He thought that if he explored his dark side in his work that as long as he got it out he'd be able to keep it from subsuming him. It worked, most of the time.

"He had a really dark side," said Mickey James. "And he traveled that road twenty-four hours a day in his work, just went back and forth between the dark and the light. He wasn't diabolic about it, but it doesn't take much to really get a glimpse of that dark area if you read any of his work, for adults or children. To him, there were never any rules. He would present them commercially to some degree but because there were no boundaries for where he would go, some of it would never get published. And he knew that."

In that way, a lot of his constant scribbling and doodling was specifically so he could get both the dark and light sides out of his brain and spelled out on stark white paper so he'd know they were real. He never staunched the flow, because he thought that would be worse, to keep them inside where they'd fester and grow but also where he couldn't see them. He *had* to get them out so he knew they were there.

His dark side manifested itself in other ways as well. Mickey and Sharon stayed at his house one night when Shel was out of town. They walked upstairs to his bedroom and found a person sitting in a chair in the dark. "We didn't know anyone was supposed to be there, so we turned on the light and saw it was a mannequin of a woman that looked like something straight out of a horror movie. When Shel came back we asked about it and he said he had conversations with her every night." While they didn't doubt that, what struck them specifically about the mannequin was that it looked evil, something from a zombie movie, along with much of the stuff he collected—the books, puppets, and knickknacks.

Though he regularly maintained that things weren't important to him, he was referring to the things that most people thought were important if you had more money than you knew what to do with. Instead of big trophy homes, expensive cars, and designer clothes, he liked to spend his money and time foraging for books and unusual items—always second-hand, he rarely bought anything new—but one suspects it was the quest and the victory of finding something rather than the item itself that drove him.

Shel loved to go to junk stores and flea markets, but because he didn't drive, he needed to find someone to chauffeur him around who also liked to dig through piles of stuff with him. More important, the candidate needed to be able to respond to Shel's whims and impatience and turn on a dime while not taking it personally. While Sharon didn't drive, Mickey did, and the couple also loved flea markets and frequently set up a booth of their own at some of the markets around the Keys.

Shel's favorite flea-market finds were books, of course, but he also loved to buy old musical instruments. Mickey cringed whenever he saw Shel pick one up, because he knew he'd have to listen while Shel played around with it for the next couple of weeks. Once he showed up at Shel's house when he was playing a clarinet he had picked up the previous weekend. "It sounded awful," said Mickey. "After Shel taught himself a new instrument, he wasn't very good at it. He wasn't a very good guitar player, either. But he loved buying that stuff and playing with it."

He also liked primitive art and homemade items that someone had obviously spent a great deal of time creating. And even though he had no patience for children's books with art that looked like it had been created by children, when it came to his flea-market finds, he treasured them. One time, when they were scouting the flea markets, Mickey spotted an oil painting of Roy Rogers chasing Indians, and it looked like a child had painted it.

"I showed it to Shel and he grabbed it and bought it immediately," said Mickey. "He said, 'I wanted it worse,' but I wasn't going to fight over it."

Another time, Shel showed up at Mickey and Sharon's house and said, "Just drive." They visited a few secondhand stores around Key West and at the last store, Shel and Sharon didn't see anything they liked, but Mickey wanted to dig through some of the stuff, so Shel and Sharon went back to the car. Once they were inside, Shel turned to Sharon and said, "I am not having a good time," and he clearly expected her to do something about it.

So Sharon got out of the car and told Mickey, "Shel is not having a good time."

"Well, then, I guess it's time to leave," he replied, and they left. "That's the way it was with Shel," said Mickey. "He was like that all the time and he never apologized for his behavior. It was impossible to keep Shel amused for more than an hour, he was so easily bored. If we were in a restaurant and the one-liners stopped coming or the sights became dull or the company he was with ceased to be amusing, he'd just stand up and walk out and find something that would hold his attention, which was usually his work. You either got used to it or you didn't hang out with the man."

At the same time, he viewed negative encounters with people as material for his work.

"He loved if somebody would rip him off," said James. "I would get pissed off at people who would rip me off, but he just loved it. Naturally, it would have ended the relationship, but Shel would look at it with a writer's eye, like a story. He thought it was amazing that anyone would do this. He could laugh about it and tell stories about it and inevitably write a song about it. I've never met anyone like that."

Because people loved his work so universally, they often showed their appreciation by giving him things. Daily, complete strangers would send or drop off gifts.

Shel couldn't get rid of the stuff fast enough. He felt that they were equating the messenger with the message, something he had always loathed, and so when fans would give him everything from clothes to pens to even decorations for his home, he treated it like poison.

"He was constantly giving his stuff away," said Mickey, "but it was only the things that people had given him because they liked his work. Some of it was pretty neat and expensive, like a mirror from India that was probably worth five hundred dollars." He gave a lot of these gifts to Mickey and Sharon, who either used them or sold them at their flea-market booth.

But he sometimes didn't like it when friends gave him things, at least those items that didn't strike a chord in him. When the gift did appeal to him, he held on to it tightly, even displaying it prominently.

Once Mickey sent Shel a batch of old postcards from the early twentieth century that ranged in value from ten to one hundred dollars apiece. Shel initially accepted them, then returned them and said it was a waste to give them to him because he didn't want them. But the time Mickey gave him a coconut with a face carved into it that was the spitting image of Shel, he loved it. Years later, Mickey and Sharon stayed in his house again and the coconut head was prominently displayed on Shel's dresser. Mickey's first thought: "We passed the test."

In the late '80s, Shel began to choose his projects more carefully, primarily because he liked the collaborative energy of watching his words come alive on stage. He continued his previous habit of getting double duty out of a work he created, but unlike before, when he most often turned a poem in one of his books into a song—or vice versa—Shel now began to adapt some of his earlier works into theater pieces. He turned "The Devil and Billy Markham," a "Robert Johnson at the crossroads" type story about a down-and-out blues singer who strikes a deal with the devil, from a *Playboy* piece into a monologue. He also chose to work with people he had worked with before, old friends, and the only person he wanted to perform the piece was Dennis Locorriere, from Dr. Hook.

Building on his experience writing plays, he agreed to collaborate with Mamet to write a screenplay for *Things Change,* a movie that came out in the fall of 1988. Starring Don Ameche and Joe Mantegna, the film is a comedy where Ameche plays an Italian-American shoeshine man with a strong physical resemblance to a Mafia don up on a murder charge, and Mantegna is a low-level mob character who is assigned to guard Ameche, who agrees to take the fall for the murder charge against his look-alike in exchange for a million-dollar payout a few years later when he's released from prison. Instead of staying sequestered in a hotel room for the weekend like they're supposed to do, the two take off to Vegas, a decision that provides lots of twists and turns as well as comic moments.

Screenwriting was a medium that Shel hadn't yet tackled. But he was still up for a challenge, especially if it was in an entirely new field.

"I think it made his writing even stronger," said Larry White. "It was a great example of how he became an excellent collaborator."

Even though Mamet had been an influential screenwriter by the time they wrote *Things Change,* with *The Verdict* and *The Postman Always Rings Twice* under his belt, he still learned something from Shel. "I asked him once about research," said Mamet. "I was doing a movie with Danny DeVito called *Hoffa* [which came out in 1992], and was complaining to Shel because I had so many books on Hoffa that I had to read. And he said, 'Never do research. When you do research, all you're doing is reading books by someone who didn't do research.' So I don't do research."

After he finished working on *Things Change,* Shel returned to writing one-act plays. In a screenplay, the writing sometimes proceeds at a snail's pace, since there are countless details to keep in mind when writing each line, among them instructing characters of specific mannerisms, camera angles, and props. Screenwriting just didn't mesh with Shel's style of off-the-cuff minimalist writing where the words are the stars, not the actors.

But as a result of collaborating on the screenplay, Shel became close with Mamet and his new wife, Rebecca Pidgeon, whom he married in 1991. Shel attended their wedding on Martha's Vineyard in the same clothes he wore every day, "impossibly baggy, vaguely military trousers, a sort of Indian shirt unbuttoned to the navel, a 1970s down-market leather jacket," as Mamet described it.

"Shel came on my honeymoon [on the Vineyard]," said Mamet. "He met us one morning for breakfast. Breakfast became lunch, and then dinner, and we saw him most of all day every day."

Squeezed in between the plays and the screenplays and his everyday writing and drawing, Shel knocked out a song called "I'm Checking Out" for the 1990 movie *Postcards from the Edge,* starring Meryl Streep and Shirley MacLaine. When the Academy Awards were announced in early 1991, Shel's song was nominated in the category of Best Music, Original Song.

As usual, Shel wanted to involve his songwriting friends. When director Mike Nichols asked him for a song for the movie, Shel called Pat Dailey to collaborate. "I told him I wasn't interested," Dailey said. "He kept bugging me about it and I kept saying no. When the song was nominated for an Academy Award, *then* I wanted my name on it."

Helen Scarborough asked Shel if he was going to attend the ceremonies. "He just grinned and said, 'Can you imagine me in a tuxedo?' "

"He had no tolerance for society," said Mamet. "He wouldn't go to parties and he didn't want to meet new people." Shel told him that a prestigious organization wanted to give him a fancy award at a gala banquet. Since he had no desire to attend a pompous ceremony, he turned it down.

When Mamet pressed him, Shel replied, "If they want me to show up and do my Shel act, let them pay me," he said.

"As he got older, he felt that everybody wanted something from him, especially after the Oscar nomination," said Dave Mapes. "He became kind of brusque and shut down whenever he sensed that somebody just wanted to glom onto him, and exploit his celebrity."

Dan Mobley discovered this firsthand. While Shel was exceedingly generous with sharing songwriting credits with collaborators, he stopped short if he sensed someone wanted to capitalize on his success with children's books. Shel offered to write some children's songs with Mobley for an album they would record and share the credit. But it never materialized because it was a lot harder to write for kids than Mobley thought, and Shel wouldn't help him. "I thought I was going to go in there and get a lot of help from the master but it wasn't like that at all," he said. "There were no gimmees when it came to that. I had to be on top of the ideas. I was trying to collaborate with Shel Silverstein on some children's songs and I was not doing the share of work he thought I should be doing. He didn't tolerate laziness in anyone and he couldn't understand why anyone wouldn't want to make the best of each day.

"He never wanted to waste a day, *ever*."

9. *Songs & Stories*

Shel had never owned a computer, and he still had old-fashioned rotary dial phones at his homes. Cell phones were not yet ubiquitous in the 1990s, but given his Spartan, technophobe existence, it's safe to say that he wouldn't have been caught dead with one.

Of course, kids were as comfortable with technology as Shel was not. "You can spend a good part of the day and never touch anything that's the way it was," he said. Quite possibly, perhaps he felt like he didn't have much in common with the children of the latter part of the twentieth century.

Shel was content splitting his time between Key West and Martha's Vineyard. Even though he didn't like the attention in the wake of his Academy Award nomination, he didn't hesitate to take advantage of the increased interest to cajole Nashville into listening to his songs. Though he didn't necessarily want or need a hit song, he knew that what was popular in country music now was worlds away from "A Boy Named Sue," "One's on the Way," and "Hey, Loretta."

As new players started to influence country music in the late 1980s, songs became more pop in style and less country. These changes had pretty much become permanent by the early 1990s. Veteran songwriter Joe Sun viewed it as a changing of the guard, which started when Garth Brooks came out with his eponymous debut album in 1989.

"The listening audience was starting to get younger and younger, and what they wanted to hear was more of a more pop sound," said Sun, adding that this change ran contrary to anybody who wrote country songs a few decades earlier.

"The kind of material the record companies and publishers were looking for was not the kind of stuff Shel was giving them," he added. Not only had the music changed, but so did the way to market them. In Shel's day, an aspiring songwriter could drop into town a few times a year and plug his songs once he got there. But with the new environment, a songwriter had to be extremely visible for the labels and artists to take him seriously, constantly hanging out at industry hot spots, dropping off demos, and generally being a pest.

Songwriters from the old school who wanted to sell their songs to Nashville did one of two things. "You either tried to figure out what they wanted and wrote like that, or you continued to write the way you were used to and see if you could manage to survive," said Sun. "I could never visualize somebody else setting the path for Shel and him trying to follow it. That definitely wasn't his way, not with all the success he had doing his own thing."

"There's a famous story about the time someone asked Chet Atkins, 'What's the Nashville sound?'" said Drew Reid. "And Chet takes a whole bunch of change out of his pocket and jingles it and said, 'That's the Nashville sound.' That pretty much sums it up and what Shel was up against."

Just as writers complain about their editors, songwriters complain about their publishers. And in Nashville, it was the norm for songwriters to grumble about the powers-that-be in country music, especially when it grew increasingly pop-oriented.

"I liked to piss and moan to Shel about the music business and how ugly it was and how it wasn't fair, and he'd always say, 'What's going to happen is going to happen,'" said Mickey James. "But one night he told me I was right about this town."

"They're not recording my songs anymore and some people don't treat me so good," he said. Though he provided few details to James, Shel realized that you're hot when you're hot, and he never became bitter about it. "He had other things going," said Mickey. "Of course, I still complained, but he'd tell me to drop it and just do what I do." His philosophy was to create these small followings for what you do and will make you happy, and he was absolutely right."

He also trusted what he was doing. "A lot of songwriters start with a really great initial idea but then they start to second-guess and doubt themselves, and pretty soon all the life is sucked out of the song," said Fred Koller. "Shel didn't work that way, his love of the language and his sheer ability to write about the absurdity of any given situation carried him through. He wasn't trying to be Cole Porter, he had a strong sense of the common man. So many of his songs were about loneliness and relationships, and why the relationship was not going to work."

He continued to write songs, but he didn't delude himself by thinking they were radio songs. The songs he wrote were more satirical story songs, and that kind of song hadn't sold in Nashville for years.

So while in earlier years, he went to Nashville to pitch some songs and hang out with friends, in the '90s, Shel primarily went to Music City to see old friends. But he still did a lot of demo sessions, because he still fervently believed that unless a song was recorded it simply didn't exist, and sometimes he wanted to hear how it sounded with a studio full of musicians. And he still held out hope that someone would want to record his songs.

Woody Allen—not the movie actor, director, and producer—was a studio musician in Key West and played on several of Shel's demo albums. The nature of a demo is to get it done as quickly and simply as possible, since studio time can be expensive and when or if it got picked up, the producer was going to change it anyway.

"He could be a bit fussy about getting the demos exactly the way he wanted," said Allen, and he asked Shel why he bothered.

"Even though I know it's just a demo, if I can give it my own clear idea right now, the more likely I am going to be happy with it when it actually gets done," Shel answered.

And he was still producing a wide range of songs. Compared with the other singers and songwriters Allen worked with, Shel really stood out.

"It was pretty astonishing that he went from clever and funny to scatological to quietly moving," he said, citing "Dopeheads on Mopeds" and another song about a man wandering around on a dance floor, and it's not until the last line of the song that it's clear he's dancing with his dead wife. "He painted a nice picture, he was enough of a poet to make it quite moving."

He still did the same things he did during his Nashville heydays. Melanie Smith Howard is the widow of singer-songwriter Harlan Howard, who died in 2002 and was close to Shel and had written "Busted," "I Fall to Pieces," and other country hits. Melanie only met Shel when she married Harlan in 1989 and she had heard the stories about Shel walking all over town, but she was amazed that he still walked everywhere in Nashville in the 1990s.

"I always offered to take him back to his hotel but he always refused, he said he liked to walk," she said. "He'd walk from his hotel to our house, which was only a couple miles, but he'd even walk at night."

Because he had cut down on his spur-of-the-moment travel, he also started to give his friends a little notice instead of just showing up on their doorsteps. "He still did sometimes just show up, but he also called to ask if we were going to be around over the next few weeks," said Howard. And when they did get together, the main topic of conversation was aging.

"Harlan and Shel would start gabbing about how shitty it was to get older," said Melanie Howard. "They'd reminisce about the old days, but mostly they'd talk about aging and what a bitch it was. I always thought Shel was in great shape because he walked so much, he didn't smoke, and he did yoga. Harlan and I thought he would live forever because Harlan was a physical wreck because he drank too much, smoked too much, and never exercised."

Despite the fact that Shel was in his mid-sixties, he was still attracting women of all ages.

"Shel was a babe magnet," said Howard. "He had women falling all over him and he still couldn't get enough. There was a certain sexiness to his brand of creative genius. He was fun to hang out with, he had done it all and was not afraid to talk about it. He was very charismatic. I think women looked past his surface and saw his heart of gold. He was a great storyteller and lived a great lifestyle, and that appealed to women young and old."

He was always trying to get Howard to set him up with her girlfriends when he came to Nashville, and she always good-naturedly refused. He also hit up his other friends to serve as matchmakers as well.

"He could be very frustrating because whenever he came to Nashville, his primary aim was to meet women," said Fred Koller. "He was very demanding about it, and it drove some people pretty crazy."

Indeed, Shel had lived large his entire life, and both close friends and strangers had come to expect him to act in a certain way; the man became the myth. But as he grew older, because he had created this image for himself he may have felt like he was obligated to continue to live up to it, even though he no longer had the energy or the desire. Perhaps that's why he began to hide out from all but his closest friends and turned down opportunities to meet new people, because he would have to turn himself into the mythical figure he no longer wanted to be.

"If I've created an image of a world traveler, an adventurer, and the fact is that I fucking want to sit down and grow roses and live with Suzie Q, then I'm going to do it," he said to Hugh Hefner in a 1989 interview. "It's funny that that's the hardest fight to win, but I have a right to do that. I'm not going to be bound by my own shit."

Even though he was tired of living up to other people's image of him, most likely his friends would laugh at the picture of Shel being married and living in a house with the proverbial white picket fence. "One day we started talking about our dreams, our fantasies," said Mickey James. "Shel said his idea of a perfect relationship would be to date a very sexual woman who would drive him all over the world in a pickup truck while he lay on a mattress in the back and did his art. And the woman had to have a very sexual name. He was very serious about it."

Shel had withdrawn from the world to some extent, but he would occasionally make new friends. One of them was Otto Penzler, a veteran of mystery publishing in New York who founded Mysterious Press and now runs his own imprint, Otto Penzler Books, at Harcourt. He also runs The Mysterious Bookshop in Manhattan, which is where he met Shel in 1994.

"I came out of my office and saw him sitting on the floor with a huge pile of books all around him," said Penzler. "We started talking about mysteries and stories and books and authors, and he asked for my advice about what to read." In time, Shel would show up at the bookstore unannounced, and they began to spend longer periods of time together.

"Shel was not a handsome man; in fact, he was very odd-looking," he said. "He had a somewhat oversized head with a truly oversized brain in it, a mind that creative needed a big dome to hold it all. Whenever I spent time with Shel, I always had the sense that I was in the presence of a towering intelligence."

He also noticed that Shel's attention span was pretty much nonexistent. "I don't think he had the patience to read a whole novel," said Penzler, adding that Shel preferred to read short stories from the turn of the century and before World War II and he liked American writers over the British. After his previous visit, he would come into the bookstore and tell Penzler, "I really like those twenty-five books I got last time except for this one." Or, "I read thirty of the forty books that I bought and I loved every one, but one of the guys writes too many stories and they all sound the same," Penzler remembered.

"He started to show up toward the end of the day. The store closed at seven, so he would show up around six and come right in and sit in my office. We'd talk until late into the night, and at that point we were talking about more than just books," said Penzler.

A favorite topic of conversation was women. Penzler's wife had recently left him when he and Shel first met, so their talk often revolved around the nature of love. "He was a talker, and he did a lot more talking than I did, but when I needed to discuss something, he was quite happy to listen," he said.

While Penzler spoke of his adoration for and need of one woman, Shel talked about the women he had known. "I don't think we brought the same definition to love," Penzler wryly noted. "Sharon Stone could beg me for sex and I'd turn her down. I don't think Shel would make the same statement as he loved women and he loved a *lot* of women, but he did seem to have that wonderful capacity to remain friends with the women who he dated."

He sensed that while Shel obviously enjoyed his company, there was something else underlying his occasional visits to the bookstore. For perhaps the first time in his life, Shel was putting his friendships ahead of his work. "I had the feeling that he had the time on his hands," said Penzler. "He wanted to fill the time and instead of going to a movie or reading a book or writing something brilliant, he just wanted to sit and talk to somebody."

Despite being in his mid-sixties, it appeared that Shel still had the capacity to pull all-nighters. One night, Penzler and Shel went out to dinner and returned to the shop afterward. It was late and Penzler had to leave because he had to work the next day. "I didn't want to be rude because I really liked him so much, but I wanted him to go," he said, noting that he used body language and subtle hints in the hopes that Shel would take the hint and excuse himself for the night.

"Body language didn't work with Shel. But once I told him he had to go, he was fine with that and left," said Penzler.

When Shel had been dropping by the store for about a year, Penzler was collecting stories for an anthology called *Murder for Love,* and he casually suggested to Shel that he contribute a story.

"I don't write short stories," Shel replied.

"Why not?" asked Penzler. "You write everything else."

Shel said he'd think about it, and a few weeks later he'd written "For What She Had Done," a short free-verse story similar in structure to his children's poems. Penzler accepted it and the anthology was published in 1996. When Penzler began working on *Murder for Revenge,* the second book in the series, he asked Shel for another story. He offered him two thousand dollars, which is what he had paid for the first story, considerably more than the average five hundred dollar to thousand dollar fees he paid.

"I don't care about money," said Shel.

"I know," said Penzler, "but I have to pay you."

Shel considered this for a moment, and finally said, "Give me credit. Give me two thousand dollars in credit for books from your store and I'll use it to buy books."

And so they struck a deal for "The Enemy," again written in a style similar to his children's poems. Shel gleefully filled six pages detailing the myriad ways a disgruntled man could do away with his worst enemy, which ranged from "impaling him on a jagged, rusted, feces-encrusted iron fence" to "skinning him alive, Then rolling his body—not gently—in rock salt and honey."

Along with the poem, Shel contributed a drawing of the head of a be-whiskered man, his eyes filled with revenge. The interesting thing about the illustration is that instead of signing it with his customary *S.S.,* he used only one *S.* to accompany it.

The third anthology, *Murder and Obsession,* was published in March 1999, and was distinctive for Shel because it represented an art form that was entirely new to him. When he presented it to Penzler, he said, "This is the first short story I have ever written."

"The Guilty Party," which fills nine pages in the book, is the story of the trial of a man named Billy Ray who is accused of rape. He refers to his penis as "Sam Johnson," noting that it's Sam that's guilty, not himself. The judge decided that Billy Ray could go free but he was sentencing Sam to twelve years in the state penitentiary.

"I'm gonna give you the opportunity to accompany your friend to Joliet, or you can stay behind and let him go on alone . . . You look pale, son."

Penzler liked the story so much that he sent it to mystery writer Donald Westlake, who was editing *The Best American Mystery Stories of 2000*, and he published it in the anthology.

Penzler did very little editing on Shel's pieces, and he encouraged him to experiment with different forms and lengths, but Shel made it clear that he created what he wanted to create when the urge struck.

"He told me he had file drawers full of stuff, that he'd write it then he'd put it away," said Penzler.

"I never really quite finish it," Shel told him. "I keep thinking I will."

While he was always extremely meticulous and painstaking when getting a story, song, or illustration ready for its final form in a book or record, Penzler quickly realized—as did other editors and producers before him—that this was Shel's least favorite thing to do.

"He didn't like doing the work necessary to turn it in," said Penzler. "He liked creating it, writing it, scrawling down some stuff and then putting it away. I always thought it was a shame, all that talent just going to waste, because I don't know if it will ever see the light of day.

"He hated the final stages of a project, of having to prepare it for the public," he said. "I told him once that if I had that kind of talent, I'd be publishing a book a year. You haven't had a book in years," said Penzler. "Why don't you do a book? Have you run out of ideas?"

"Are you kidding me?" Shel replied. "I've got file drawers and cartons and desks full of stuff."

"So why don't you do another book?" Penzler asked.

"I will. I'll get to it, but I hate that part of having to organize and put it into a book and doing the work."

"He made it sound like *that* was the work and that doing the doodles and writing the poems and the songs was fun for him," said Penzler. "Making it coalesce into a cohesive whole was hard work for him, and he didn't like doing it at all. He always told me he was going to do it at any moment and he was really going to pull it together. But that's like an alcoholic saying this time, he's really going to quit. I didn't believe him, because I knew he hated it, but every once in a while he would pull it together and do it."

Despite his international success and recognizable appearance, there were still times when some people avoided Shel because of his appearance, even surprisingly, in a bookstore in his own backyard.

"He once went into a bookstore in Key West and tried to buy some books," said Pat Dailey. "The clerk came back and told him his credit card was no good. The next day Shel gets a call from his accountant asking him if he'd lost his wallet recently. The guy from the bookstore called the credit card company saying some homeless guy was trying to pass himself off as Shel Silverstein."

The clerk's suspicions weren't entirely off-base; Fred Koller said there were usually at least four guys down in Key West who were all trying to pass as him.

"Another time," Dailey continued, "we had finished dinner at a fancy restaurant in Manhattan and Shel had gone outside to wait for us. A woman gave him her doggie bag and said there was half a sandwich in the bag. We laughed about that a lot."

Once, Shel was in San Francisco and he saw a cat run under a car that was about to move. "He ran up to the door of the car and pounded on the window, and said, 'stop, don't move the car' to the guy inside," said Kerig Pope. "The guy thought he was a homeless man and he got scared and drove away. But the cat was not hurt."

Shel was starting to lose lifelong friends as one by one, they began to die. First, Bob Sweeney, his old army buddy, died in 1993. And then on

May 9, 1993, his mother, Helen, died at the age of ninety-four. His primary cheerleader from the time he was just a kid, who always stood up for Shel to his father, the one person who had always believed he could do anything he wanted to and told him so, was gone.

Even though she had lived a long, full life, Shel was crushed.

"He was very worried about dying, especially once his friends began to die and his mother passed on," said Dan Mobley. "Then Bob Gibson got sick, and that's when Shel really started to become very aware of his health."

Gibson was diagnosed with a rare form of Parkinson's disease called progressive supranuclear palsy. Shel helped Gibson in many ways through the years, and even though his illness had progressed to where he could no longer play the guitar, Shel believed that the best thing to do for each other, and to serve as a testament to their decades-long friendship, was to make one last album together and bring many of their old friends along for the ride. The decision made, Shel immediately began working on *Makin' a Mess, Bob Gibson Sings Shel Silverstein.*

He kicked into high gear, calling Tom Paxton, Emmylou Harris, Peter Yarrow, Dennis Locorriere, John Hartford, and other longtime mutual friends to invite them to the recording session. Then he started going through songs he had written years earlier and writing new ones as production on the album neared. "It was hard to narrow it down because Shel had so many good songs," said Gibson. "There's the straight-ahead, vulnerable Shel of "Whistlers & Jugglers" and "Stops Along the Way," and the funny, caustic Shel of "Still Gonna Die," "Killed by a Coconut," and "Makin' a Mess of Commercial Success." The thing about Shel is he's always kept his integrity. I attribute all my success to him, as he does me."

"Shel was instrumental in making the whole thing happen," said Meridian Green, Gibson's daughter. "It was difficult to get the project off the ground, especially since my dad couldn't play the guitar anymore. But Shel recognized that my father could still get up there and put a song across, and the project was an acknowledgment of who they were to each other. Their friendship straddled my father's entire life, through all of his ups and downs. There is nobody else who comes close."

Shel wrote the title track, "Makin' a Mess of Commercial Success," with Mickey James, who said that when he wrote the song it had only four verses, but after Shel got his hands on it he added twenty more overnight. It was yet another example of how Shel took an annoying real-life event and twisted it into a humorous song.

"We were playing at Sloppy Joe's, and a camera crew was shooting a beer commercial across the street," said James. "They were pulling people off the street to sit at the bar and drink beer for a few hours, and paying everyone a hundred bucks."

Just how far removed Shel had become from the way most Americans live their lives was revealed in an intimate interview that Shel and Bob did with their old Chicago friend Studs Terkel to promote the *Makin' a Mess* CD. Twenty years earlier, Shel had sworn off doing media interviews, but he made an exception because they were sitting in the living room with two of his closest lifelong friends, telling stories about the good old days as well as some from more recent times.

In the interview with his buddies, Shel pulled back the curtain on how he observed the events and people of everyday life and spun them into his art. His words also revealed his thinly disguised contempt for what passed for culture among the majority of Americans in the 1990s.

At times, the discussion deteriorated into a fist-shaking, what's-wrong-with-these-kids-today diatribe. In discussing the real-life inspiration for the title song on the CD, about a TV crew filming a commercial that comes to Key West and disrupts life there for a day while others gawk because they're making a TV commercial, Shel's venom towards the medium was front and center.

"The [camera crew] assumes you should be honored that they are shooting on your street and blocking off traffic. They couldn't get away with it for any other reason. People worship TV that much so it just becomes a holy experience," he said.

Shel's song about how technology has taken over everything, "The Man Who Turns the Damn Thing Off and On," reveals him to be somewhat of a Luddite. "[It's about] the last working man," he said. "This is pretty positive, too. We're assuming that they're still gonna need one person to start the machine. They may not, though, they might be able to beat that."

In describing the inspiration behind the song "You're Still Gonna Die," Shel said, "I'm very healthy in my diet, I just don't want to kid myself that it's gonna do more than I think. I think we have too much information, that anything pleasurable can kill us. When you didn't know, you could just have some fun, and if you keeled over that was okay. Now we know that everything can hurt us, so I think that stops us from having total pleasure."

The CD was released in early 1995. Gibson's health continued to deteriorate for the rest of the year and into 1996. When it was clear that Gibson didn't have long to live, Shel and his friends and family held a farewell party for him on September 20, 1996.

"Shel was very present during the farewell party," said Meridian Green. "And that must have been really hard for him, because there was no clue when you looked at him that he was not in great shape. Shel looked like he was in fantastic shape."

One week after the farewell party, on September 28, 1996, Bob Gibson died.

Old friends were so important to Shel that he agreed to do things he would automatically have turned down if his friends didn't happen to be involved.

A few months before Gibson's death, Drew Reid was organizing a country music songwriting festival in Key West. Though he hoped it would become an annual event, he realized it might only be a one-shot deal. "We were flying by the seat of our pants," he said. "We had zero budget."

But he knew people with names that could draw an audience, like legendary songwriter Mickey Newbury, who wrote songs for Eddy Arnold and Tom Jones and was inducted into the Nashville Hall of Fame in 1980, and who agreed to headline the event. "Once word got out, people started calling me up to ask if Shel was going to be there, too. 'If Mickey's there, you've got Shel booked, don't you?' "

Drew laughed. "You don't book Shel," he told them.

But he did talk to Shel about the festival and hinted that Newbury would show up. Shel said that he'd love to see Mickey, but he didn't commit to being there.

On the first day of the festival, a few hours before the first show, Shel called to ask Reid if he thought Mickey would mind if he played a few songs before he started his set. "I told him I thought it would be okay, and it just about blew my mind," said Reid. "Everybody else in Nashville would show up with entourage in tow, but Shel called up and asks permission."

Shel rarely made public appearances, but he did it just to see Mickey, though he didn't hesitate to play around a bit first. "Shel did four or five songs and people were just going nuts," said Reid. "This was the icing on the cake, everyone was there for Mickey and Shel showed up to play and just kills them. And then for an encore, he looked around and asked if there were any kids around. There weren't any, so then he pulled out a couple of real raunchy songs and just laid them dead. He and Mickey were just all over each other hugging and talking and laughing."

As it turned out, it happened to be Newbury's birthday.

Fifteen years had elapsed since Shel's last children's book, *A Light in the Attic,* was published. In 1995, he decided he was ready to do another one, entitled *Falling Up*.

Why the lengthy gap between books?

"He wasn't ready to do another book," said Joan Robins. "He would suddenly drop in and show me some of his work and then drop out for another year, though he would call from time to time. And he was working on *Runny Babbit* all those years as well."

Robins had retired in 1988, but Shel insisted that she work with him as a consulting editor on *Falling Up* along with Robert Warren, who had been part of the team on *A Light in the Attic.*

Undoubtedly, Robins and Warren had felt pressure through the years to encourage Shel into producing another book. By this time they were intimately familiar with how he worked and brushed off the higher-ups' concern. "Though we would never think of pressuring him, once he said he was ready to publish, I felt a real responsibility to keep him on track," said Robins. "Once it was in the catalog, then he took it seriously and I took it seriously."

Though book publishers generally expect their authors to abide by the terms spelled out in the contracts they issue, no one at Harper paid much attention to Shel's contract. "He was the boss and he knew it," said Robins. "No publisher would ever be his boss, and the publisher knew it. Whatever was in his contract didn't matter." And if someone at Harper did decide to enforce the contract, there was a chance they could lose him to another house.

"His relationship with Harper was akin to a married couple who are constantly in some kind of conflict," she said. "Nevertheless, the marriage works even with all that strife. Any publisher at that time would have done just as well for him."

Indeed, he was loyal in his own way to Harper most likely because they agreed to publish *Different Dances* years earlier. "He was a pretty loyal person," said Robins. "He could be very brutal about telling you what he would and wouldn't do, but he never went behind your back. If he attacked you, he attacked you to your face because you had done something wrong."

As before, Shel moved into the conference room at Harper so he could work without distractions, and a flurry of editors, designers, and gofers on Shel Patrol surrounded him, ready to fetch copies of page mock-ups and sushi takeout at a moment's notice.

His editors still marveled at what he could do.

In the middle of production, Shel was reviewing the list of poems he wanted to include in the book, matching the poem with the accompanying illustration when he came upon the poem called "Cereal." He couldn't find the drawing. It also happened to be Joan's favorite poem in the whole book, though he didn't know it.

When Shel discovered he had no illustration for "Cereal," he frowned. "Then he leaned over and drew this little bowl with the big spoon right under the poem," she recalled. "I stood behind him watching him. I love that! It was this kind of magic he did that made the whole book come alive, and that made his endless changes worth it."

Though Robins didn't agree with all Shel's decisions, they were his alone to make. Sometimes he was ambivalent about a particular poem, whether to keep it in or take it out, and he voiced his concern to Robins. "I told him that sometimes I'll look at a poem for months and it doesn't appeal to me and suddenly I look at it and I know that I love it," she said.

"Well, that happens to me, too," he replied.

"I think he appreciated the fact that people were variable and their moods were variable, and that his own were as well," said Robins. "As a result, everything was a production as of the moment and was the best that he could give it at that time, and that was the case right up to the very end stages of publication."

Of course, as before, Shel was still making changes large and small up until the very last minute before the deadline. "All of the changes he made improved the book as a whole," said Warren. "There was always something he could do a little bit better. From a production standpoint it was exasperating, but it was so wonderful that he cared so much about his work."

It's an editor's job to gently suggest to an author changes that could improve a book in terms of both the large and small picture. At the same time, editors have to continually remind themselves that it's not their own work, it's the author's and they have to respect this. Warren rarely suggested changes during production of *Falling Up* and when he did it was more along the lines of changing the order of a couple of poems so that the book flowed more easily. He did it sparingly and he had to be able to state his case very succinctly. But Shel needed very little of that; he instinctively knew what he needed to do to improve the book, more than anyone else.

When *Falling Up* was published in May 1996, it wasn't as well-received as either *Sidewalk* or *Light in the Attic*. Though it appeared on *The New York Times* best-sellers list shortly after publication, it dropped off just after the new year, 1997. Of course, most writers would love to have a book with this kind of tenure on the list.

But to Shel, as usual, either way it didn't matter.

10. *I'm Checking Out*

I'm counting the years, counting the friends gained and the friends lost," said Shel. "Closeness with real friends is becoming the most valuable thing of all. It always was valuable for me, but in my younger days, getting the new fuck that night would break up any conversation. Not that it still wouldn't, but she might not be invited two out of three nights."

In the late '90s, with another collection of children's poetry under his belt and a body of work behind him that was beyond prolific, Shel had nothing left to prove. His life was about to become as simple as his art. And with the loss of his mother and several good friends in the last few years, he stepped up his efforts to connect with those remaining friends from the past.

One of them was Lynne McCalford, who first met Shel in 1981 when she was interning with Ensemble Studio Theatre in New York. They had been out of touch since the early '80s and met up again at the twenty-fifth anniversary party for the theater in 1997. They recognized each other at once.

"We hit it off immediately," she said. "It was the revival of a friendship that was much stronger the second time around, and we enjoyed each other's company tremendously." Soon she was spending time with Shel in his house in Key West and traveling to see him when he was in another city. McCalford estimated that they saw each other about once a month, and she always looked forward to their meetings with great excitement, coming away from them "swimming with insight," as she described it, usually with a humorous bent.

"He had the ability to come up with a phrase that would just succinctly sum up the situation, and that was part of his talent," she said. "This was a man in his sixties who was kind of a loner who had accomplished a lot, he had no money worries, a great life, and was happy with it. I didn't find him obsessed with anything."

The way he spent time with women also mellowed. In the earlier years, he was primarily interested in bedding them, seeing them primarily at night after he had finished his work. Now he was more interested in spending time together day or night, focusing his entire attention on her.

Shel was still writing plays, and they were still being produced and performed, but he was increasingly content with just seeing them staged as informal readings or in a workshop, without exposing them to the scrutiny of a live audience and critics.

He was still writing songs for the sheer joy of it, especially after he realized that Nashville was not the same place that it once was. But he was always up for a challenge, particularly when tossed out by one of his oldest and dearest friends, Bobby Bare.

"Shel was in town and we were talking about how radio wasn't for old farts like us anymore," said Bare. "I said to Shel, 'Why don't you write me an album of songs for people our age that we can relate to?' So he did," said Bare.

The result was *Old Dogs*. For the recording session, they brought Waylon Jennings, Mel Tillis, and Jerry Reed on board. It was another one of Shel's concept albums, but none of the "old dogs" who had teamed up to make the album—Bare, Jennings, Tillis, Reed, and Shel—deluded themselves into thinking it would even sell 1 percent of Shel's most successful concept album, *Lullabys, Legends and Lies*. They were doing it for the pure fun of it.

Then life imitated art. When they were in the studio recording *Old*

Dogs, Bare and Shel were in the control room, headphones on, offering direction to Tillis, who was singing his part.

Whenever Bare suggested a change for Tillis to try on the next take, Shel repeated Bare's words almost exactly. At first, Bare thought Shel was putting him on, but it soon dawned on the veteran country singer exactly what was going on. "Shel," said Bare, "put your hearing aid in. You're repeating me word for word."

"Aw, that's embarrassing," Shel replied. "I can't hear a word you're saying."

The album came out in December of 1998. Songwriter Mike Settle spoke with Shel about the time the album was released, and remembers thinking that his old friend had mellowed. "He told me that he wasn't trying to compete with the young guys anymore," said Settle.

"These days, a guy like me has to come up with a project, write all the songs, sell the project, and then put it all together," Shel said, which is exactly the process he followed for *Old Dogs.*

Shel was also serving as mentor to Bare's son, Bobby Bare Jr., who had long regarded Shel as an uncle, much like Dave Mapes and Sarah Sweeney McCann before him. Bare Jr. had a minor radio hit in 1999 with the indie rock song "You Blew Me Off."

"From the time he started writing, Bobby would always run everything by Shel," said Bare Sr. "Shel would call him up and encourage him. It was an ongoing thing." Indeed, he included Shel's "Painting Her Fingernails" on his album *Bobby Bare Jr.'s Young Criminals' Starvation League* and co-wrote "I Hate Myself" with Shel for *Boo-Tay,* his first album.

"Kristofferson looked at Shel as an equal," said Bare Jr. "Sometimes people don't understand that, because he wrote so many songs that people thought of as 'novelty.' He had stuff that could tear your heart into a thousand pieces, but it was the novelty stuff—that kept people from taking it too seriously."

At the same time, Shel was also mentoring another youngster: his own son, Matthew, who had started his own band at the age of fourteen. "We talked about Matt's band and how he was learning the trombone," said Fred Koller, who occasionally visited Shel on Martha's Vineyard. "He was really happy that Matt was getting into music."

Matt was starting to spend more time with his father, particularly during summers in the Vineyard. "He was thrilled when Matthew visited him on the Vineyard," said Koller. "He thought it was the greatest thing ever. Shel seemed to be in a very good place. He was doing yoga every day and Matthew was with him a lot."

But Shel struggled with having a child around, especially a teenage boy. After all, by this time Shel was in his late sixties and never had to raise a child on a full-time basis.

"He was having a few teenager problems with Matt," said Helen Scarborough, who said that Shel often confided in her late husband. "They talked a lot, and it was often man talk. But I know that Shel also told Henry that Matt was becoming a handful as a teenager and he didn't know how to handle it."

After living in the Vineyard part-time for a couple of decades—Shel usually arrived at his cottage in the campground in mid-May and returned to Key West by the end of October—Shel was thinking of finding a new place to spend his summers. "The last time I spoke with him he said that he was going to try to find another island to live on," said Scarborough. "He thought Martha's Vineyard was getting too crowded."

Even though he hadn't contributed to *Playboy* in years, he was still welcome at the Mansion West. Shel was such a part of Hef's world that he was one of the few people who didn't need to call in advance to make sure it was okay for him to show up. As before, sometimes when he showed up he would stay for only a day or two and sometimes he'd camp out there for weeks.

But in the late '90s, it was clear that his health was his primary concern, particularly yoga. He practiced bikram, or hot yoga, where the temperature of the room is kept between 95 and 100 degrees for the entire class. Larry DuBois ran into him on one of Shel's rare trips to the Mansion West in 1999. "He was really into yoga and meditation," he said. "He looked like a million bucks and he was more radiant than I had ever seen him. He talked about how much he loved yoga and meditation and how high he was getting from it. He just loved it."

DuBois thought Shel's gushing about yoga was a bit out of character for him.

"Shel was not a self-destructive guy," he said. "He took pretty good care of himself, but he wasn't a naturally high, radiant kind of guy like he was when I last saw him. So it came as a bit of a shock to me when he was just so high off the yoga and meditation."

"He did a three-hour hot yoga class every day whenever he was in Key West," said Mickey James. "I joked about it a lot, and did a couple of classes with him. It was horrible. It was awful. I asked him, 'Does this yoga ever feel good?' And he said, 'Yeah, every time you stop.'"

Drew Reid and Shel were catching up on the phone in May 1999. In the middle of the conversation, Shel blurted out a question that was out of character for him.

"Are you having any fun?" he asked.

"I said, 'Yeah, Shel, I'm having fun,'" said Reid.

Shel's answer surprised him. "I'm not having as much fun as I used to," he said.

"I told him that the world is not as much fun as it was back in the seventies, so he should just hang in there and something will come along," said Reid. "He really wasn't complaining; it was almost like he was world-weary. He was slowing down a little bit and getting a little grayer. I thought he sounded a little lonely, like he felt he had done it all, so what was left."

Other longtime friends picked up on this more pensive, slightly morose trait in Shel. For one, he began to worry about the legacy of his work. Dennis Locorriere was in New York over the Christmas season in 1998 and ran into Shel in Greenwich Village. They spoke for a while, and

Dennis told Shel of his plans to move to England. Shel asked, "Do you think they remember me over there?" Locorriere thought Shel appeared distracted, but he was more disturbed by his question, which seemed totally out of character.

On May 9, 1999, it was six years since his mother Helen had passed away. Bobby Bare spoke with Shel on the phone, a daily habit that they had continued for years. Shel was in Key West and was making plans to head north to his cottage on Martha's Vineyard. He told Bare that he thought he was coming down with the flu and that he was going to wait until he felt better before making the trip. When Shel said that he was in bed and it was six o'clock in the evening, Bare immediately knew something was wrong. "Damn, you must be sick," Bare remembered telling Shel. "There was no way Shel would be in bed at six o'clock."

The next day, the word quickly spread: Shel Silverstein had died of a massive heart attack. His cleaning ladies found him beside his bed, where his work was spread out, next to his nightstand where his phone was. He had obviously tried to call for help but didn't make it.

His friends were in shock.

"Shel was the only person I knew who took care of himself," said Bobby Bare. "He ate right, and he wasn't doing drugs or alcohol."

A week before Shel died, Kris Kristofferson went into the hospital for bypass surgery. He had been having trouble breathing for years. "The day I got out of the hospital, Shel died of the same thing," he said. "I felt very lucky."

When Dan Mobley heard the news, he immediately headed over to Shel's house, where he found a group of other friends. When he wandered into the house, he found a song on the kitchen table that Shel had written for Mobley in the last couple of days called "We Have Fish."

Mobley regularly played at the Hogs' Breath Saloon, and he and Shel had a fish dinner there about a week before he died; the song was a riff on their conversation that night. When he looked at the song written out, Mobley thought it almost didn't look like Shel's handwriting; the letters were a little shaky. "He may have been already slipping a bit at the time, maybe he was sick that week."

People magazine eulogized him by referring to him as a "rare contradiction: a recluse totally engaged in life." Cartoonist Jules Feiffer said, "He imagined things the way kids do when they're little, and it goes away when they're older—only in his case it didn't go away."

"He was one of the most amazing observers of human nature I ever knew," said former *Playboy* Editorial Director Arthur Kretchmer. "He had a protean sensibility. He never let himself lie to anybody, and he never let anybody lie to him."

"To millions of children and adults, Mr. Silverstein was a master of whimsy and light satire, which he delivered in verse—sometimes downright goofy—that tapped a universal sense of the absurd," wrote Bart Barnes in *The Washington Post*. "His writing was accompanied by line drawings of confused and befuddled people and other creatures with human attributes, and he had an uncanny knack for making nonsense funny."

"Dr. Seuss plays with language, and makes up funny words," children's author Donna Jo Napoli said in Shel's obituary that appeared in the *Philadelphia Inquirer*. "What Shel Silverstein does is a lot harder. He uses ordinary words that roll off the tongue."

His country-music friends held a memorial service for Shel in Nashville on May 13. Mickey James, Chet Atkins, Bobby Bare, Jack Clement, Harlan Howard, and about a hundred other people showed up to tell stories, laugh, and sing Shel's songs.

Shel's son, Matthew Silverstein, was fifteen when Shel died, and is the sole heir to his estate. The estimated amount of the so-called "liquid securities" in Shel's estate was valued at twenty million dollars in 1999. An estimate of the value of the non-liquid securities—the rights and continuing royalties to Shel's books—was not given, but over the years the royalties will undoubtedly add up to many times the liquid securities.

For the time being, Matthew is not involved in perpetrating Shel's legacy. Instead, Shel's nephew, Mitch Myers, is serving as the media spokesman for Shel's body of work, as well as arranging with publishers and music companies to produce new and revised versions of his works. For instance, *The Best of Shel Silverstein: His Words, His Songs, His Friends,* a CD compilation of his songs performed by Shel and other singers including Bobby Bare, the Irish Rovers, and Dr. Hook, came out in 2005.

In the spring of 2005, *Runny Babbit,* the book of spoonerisms that Shel had been working on for fifteen years when he died, was finally published by HarperCollins. Critical reviews were positive, and the book won a Quill Award in 2005. It was the first book with his name on it that wasn't produced under Shel's always-critical eye over two or three months of intense production work in the HarperCollins conference room. As a result, some feel that because he wasn't around to supervise and micromanage every aspect of the book's production, the book that was published turned out much differently than it would have otherwise. The first printing for the book was 500,000 copies, and the audiobook version was voiced by none other than Shel's old friend from Dr. Hook, Dennis Locorriere.

In the meantime, some of Shel's friends are helping Matthew Silverstein to explore his father's legacy, whether or not he decides to follow in Shel's footsteps.

Larry White helped show Matthew around New York one of the first times he came to New York by himself after Shel's death. "He wanted to have somebody show him around and give him an idea about what was happening in the Village and the Upper West Side in terms of music," said White. "We didn't spend much time together, it was just a way to help make him feel like he wasn't totally alone in the city, and that he had someone to call if he needed anything."

He said he didn't notice any real similarities between Matthew and Shel, at least on the surface. "If you saw me and my father together you wouldn't necessarily see any similarities between us either," said White. "But the main thing I noticed about Matt was that he has a real desire to be creative. And that's what Shel passed on to his son."

The legacy Shel left to his friends was that of generosity. "He was a very giving person to the people he respected and loved," said Chris Gantry. "He gave his time and occasionally his money, but more than that, he was willing to share his art with anyone who was truly interested in learning. He wasn't the kind of friend to drop in for coffee every day at a certain time, and there were times when you wouldn't see him for months. But when you were with him, he was there in the moment one hundred percent, and having fun."

"Where everyone else stopped, that was where Shel began," said Bobby Bare.

And whenever Shel began a project, he always knew where he was going to end up. Dan Mobley said that was the most important thing Shel taught him about songwriting. "Anyone can start writing a story or a song, but the fact is you need to know where it ends before you can even start," he said. "I didn't realize that if you start a song where Carl the crab crawled out of his cave on a coral reef one day, you need to know where Carl is going or else you have no story."

Even though Shel had a love–hate relationship with writing and drawing for kids, his life was absolutely sealed by the children's books. It's what gave him credibility, and they certainly gave him a means to live the kind of life he wanted. *The Giving Tree, Where the Sidewalk Ends* and his other books for children made him very famous. While *Playboy* put him on the map, the children's books enshrined his talent forever. If he hadn't done the children's books, he would have been just another hustling cartoonist. His books have been translated into twenty different languages and have sold well over twenty million copies.

Did he spend his life running from an ending that was inevitable? Larry DuBois doesn't think so.

"I don't think of Shel as running from something, I think of him as always wanting to run *farther* and find more," he said. "He was always on some quest. He was always trying to find answers, he was always pushing forward. He was looking for some kind of truth. He was a great artist."

And like most great artists, Shel could simultaneously seem young and old beyond his years.

"I was always convinced that he was a million years old, but at the same time, there was a child inside him, an adolescent soul," said Larry White. "He was a timeless man who would always have a childish essence. I also felt he was impervious to age, unlike the rest of us."

Marty Stonely, a fellow musician in Key West, tells a story that sums up Shel in a nutshell. He had been giving Shel a few clarinet lessons and one day showed him how to play a particular scale. "He started playing it the wrong way," said Stonely. "So I stopped him and said, 'Hey, Shel, you're missing a note here, you gotta play it like this.'

"Shel just looked up at me and said, 'I know, but I like the sound of this better.'"

Notes

Introduction

1. *A Boy Named Shel*

16 "in his native Chicago": Ibid.

17 "the fellows he wanted most to please": Ibid.

2. *Wild Life*

20 "that's all there is to it": Studs Terkel interview, WFMT, December 12, 1963

20 "I was mad at everybody who was": Studs Terkel interview, WFMT, December 6, 1961

22 "which is a legitimate concern" *Playboy,* January 2006

22 "he won't be there": Ibid.

25 "more than I had in myself": Ibid.

27 "something goofy and strange?": Studs Terkel interview, WFMT, December 6, 1961

30 "might get absolutely nowhere": *Aardvark,* Fall 1963

30 "won't be doing it very long": Ibid.

31 "were the social directors": *Bob Gibson & Bob Camp at the Gate of Horn* liner notes, 1st edition

32 "Gibson's chord changes": *I Come For To Sing,* p. 44

32 "and introduced it": *Bob Gibson & Bob Camp at the Gate of Horn* liner notes. 2nd edition

34 "pictures of naked women." Ibid.

35 "never create the magic in her": *Playboy,* January 2006

36 "a master at that": *Playboy,* January 2006

38 "screened through a Brillo pad": *Weekender,* May 21 1999

3. *No Grown-ups*

48 "to make our own schedule": *Inside the Playboy Mansion,* p. 82

50 "funny situation about two guys": Studs Terkel interview, WFMT, December 6, 1961

51 "just hints at these things": Ibid.

51 "watch out for those fairy tales": Ibid.

52 "change my mind about *Uncle Shelby's ABZ*": *The Los Angeles Times,* November 11, 1962

52 "it isn't clear enough": *Aardvark,* Fall 1963

54 "because he shaved his": *Playboy,* January 2006

56 "they'll think you are out of your skull": *And You Were on My Mind* liner notes, Jo Mapes, 1963

57 "have all the junket I wanted": Ibid.

58 "do the work that you think is right": *Aardvark,* Fall 1963

58 "they are *not* draftsmen": Studs Terkel interview, WFMT, December 6, 1961

59 "look at his work. That's enough": *Aardvark,* Fall 1963

60 "muddle it by talking about it": Ibid.

60 "that's tough shit": *Aardvark,* Fall 1963

60 "looking inside their brains": Studs Terkel interview, WFMT, December 6, 1961

61 "because you can't solve that problem": Ibid.

61 "you can't separate a man from his work": Ibid.

61 "unzip your fly for you": *Aardvark,* Fall 1963

62 "aspiring songwriters in Nashville": *The Best of Shel Silverstein* CD liner notes

62 "sing something that more fits what they know": Studs Terkel interview, WFMT, December 6, 1961

62 "the dumbest things in the world": *Aardvark,* Fall 1963

62 "singing folk songs and drinking hot chocolate": Ibid.

65 "some of the wonderful stuff there is in life": *Publishers Weekly,* February 24, 1975

65 "I guess I'll keep traveling": *Chicago Tribune,* February 21, 1960

66 "a spider who's getting ready to die": William Price Fox, *Free Times*

66 "I never saw no swimming hole": Studs Terkel interview, WFMT, December 12, 1963

67 "It has more story in it": *The New York Times,* April 30, 1978

67 "if the ideas are all laid out": *Publishers Weekly,* February 24, 1975

67 "ideally what kids want, she'll buy it": Studs Terkel interview, WFMT, December 12, 1963

68 "he doesn't want to see that": Ibid.

68 "it isn't for adults, too simple": *The New York Times,* September 9, 1973

68 "writing books a long time ago": Studs Terkel interview, WFMT, December 12, 1963

68 "it means you don't want to do it": *Aardvark,* Fall 1963

69 "It turns out twice as filthy": Ibid.

4. *Different Dances*

71 "then you get sick of writing songs": Studs Terkel interview, WFMT, December 12, 1963

71 "one job or one town": Ibid.

72 "changing all the time": Ibid.

72 "different door from most songwriters": *Brother, Can You Spare a Rhyme?* p. 151

73 "It has a pretty sad ending": Studs Terkel interview, WFMT, December 12, 1963

73 "one gives and the other takes": *The New York Times,* April 30, 1978

73 "I hope they can find enough in it": *Aardvark,* Fall 1963

73 "they'll really dig it now": Studs Terkel interview, WFMT, December 12, 1963

74 "because Mom wasn't there to give it": *Chicago Tribune,* August 4, 2002

74 "the further you get from marriage": *Chicago Tribune,* June 14, 1964

77 "but you'll never have it, either": *Playboy,* January 2006

78 "the things I care about": Studs Terkel interview, WFMT, December 12, 1963

78 "I started out with what I had to say": Ibid.

78 "And spit at what you don't like": Ibid.

79 "what began Jean Shepherd's writing career": *Excelsior,* p. 320

79 "no reason for me to write any songs": Studs Terkel interview, WFMT, December 12, 1963

79 "It was the white man's blues music": Ibid.

80 "Shel was kind of freaky looking": *Playboy,* January 2006

82 "I like the way I sing": *The Chicago Tribune,* March 4, 1973

82 "anybody with a deal like that": *I'm So Good That I Don't Have to Brag* liner notes

83 "and woke that woman up": *Playboy,* January 2006

83 "close to deciphering the Rosetta Stone": *Ram Magazine,* Australia, June 3, 1977

83 "they'd all speak warmly of him afterward": *Salon.com,* May 27, 1999

84 "he used it as his mood light": *Playboy,* January 2006

86 "they were very attracted to him": Ibid.

91 "Not even a postcard, you rat": *Dear Genius: The Letters of Ursula Nordstrom,* p. 255

92 "someone else had created especially for him": *Where the Sidewalk Ends* CD liner notes

93 "so wiry?": *Excelsior,* p. 44

5. Drain My Brain

100 "being a writer was the best job in the world": *Cleveland Plain Dealer,* December 26, 1999

100 "Nobody in Nashville was recording that kind of stuff": *I Come For To Sing,* p. 108

104 "especially when it got to be Number One": *Coal Miner's Daughter,* Loretta Lynn, p. 159

107 "the guys to do Shel's songs for *Kellerman*": *Rolling Stone,* November 9, 1972

107 "they brought it off": Ibid.

108 "spoiled it with a sledge hammer": Ibid.

108 "made me so much more of a singer": *Brother, Can You Spare a Rhyme?* p. 151

111 "it was 'The Cover of the Rolling Stone'": Ibid.

111 "he's saying a whole lot more than people can grasp": *ZigZag Magazine,* June, 1974

112 "he never had to fight over percentages again": *Salon.com,* May 27, 1999

112 "And that causes a lot of pain": *I Come For To Sing,* p. 273

112 "The song would not exist without them": Ibid.

113 "but it may not be very good": Ibid.

113 "avoiding pain at every turn": Ibid.

114 "requiring replacement and/or reupholstering": *Hef's Little Black Book,* p. 75

116 "and nobody could do it": *Gritz,* November 2005

116 "a charismatic figure to be reckoned with": Ibid.

116 "it was so radical for the time": Ibid.

118 "I continue the legend of the tooth fairy": *The New York Times,* April 30, 1978

119 "We didn't want them thinking we'd gotten VD as well": *I'm So Good That I Don't Have to Brag* liner notes

119 "You want people to allow for all of you": *Chicago Tribune,* March 4, 1973

121 "thousands of pieces of paper and millions of changes": *Dear Genius: The Letters of Ursula Nordstrom,* page 367

123 "as close to final form as he said over the phone, it can be": Ibid., Page 368

123 "And I won't give any more interviews": *Publishers Weekly,* February 24, 1975

6. *Underwater Land*

125 "the disturbing part of it": *The New York Times,* April 30, 1978

127 "She laughed, 'I already did'": William Price Fox, *Free Times*

7. *The Lifeboat Is Sinking*

147 "he wrote it for himself first": *Chicago Tribune,* October 18, 2001

149 "The answer is that it's just different": *The New York Times,* February 8, 1985

150 "your friends stop throwing you going-away parties": Ibid.

156 "so completely happy and alive": William Price Fox, *Free Times*

161 "I have to be prepared for failure too.": *Publishers Weekly,* February 24, 1975

161 "It was a ten-minute operation.": *Wisconsin State Journal,* June 30, 1999

162 "I don't think he ever really recovered from it": *Playboy,* January 2006

164 "And we all knew who it was": *The New York Times,* October 14, 2001

164 "quoting Kipling to each other": Ibid.

165 "and making something good out of it": *The New York Times,* February 8, 1985

165 "They're challenging them on it": *Chicago Tribune,* October 18, 2001

167 "if I was giving him excuses": *Cleveland Plain Dealer,* December 26, 1999

168 "He said, 'Look how lucky that guy is' ": Ibid.

8. *The Empty Room*

177 "and do to myself daily": *Playboy,* January 2006

178 "and the constant battle in your head": *Cleveland Plain Dealer,* December 26, 1999

182 "So I don't do research": *San Diego Union-Tribune,* November 10, 2001

183 "we saw him most of all day every day": Ibid.

183 *"then* I wanted my name on it": *Cleveland Plain Dealer,* December 26, 1999

184 "let them pay me": *The New York Times,* October 14, 2001

9. *Songs & Stories*

189 "I'm not going to be bound by my own shit": *Playboy,* January 2006

194 "trying to pass himself off as Shel Silverstein": *Cleveland Plain Dealer,* December 26, 1999

194 "We laughed about that a lot": Ibid.

195 "all my success to him, as he does me": *I Come For To Sing,* p. 203

197 "it just becomes a holy experience": *Makin' a Mess* promotional CD

197 "they might be able to beat that": Ibid.

197 "that stops us from having total pleasure": Ibid.

10. *I'm Checking Out*

203 "invited two out of three nights": *Playboy,* January 2006

204 "wasn't for old farts like us anymore": *Gritz,* November 2005

204 "So he did": *Chicago Tribune,* September 22, 1999

205 "I can't hear a word you're saying": Ibid.

205 "It was an ongoing thing": *Tennessean,* May 11, 1999

205   "from taking it too seriously": *No Depression*, July/August 2004

208   "Do you think they remember me over there?" *Playboy*, January 2006

208   "Shel would be in bed at six o'clock": Ibid.

208   "he wasn't doing drugs or alcohol": Ibid.

208   "I felt very lucky": *Tennessean*, December 12, 2003

209   "a recluse totally engaged in life": *People*, May 24, 1999

209   "in his case it didn't go away": Ibid.

209   "an uncanny knack for making nonsense funny": *The Washington Post*, May 11, 1999

209   "ordinary words that roll off the tongue": *Philadelphia Inquirer*, May 11, 1999

211   "that was where Shel began": *Gritz*, November 2005

List of Shel Silverstein's Work

Books

1955: *Take Ten*

1956: *Grab Your Socks!*

1960: *Now Here's My Plan: A Book of Futilities*

1961: *Uncle Shelby's ABZ Book: A Primer for Tender Young Minds*

1963: *Lafcadio: The Lion Who Shot Back*

1963: *Playboy's Teevie Jeebies*

1964: *Uncle Shelby's Zoo: Don't Bump the Glump! And Other Fantasies*

1964: *A Giraffe and a Half*

1964: *The Giving Tree*

1964: *Who Wants a Cheap Rhinoceros?*

1965: *MORE Playboy's Teevie Jeebies: Do-It-Yourself Dialogues for the Late Late Show*

1974: *Where the Sidewalk Ends*

1976: *The Missing Piece*

1979: *Different Dances*

1981: *A Light in the Attic*

1981: *The Missing Piece Meets the Big O*

1996: *Falling Up*

1998: *Draw a Skinny Elephant*

2005: *Runny Babbit*

2007: *Playboy's Silverstein Around the World*

Albums

1959: *Hairy Jazz*

1961: *Shel's Stag Party* (A reissue of *Hairy Jazz*)

List of Shel Silverstein's Work

1962: *Inside Folk Songs*
1965: *I'm So Good That I Don't Have to Brag!*
1967: *Drain My Brain*
1969: *A Boy Named Sue and His Other Country Songs*
1970: *Inside Shel Silverstein* (A reissue of *Inside Folk Songs*)
1972: *Freakin' at the Freakers Ball*
1973: *Crouchin' on the Outside* (A reissue of *I'm So Good That I Don't Have to Brag!* and *Drain My Brain*)
1978: *Songs & Stories*
1980: *The Great Conch Train Robbery*
1984: *Where the Sidewalk Ends*
1985: *A Light in the Attic*
2005: *The Best of Shel Silverstein*

Movie Scores

1970: *Ned Kelly*
1971: *Who is Harry Kellerman and Why is He Saying Those Terrible Things About Me?*
1972: *Payday*
1977: *Thieves*

Screenplays

1988: *Things Change*

Plays

Shel wrote well over one hundred one-act plays. Except for *The Devil and Billy Markham*, the following are the plays that were published in two collections: *An Adult Evening of Shel Silverstein*, and *Shel's Shorts*, both available from Dramatists Play Service, Inc., (www.dramatists.com).

Abandon All Hope
All Cotton
The Best Daddy
Blind Willie and the Talking Dog
Bus Stop
Buy One, Get One Free
Charades
Click

The Crate
The Devil and Billy Markham
Do Not Feed the Animal
Dreamers
Duck
The Empty Room and Other Short Plays
Feeding the Baby
Garbage Bags
Going Once
Gone to Take A
Gorilla
Hamlet
Hangnail
Happy Endings
The Happy Hour
Hard Hat Area
Have a Nice Day
I'm Good to My Doggies
The Lady or the Tiger Show
The Lifeboat Is Sinking
Little Feet
New Living Newspaper
No Dogs Allowed
No Skronking
No Soliciting
Nonstop
One Tennis Shoe
Remember Crazy Zelda?
Smile
Thinking Up a New Name for the Act
The Trio
Very, Very Serious Plays
Wash and Dry
Wild Life

Acknowledgments

As *always*, thanks must first go to Superagent Extraordinaire Scott Mendel for shepherding this book through its various hoops and barrels.

Next at bat are editors Sean Desmond, who acquired the book, and Peter Joseph, who inherited it. Many thanks for seeing the need for a long-overdue biography of Shel.

Two Web sites were invaluable in getting me up to speed on Everything Shel in the beginning of my research: Carol's Banned Width (banned-width.com), and Sarah Weinman's Shel Silverstein Archive (shelsilverstein.tripod.com).

Transcriptionists Judy Reynolds, Sarah McKinnon, and Paula Hancock made sense of hours upon hours of interviews as Shel's friends talked, reminisced, and burst into tears.

Chicago genealogist Jeanne Larzalere Bloom went way above and beyond when it came to digging up those little nuggets that helped me put Shel's early days in perspective.

Thanks to Shel's friends, acquaintances, business associates, and assorted others, including Woody Allen, Franklin B. Ashley, Dianne Chandler, Jonathan Dolger, Ellen Dominique, Larry DuBois, Gretchen Edgren, Fred Foster, Chris Gantry, Meridian Green, Rick Grumbecker, Judy Henske, Jac Holzman, Melanie Smith Howard, Arnold Hyman, Jef Jaisun, Mickey and Sharon James, John Kendall, Fred Koller, Frank Laidlaw, Lenny Laks,

Acknowledgments

Jay Lynch, Dave Mapes, Hillary Mapes, Lynn McCalford, Sarah Sweeney McCann, Michael Melford, Dan Mobley, Mike Mulvaney, Joe Muranyi, Lois Nettleton, Leon Oakley, Arthur Paul, Otto Penzler, Kerig Pope, Drew Reid, Joan Robins, Helen Scarborough, Terry Schmida, Mike Settle, Jim Skofield, Marty Stonely, Joe Sun, Bob Thompson, Robert Warren, Larry White, and Skip Williamson.

Kudos to the Buddies for never knowing how I'm going to walk in the door when I'm in the throes of a deadline, and not holding it against me: Dianne Burrington, Leslie Caputo, Mark d'Anjou and Sarah McKinnon and critters, Bob DiPrete, Doc and Nancy Gerow, Dean Hollatz, Don McKibbin, Cary and Paul Rothe, and Sara Trimmer.

Eternal thanks to the gang at the Salt Hill Pub in Lebanon, New Hampshire, for slinging the many burgers and myriad distractions that sustained me through the last brutal haul.

Finally, a big thank-you must go to fellow Granite Stater Dan Brown, author of *The Da Vinci Code*. My biography of Brown, published in the United States and all over the world, made it possible for me to put my full energies toward researching Shel's life.

Index

Index

Index

Index

Index

Index